AEGEAN TURKEY
AN ARCHAEOLOGICAL GUIDE

AEGEAN TURKEY
AN ARCHAEOLOGICAL GUIDE

GEORGE E. BEAN

FREDERICK A. PRAEGER, *Publishers*

NEW YORK · WASHINGTON

BOOKS THAT MATTER
Published in the United States of America in 1966
by Frederick A. Praeger, Inc., Publishers
111 Fourth Avenue, New York 3, N.Y.

Printed in Great Britain

Foreword

FEW PEOPLE, I believe, can pass a pile of ruins without some stirring of interest or curiosity. Turkey is remarkably rich in the remains of antiquity, and especially since the Second World War has been the scene of great archaeological activity, which shows no signs of abating. For the ordinary traveller the west coast in particular is full of interest, but without help much of the interest is lost to him. Many times, in the twenty years I have lived in Turkey, I have been asked, 'Is there no book to tell us about these things?'

Of course there are books. The reports of the old eighteenth- and nineteenth-century explorers, Chandler, Arundell, Hamilton, Fellows and others, are still excellent reading, but knowledge has naturally advanced since then. In recent times many people have written their 'Turkey books' after longer or shorter visits to the country; most of these are bright and entertaining, but generally unreliable on the antiquities. Two other books have appeared in the last ten years which are addressed to the general public and deal especially with the Greek period in western Asia Minor. The more recent is J. M. Cook's *The Greeks in Ionia and the East,* a scholarly and readable account, from the archaeological point of view, of Greek civilisation in Asia. The other is Freya Stark's *Ionia: a Quest.* Miss Stark describes her own journeys, recapturing most sympathetically and successfully the atmosphere of the country; she deals with the historical and literary background more than with the actual extant remains. On the other hand, the *Hachette World Guide* supplies a mass of facts—mostly, but not always, accurate—but has naturally little space for the background.

There seemed to me accordingly to be room for a book, addressed especially to those who have, or would like to have, an opportunity for travel in western Turkey, which should concern itself particularly with the actual standing ruins, letting the traveller know what things there are to be seen and what matters of interest attach to them. This book, therefore, is not written for specialists, who will find in it too much that

5

they know already; rather, the reader is assumed to have an interest in these matters, but no special knowledge concerning them.

My lower limit of time is in general about A.D. 300. Of the Byzantine and Turkish civilisations I have no qualification to write.

The area covered is roughly that which is in comfortable reach from Smyrna. Roads in Turkey are now vastly improved; those shown on the map are all fit for a private car, and others are continually becoming so. A jeep will take the traveller, at least in summer, within a very short distance of all the places discussed. I have myself visited all of these within the last few years, but excavation is proceeding apace and on a number of sites considerable changes will very soon be found to have taken place. Hotels also have improved, and country towns like Bergama or Söke now provide a perfectly tolerable, though simple, night's lodging. Turkey is at last becoming tourist-minded, but it will be many years yet before the atmosphere of the country is seriously spoiled.

Some of the sites included here have very little to show in the way of tangible ruins; but even if the ancient city be regarded merely as a pretext for a picnic and a bathe, so beautiful is the landscape in itself that few, I think, will come away disappointed.

My obligations are for the most part to the published works of numerous scholars in the learned journals and elsewhere. I have not thought it necessary, in a book of this kind, to give references for individual statements; in general, these may be found if required in the works listed in the bibliography at the back. I must, however, express my gratitude, first, to Professor J. M. Cook of Bristol University, with whom I have discussed a number of problems, and second, to my wife; the line-drawings, and most of the photographs, I owe to her.

In the spelling of Greek proper names I have used the Latin and English forms which come most naturally to the English tongue. To write Homeros or Alexandros or Eukleides seems somehow to make a stranger of an old friend. Inconsistently, I have written Claros, not Clarus; but this is simply because in practice no one ever says Clarus.

For Turkish names I use the modern Turkish spelling. In this, as a general rule, the vowels are pronounced as in German, the consonants as in English, except that: c = English j; ç = English ch; ş = English sh. ı is a sound not unlike the indeterminate vowel-sound in 'col*ou*r' or *a*gain'. ğ is virtually not pronounced at all. In speaking Turkish names spread the stress more or less evenly over the syllables; in particular, avoid stressing the penultimate syllable.

Contents

List of Plates

[*In one section between pages* 80 *and* 81]

11

List of Illustrations in Text

Glossary

Agonothete. Official charged with the organisation of the public games.

Agora. Market-place; the civic centre of an ancient city.

Archaic period. Approximately the seventh and sixth centuries B.C.

Ashlar. Masonry of rectangular blocks laid in horizontal courses.

Cavea. Auditorium of a theatre.

Cella. The main chamber of a temple, in which the cult-statue stood.

Classical period. Approximately the fifth and fourth centuries B.C.

Composite capital. A late style of column-capital combining the Ionic volute with the Corinthian acanthus-leaves.

Corbelled arch. A form of arch in which each course on either side projects beyond the course below, till the two sides meet or nearly meet; the projecting angles of stone are normally cut away.

Corinthian order. A style used in temples and other buildings. The columns are similar to those of the Ionic order, except that the capitals, instead of the Ionic volute, have a drum adorned with sprays of acanthus-leaves.

Cuneus. One of the wedge-shaped sections into which a theatre is divided by the stairways.

Cyclopean. A style of masonry using large blocks of irregular shape laid together without mortar and without courses.

Diazoma. A passage across the cavea of a theatre, dividing it into horizontal sections.

Doric order. A style used very frequently in the temples of Greece, but rarely in Asia Minor. The columns stand directly on the platform without any base, and have normally

AT—B   17

twenty flattish flutes meeting at a sharp angle. The capitals are of saucer or 'inverted Eton collar' shape.

Hellenistic period. The period from the time of Alexander the Great to that of Augustus—roughly the last three centuries B.C.

Ionic order. The style most used in the temples of Asia Minor. The columns stand on moulded bases and are more slender than the Doric; they have normally twenty-four deep flutes separated by narrow ridges. The capitals are flat; at the front and back (and sometimes on all four sides) they end on right and left in volutes ('rams' horns'), which are the especial characteristic of the order.

Opisthodomus. Rear chamber in a temple, often used to house the temple treasure. Some temples have no opisthodomus.

Orchestra. The dance-floor in a theatre, where the chorus performed, between the stage-building and the cavea.

Parodoi. The side-entrances to a theatre, between stage-building and auditorium.

Pronaos. Front chamber in a temple, usually on the east, giving access to the cella.

Propylon, Propylaea. Monumental entrance gateway.

Proscenium. The part of the stage-building in a theatre which projects in front towards the auditorium; used as a stage in post-classical times.

Stadium. (1) A measure of length, about 180 m., but variable. (2) A foot-race of this length. (3) The long building in which foot-races and other athletic contests took place.

Stele. A narrow slab of stone set upright, generally bearing writing or decoration or both.

Stoa. A long covered portico beside a street or agora or elsewhere.

Vomitorium. Covered passage by which the audience entered and left a Roman theatre.

CHAPTER ONE

Historical

F O R T H E ancients history began in effect with Homer and the
Trojan War. Of the two great civilisations of the second millennium lately revealed by archaeologists, the Minoan and the
Hittite, only the vaguest memories survived in classical times.
There were indeed legends concerning a king of Crete by the
name of Minos, who reigned two generations before the
Trojan War, conquered much territory and gained control
of the Aegean islands. But of the great Hittite power in central
Anatolia virtually nothing was known. Some modern scholars
have thought that the stories of the Amazons, who appear in
many parts of Asia Minor, may perhaps preserve a confused
tradition of the Hittite armies. On Egyptian monuments
Hittite soldiers are represented as wearing a long robe reaching
to the feet, which gives a distinctly feminine appearance. This
is not the case on the monuments of the Hittites themselves,
where they are shown dressed in a short tunic; nevertheless,
it may help to explain the curious tradition of the formidable
female warriors familiar in Greek literature.

That the Trojan War is an historical event has long been
recognised. Its traditional date, 1194–1184 B.C., is now thought
to be a little too late, but of the central fact—the destruction
of Troy by an expedition from Greece—there is no doubt.
Legend told that the Argonauts had recently made their way
into the Black Sea, and it may be that reports of the potential
riches of that region, to which access was controlled by the
Trojans, furnished the motive for the Greek enterprise. At
least it is hardly likely that the recovery of Helen was their
only purpose. However this may be, the Greeks surprisingly
took no steps to exploit their victory. The next appearance of
Greeks in Asia was due to entirely different causes.

Perhaps a century after the Trojan War, Greece was invaded from the north by a race called Dorians, who brought
to an end the civilisation of the Mycenaean kings who had
fought at Troy. Under the southward pressure of the invaders
many of the Greeks left their homes and migrated across the
Aegean. The first to make the move were the Aeolians from
Thessaly and Boeotia, who settled in the island of Lesbos and
in the region between the Troad and the gulf of Smyrna, which
henceforth bore the name of Aeolis. They were followed by the
Ionians, led according to tradition by the sons of Codrus, king
of Athens. These occupied the district south of Aeolis as far as
the River Maeander. These settlements seem to have begun in
the tenth century, and were certainly spread over a considerable period. It is unlikely that they met with any serious
opposition; since the break-up of the Hittite power about
1200 B.C. there was no organised government in Asia Minor,
and such resistance as the native inhabitants could offer would
be merely local. About a century later the Dorians, too, sent
settlers to Asia; these took the islands of Rhodes and Cos and
the adjacent coast of Caria to the south of the Maeander,
beyond the limits of the present work. The cities founded in
the course of these migrations were all on or near the coast.
Their relations with the native towns seem to have varied;
some at least accepted Anatolians as citizens, but all regarded
themselves as Greek cities, and their institutions were throughout antiquity purely Greek.

Herodotus says that the climate of Ionia is the finest in the
world; Aeolis has better soil, but inferior weather. Either for
this or for some other reason, the development of the Aeolian
and Ionian cities was markedly different. Of the eleven
Aeolian cities the very names of the majority are unknown to
most people other than specialists, and their history is a blank.
They remained small, attending to their own affairs and playing little or no part in the main current of events. Smyrna was
at first an Aeolian city, but became Ionian at an early date.

Ionia, on the other hand, developed a civilisation of quite
exceptional brilliance. While Greece was still hardly out of the
dark age that followed the Dorian invasion, the Ionian cities
were laying the foundation of Greek literature, science and

philosophy. Of the early literary works only those of Homer have survived; they testify to a long tradition behind them. Homer's date and birthplace, and even his existence, have been endlessly disputed; but it is now fairly generally agreed that the *Iliad* and *Odyssey* were composed, or compiled, by a single poet in the latter part of the eighth century, the *Odyssey* no doubt rather later than the *Iliad*. Tradition said that this poet was called Homer and that he was an Ionian, and the strongest traditions connected him either with Chios or more especially with Smyrna. The civilisation depicted in the poems is a mixture of the Mycenaean and that of the poet's own time.

Science and philosophy were at first the same thing, and were concerned with the basic structure of matter and the constitution of the physical world. When Thales of Miletus about 600 B.C. made the startling assertion that all things are water, he began a chain of speculation that has led in our time to nuclear theory and the atomic bomb. His successors preferred other basic principles, such as air or fire or even the infinite; the boldness of these conceptions is remarkable at this early date. But Thales' most famous achievement was his prediction of the solar eclipse of 585 B.C. (28 May 585, by modern reckoning). This was not really quite as impressive as it sounds. No one at that time was capable of calculating an eclipse of the sun, but the Babylonian astronomers had noticed that eclipses tended to recur at intervals of about eighteen years, and Thales had his information from them. He predicted in any case only the year of the eclipse.

With regard to the government of the cities at this period we are very inadequately informed. The original system of hereditary kingship did not last very long, and by the seventh century it appears that most of the cities had a primitive kind of democracy, with a council and magistrates whose functions were laid down by law. At the same time the influence of the richer citizens and the nobles who claimed descent from the early kings was undoubtedly strong; and in a number of cases the power came into the hands of a tyrant. The word tyrant denotes merely a monarch whose claim to rule was not hereditary; he might have seized power for himself, or he might have been chosen by the people, and his rule might be good or bad. The general standard of living was probably high; populations were modest, not above a few thousand, and most citizens owned slaves; and the art of gracious living was one that came easily to the ancient Greek.

At an early date, apparently before 800 B.C., the twelve major Ionian cities had formed themselves into a Panionic league. The coastal territory was divided among these twelve; the smaller places continued to exist, but without political importance. The league had its religious centre at the Panionium on the territory of Priene, but this bond in no way restricted the independence of the individual cities, who remained free to pursue their own policies and to quarrel among themselves.

, The twelve cities were:

Miletus	Ephesus	Teos	Phocaea
Myus	Colophon	Clazomenae	Samos
Priene	Lebedus	Erythrae	Chios

To these Smyrna was later added as a thirteenth.

A number of these cities in due course—mostly in the seventh and sixth centuries—sent out colonies of their own to various parts of the world. The most energetic in this respect was Miletus; in the Propontis (Sea of Marmara) and along the south shore of the Black Sea a string of Milesian settlements grew and flourished. Among the best known are Sinope, Amisus and Trapezus, all of which have kept their names hardly altered as Sinop, Samsun and Trabzon. In all Miletus was said to have led no fewer than ninety colonies.

Inland from Ionia lay Lydia, with its capital at Sardis, and beyond this the kingdom of Phrygia. In the eighth century Phrygia was the more powerful of the two; the legend of its King Midas and his golden touch is evidence of its prosperity, and the rock-cut monuments still standing in Phrygia, with their elegant decoration and inscriptions, show that art and literacy were well developed. About the end of the eighth century a new dynasty came to power in Lydia under King Gyges, who at once set about extending his dominion to the north, and also attacked the Greek cities of the west coast.

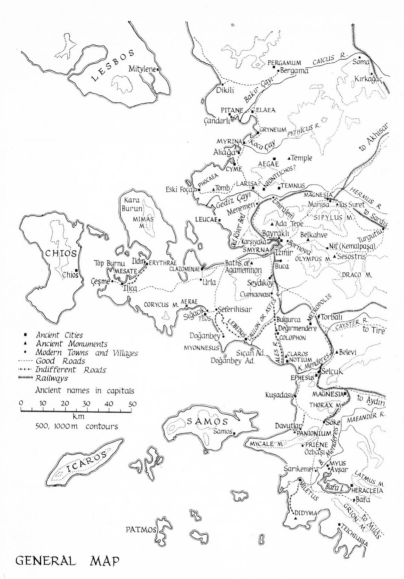

GENERAL MAP

FIG. 1 General Map, showing area covered by this book
[*Also facing page 272 on a larger scale*]

23

But his plans were interrupted by a sudden invasion of Asia
Minor by a horde of barbarians from the north, who for a
great part of the seventh century put the civilisation of
Anatolia in peril.

These were the Cimmerians. Displaced from their home on
the north shore of the Black Sea, they moved southward and
overran much of Asia Minor. The Phrygian kingdom succumbed
to their attacks and never recovered; Sardis also fell to them,
and even the Greek cities suffered. The danger of a new dark
age was imminent. Deliverance was due to Gyges' successor
Ardys, who succeeded in defeating the invaders and expelling
them once for all. The Cimmerians disappear from history, but
their name survives in Crim Tartary and the Crimea.

Freed from this peril, the Lydians renewed their attempts
upon the Greek cities. Priene fell to Ardys, Smyrna to his
successor Alyattes; finally Croesus in the middle of the sixth
century reduced them all except Miletus. Long before this
there had been intercourse between Greeks and Lydians, and
the latter are never spoken of by Greek writers as complete
barbarians. The Lydians are, for example, credited with the
invention of coinage. Croesus in particular, despite his hostile
activities, was regarded more as a friend than an enemy. He
made handsome offerings to the Greek temples and oracles
both in Greece and Asia; the sculptured column-drums which
he presented to the temple of Artemis at Ephesus are now in
the British Museum. And it was related (unhistorically, for
the dates do not fit) that the Athenian lawgiver Solon visited
and conversed with him at Sardis.

But the Lydian supremacy was short-lived. A new enemy
appears upon the scene, destined for more than two centuries
to overshadow the lives of the eastern Greeks. The Medes and
Persians had indeed long been there in the background, and an
indecisive war between Medes and Lydians had been fought
early in the sixth century; but Croesus now conceived the idea
of extending his empire to the east at their expense. He chose
his time badly, for Cyrus the Great had recently usurped the
Median throne. Croesus' invasion of Persia was a total failure;
Cyrus drove him back into Lydia, defeated him severely before
Sardis, and sacked the capital (546 B.C.).

Greeks and Persians were now for the first time face to face. Cyrus rejected all overtures of friendship, and the Persian forces at once advanced to the attack. The Ionians were hopelessly disunited and incapable of a common resistance; the Panionian league was neither a political nor a military union, and the cities were easily captured one by one. Within a few years the whole of Asia Minor was incorporated in the Persian empire.

Persian dominion was not in practice onerous for the Greeks of Asia. The country was put under regional governors called satraps, whose functions normally involved little more than seeing that tribute was duly paid; the cities were left to manage their own affairs, and most of them were actually ruled by Greek tyrants approved and supported by the Persian king.

One attempt was made by the Ionians to regain their independence. It was instigated, from personal motives, by the tyrant of Miletus, Aristagoras. In 499 B.C. the cities expelled their pro-Persian tyrants (Aristagoras resigning his own position) and established democracies; with some help from Athens, now a rising power in Greece, they raised an army and advanced to the satrap's capital at Sardis, which was sacked and burnt. But again their lack of unity proved fatal. The revolt was half-heartedly pursued, and the sack of Sardis only provoked the new king Darius to energetic measures. The Greeks at once withdrew to the coast; following a naval defeat off the island of Lade, Miletus was besieged and captured, and the Ionian revolt was at an end (494 B.C.).

Nevertheless, this ill-conceived and ill-managed venture did, in fact, lead indirectly to the liberation of the Greek cities of Asia. The part played in it by Athens induced Darius to embark on a project which he may have had in mind for some time, the subjugation of Greece. The failure of this enterprise, and the Persian defeat at Marathon by Athenians and Plataeans are familiar (490 B.C.); not less so is the failure of the second attempt by Xerxes ten years later, which came to grief at Salamis and Plataea. The immense prestige gained by Athens in these Persian wars left her as the equal of Sparta in the leadership of Greece, and in particular as the undisputed mistress of the Aegean. The Asiatic Greeks at once placed themselves under her protection, and a league was formed, under Athenian control, with the professed object of maintaining freedom from Persia.

This league, known as the Delian Confederacy, was nominally a voluntary association, and included nearly all cities, Greek and barbarian, on the Aegean coast. Each was required to contribute either ships or an equivalent sum of money. Xerxes, licking his wounds in his distant capital at Susa, had little heart for opposition, and the original purpose of the league was quickly achieved. It might then have been dissolved, but the Athenians were unwilling to forgo the tribute which came in annually from the member states; they severely repressed all attempts to secede, and the league turned gradually into an Athenian empire.

The amounts of tribute collected were recorded at Athens on stone stelae, many of which have survived; they afford interesting information as to the relative prosperity of the various cities at that time.

In 431 B.C. Athens became involved in the Peloponnesian War with Sparta. When this ended twenty-seven years later with a complete Spartan victory, the Delian Confederacy passed into the hands of the victors. But the Spartans had not the qualities required for ruling an overseas empire; the Persians reappeared on the west coast of Asia Minor, and eventually, by the King's Peace of 386 B.C., all the Greek cities of Asia were recognised as belonging once more to Persia.

During this period occurred an episode which, though it had no lasting effects, made an immense impression at the time. In 401 B.C. Artaxerxes had lately succeeded to the Persian throne. His younger brother Cyrus, however, desired the throne for himself; collecting a large army, including some 13,000 Greek mercenaries and volunteers, he set forth from Sardis to depose his brother. Among the Greeks was the Athenian Xenophon, who has left us a detailed account of the whole expedition. Slowly the army advanced through Asia Minor and on into the heart of the Persian empire. At length, at a spot called Cunaxa in Babylonia, the two brothers came face to face. In the ensuing battle the Greek troops were in a

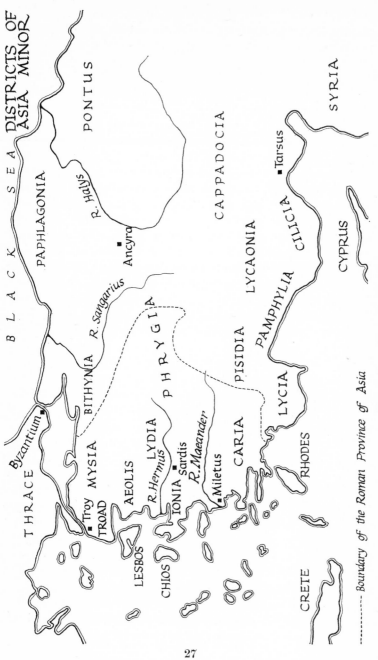

DISTRICTS OF ASIA MINOR

BLACK SEA

THRACE

Byzantium ■

Troy ■
TROAD

MYSIA

AEOLIS

LESBOS

CHIOS

IONIA

Sardis ■

R. Hermus

LYDIA

R. Maeander

Miletus ■

CARIA

RHODES

CRETE

PAPHLAGONIA

R. Sangarius

BITHYNIA

PHRYGIA

Ancyra ■

R. Halys

PONTUS

CAPPADOCIA

PISIDIA

LYCAONIA

LYCIA

PAMPHYLIA

CILICIA

Tarsus ■

CYPRUS

SYRIA

------ Boundary of the Roman Province of Asia

Fig. 2 Districts of Asia Minor

27

fair way to win the victory, but Cyrus himself was killed, and
his Asiatic forces at once fled and dispersed. The surviving
10,000 Greeks, finding themselves alone and leaderless, refused
to surrender to Artaxerxes and formed the plan of marching
northwards, through utterly unknown territory, to the Black
Sea. Led by Xenophon himself, overcoming every difficulty
and danger from the weather and from hostile barbarians, they
finally reached safety in the Greek cities of the coast.

For half a century after the King's Peace the Asiatic
Greeks lived quietly and contentedly enough under the
Persian dominion. Only for a short while was peace disturbed
by the activities of Mausolus in Caria. Mausolus' official position was that of Persian satrap, but he had made himself in
effect an independent despot and won the allegiance of the
Greek islands, allies of Athens, off the coast of Asia. Athenian
efforts to recover the islands were repelled, and for a time it
looked as if Ionia, too, might be drawn into a Carian empire.
But Mausolus died young (353 B.C.) and his ambitions were
never fulfilled. He was an able and enlightened man; he re-
organised the cities of Caria on the Greek model, and his tomb
at Halicarnassus, the Mausoleum, stood throughout antiquity
as one of the seven wonders of the world.

With the coming of Alexander a new era opened for Asia
and for the whole world. The Macedonians were on the border-
land between Greek and barbarian; Philip, by force of arms,
had won recognition as a Hellene, and had announced his
intention of leading a united Greece to overthrow once and for
all the power of Persia. For this purpose he was elected general
by the Greeks at Corinth, but he was murdered shortly afterwards and the achievement of his ambition was left to his
son Alexander. At the head of an army of some 35,000 Macedonians and Greeks, the young king crossed the Hellespont
in 334 B.C. His first act was to visit Troy, where he dedicated
his armour to Athena and placed a crown on the tomb of
Achilles, whom he regarded as his ancestor.

The conquest of Persia, thus marked as a sequel to the
Trojan War, proceeded with extraordinary speed and success.
A first engagement with the Persian forces at the River
Granicus east of Troy opened the way into Asia Minor. In that

same summer and the following winter Alexander overran the whole of the west coast, together with Lycia and Pamphylia; here and there, as at Miletus and Halicarnassus, the Persian garrisons offered resistance, but most of the country submitted readily. A second great victory at Issus in the following year was the prelude to the conquest of Syria and Egypt, and a third at Gaugamela in 331 B.C. brought the final downfall of the Persian empire. The Great King Darius was present in person at both battles, but escaped from both. Alexander went forward to the Persian capitals at Susa, where he laid hands on vast treasures, and Ecbatana; thereafter, induced partly by the course of events and partly by his own instinct for conquest and discovery, he advanced farther and farther into the unknown lands of the east. From the neighbourhood of the Punjab he was forced to turn back when his soldiers refused to advance any longer; on reaching Babylon he was seized by a fever and died (323 B.C.).

Alexander had crossed into Asia as a Greek against barbarians, to avenge the wrongs inflicted on Greece by the earlier Persian kings; but as he saw more of the Persian civilisation his views changed, and he began to think of a world empire where Europeans and Asiatics should be on an equality, ruled by a monarch whom all mankind should regard as their own king. It was a new and bold conception, but one which only its originator might possibly have realised.

His successors had other ideas. Upon Alexander's death his generals held a conference at Babylon to determine how to control the vast new empire that had just been won. Alexander was 32 when he died, and left as possible successors from his own family only a mentally deficient half-brother and an unborn son. A move was at first made to reserve the succession for these jointly, but neither was more than a figure-head and before long both were murdered. The power was in the hands of the generals, who proceeded to divide the conquered territories among themselves. For a generation they warred with one another, until finally three main kingdoms were established. The most permanent and stable of these was that of Ptolemy in Egypt; it continued under a succession of kings, all of whom took the name Ptolemy, down to the time of

Cleopatra. The second was that of Seleucus, which comprised Syria and, at first, all the eastern regions as far as India; but these latter gradually fell back under various oriental powers. The Seleucid dynasty, under kings named Seleucus or Antiochus, lasted till 65 B.C., when Syria became a Roman province. The third was Macedonia, including Greece. The north of Asia Minor, along the south coast of the Black Sea, where Alexander never set foot, was occupied by smaller kingdoms, non-Greek in origin and established before the Macedonian conquest, notably the kingdoms of Bithynia and Pontus; these maintained themselves against all opposition till the first century B.C., when they, too, were incorporated in the Roman dominions.

Western Asia Minor belonged properly to none of the kingdoms mentioned, but was contested at different times by all of them. After Alexander's death it fell to Antigonus; but his ambitions united the other generals against him, and he was defeated and killed at the battle of Ipsus in Phrygia in 301 B.C. The west coast then passed into the hands of Lysimachus, another of Alexander's generals, who held it till he in his turn was killed in battle in 281 B.C. and his territory annexed to the kingdom of Syria.

At this point a new actor appears on the scene. A certain Philetaerus, finding himself at Pergamum in possession of Lysimachus' treasure, used it to establish a dynasty there.[1] This Attalid dynasty, as it was called, grew rapidly in power, and Pergamum was before long to be reckoned as an equal to the three main kingdoms. The history of western Asia Minor for the next century is that of the attempts by the various kings to extend their dominion over it. For a time in the third century they were distracted by the activities of the Gauls, a European tribe who had settled in the interior of the peninsula; their incursions, which reached at one moment as far as Miletus, gave the kings much trouble until they were finally suppressed by Attalus I of Pergamum.

Though Alexander's vision of a political union of mankind remained unrealised, his conquests had nevertheless changed the face of the world. One outcome was the great increase in

[1] See below, p. 69.

wealth, as the immense treasures of the Persian kings were released; but a more far-reaching result was the permeation of the east by the Greek language and culture. The Hellenistic kings were active in founding new cities of Greek form, named mostly after the kings themselves and members of their families; hence the constantly repeated names on the map of Asia such as Antiocheia, Seleuceia, Ptolemais and many others. In these Greek was the official language, and in the third century the whole of the hitherto barbarian world was busily learning the tongue of Demosthenes and Plato.

The cultural centre of the Hellenistic world was at Alexandria in Egypt. The vast library assembled by the Ptolemies, variously estimated at 400,000 or 700,000 volumes, afforded unique facilities for literary research and criticism; and if the original works of the Alexandrian poets and prose-writers are not equal in genius to those of the classical Greek age, the achievements of their mathematicians and scientists are impressive. Euclid's *Geometry*, written in the early third century B.C., was still a school textbook in the present writer's youth. To the same century dates the invention of the first primitive machine driven by the power of steam. Alexandrian astronomy is even more striking. That the earth is a sphere was known since before the time of Aristotle; but about 225 B.C. Eratosthenes succeeded in measuring its circumference to within some 200 miles of the truth. There were, in fact, errors in his data, but these happened to cancel out, and his method was absolutely sound (Appendix I). Heraclides maintained a belief in the daily rotation of the earth, and that Venus and Mercury were satellites of the sun; Aristarchus went further and suggested that the sun was the centre of the entire system of planets. Hipparchus calculated the distance of the moon from the earth as thirty-three times the earth's diameter; the true figure is a little over thirty. Seleucus believed that the tides were caused by interaction of the earth and moon, and was well on the way to discovering the law of gravitation. But the trouble was that in most cases these theories were not at that time capable of proof; they were accordingly not generally accepted, and remained to be rediscovered in comparatively modern times. It is not always realised that most of the major discoveries up to the present century were in fact anticipated by the Alexandrian scientists.

Towards the end of the third century the scene began to be overshadowed more and more by the growing power of Rome. Not that the Romans were eager for conquest in Asia; they were, on the contrary, reluctant adventurers in the east. It was the restless ambition of Antiochus III of Syria that first brought a Roman army across the Aegean. Lately released from their conflict with the Carthaginians under Hannibal, the Romans became embroiled with Philip V of Macedonia, whom they defeated in a pitched battle in 197 B.C. Certain Greeks, dissatisfied with the settlement then imposed by Rome, invited Antiochus to liberate Greece. Antiochus, urged on by Hannibal, who had fled to his court, accepted the invitation. Meeting with no success, he retired to Asia, whither he was followed by a Roman army and decisively defeated at Magnesia-under-Sipylus (now Manisa) in 190 B.C. In the settlement which followed most of Asia Minor was granted to Eumenes II of Pergamum, the Romans having no desire to annex it for themselves. This state of affairs continued for half a century, till the last king of Pergamum, Attalus III, brought his kingdom to an end by bequeathing it to Rome (133 B.C.).

This time the Romans did not refuse. Quickly suppressing a revolt by a pretender named Aristonicus, they organised the territory as the Roman province of Asia. Rome was at this time a republic, immensely powerful in the field of battle, but indifferently equipped for governing a distant province. There is no doubt that Asia was at first badly administered. The supreme authority was in the hands of the governor, appointed normally for one year with proconsular status and assisted by a team of junior officials. In administrative and judicial matters his word was law. Some few governors were honest and upright men, but the majority saw in their province chiefly a means of enriching themselves. A governor was in theory liable to prosecution in Rome for any misdeeds, but his judges were politicians who might one day find themselves in his position, and convictions were hard to secure; a judicious distribution of gifts was normally enough to ensure his safety.

A political career at Rome was an expensive business, and it was commonly said that a governor needed to make three fortunes out of his province—one to pay his debts, one to bribe his judges, and one to live on. But a worse infliction for the provincials was the exactions of the tax-gatherers. The taxes themselves were fixed by law, and were probably no higher than had formerly been paid to the kings of Pergamum; but the method of collecting them was unfortunate. The taxes were farmed out at Rome for periods of four years to the highest bidder among the companies of 'publicans' (tax-gatherers); these were left to collect the money for themselves, and any surplus was for their own profit. It was therefore to their advantage to extort the maximum possible; we hear repeatedly of cases where the publicans attempted to tax land which was not properly liable, such as the territory of 'free cities' (see below), or the revenues of fisheries and salt-pans belonging to the temples. On a few occasions their claims were disallowed on appeal to the governor, but in general there is no doubt that they were a sore trial to the province.

Others who found in the province a source of gain were the Roman merchants and bankers who settled in Asia in great numbers. Many of the provincials, both cities and individuals, were before long deep in debt, and were obliged to resort to these companies for loans; security being poor, rates of interest were very high.

Financial matters apart, it was in general the Roman policy to interfere as little as possible in the administration of the individual cities. Everywhere the daily management of affairs was controlled, as before, by the city council and assembly, and only if the situation grew seriously out of hand did the Roman governor appoint an official to set things right. Certain cities indeed were, in theory at least, entirely independent of the Roman power. Those which had been free under the kings continued for the most part to enjoy their freedom as 'friends and allies' of Rome. These were not subject to the governor's orders and were exempt from tax. Nevertheless, they felt themselves to be very much a part of the province, and most of them possessed a temple and cult of the deified Rome; in some cases this cult had been established before the

AT–C

formation of the province. It was in these cities also that the governor sat to administer justice. Such was the case in Asia with Pergamum, Sardis, Smyrna, Ephesus and Magnesia.

One last attempt was made to expel the Roman power from Asia. Mithridates VI, king of Pontus, was a man whose huge physique was matched by his ability and ambition. In the course of enlarging his kingdom at his neighbours' expense he had clashed with a number of petty monarchs who enjoyed the support of Rome. Finding himself committed to a struggle with the Romans, Mithridates in 88 B.C. advanced into the province with an army estimated at the unlikely figure of a quarter of a million. Such was the dissatisfaction with the Roman administration that he was almost everywhere welcomed as a liberator; the Roman defence was feeble and the whole of the province was soon in the king's hands. He then proceeded to the step which has made his name infamous. He ordered the massacre of all Romans and Italians in the province, without distinction of age, sex or status. The order was carried out, apparently with enthusiasm, and in this 'Asian Vespers' 80,000 persons, bankers, merchants, publicans and their families, are said to have perished. Still not content, Mithridates sent an army across the Aegean to occupy Greece, which now formed the Roman province of Achaea. The Romans, moved to energetic action, sent an army to Greece under Sulla, and the king's forces were quickly expelled. In consequence, however, of political changes at home, Sulla was deprived of his command and even proclaimed an outlaw; a second army was sent under a new commander, Flaccus. But Flaccus was murdered and his command usurped by his subordinate Fimbria; Sulla declined to give up his army, so that the war against Mithridates was carried on by two generals, neither of whom was officially in command. Fimbria defeated the king in Asia, and peace was signed in 85 B.C. on the terms that Mithridates should surrender all his conquests and pay an indemnity, but should be recognised as king of Pontus. Fimbria, afraid to return to Rome, committed suicide at Pergamum.

Twelve years later Mithridates made another attempt, but

this time the Romans were better prepared, and the king was unable to advance beyond Cyzicus. The Romans in their turn assumed the offensive, and Mithridates was driven from his kingdom. With the help of Tigranes, king of Armenia, however, he was able to prolong the war until in 66 B.C. Pompey the Great was appointed to the command. Decisively defeated in the field, the king retired to the Crimea, where he died by his own hand in 63 B.C.

This was not Pompey's first success. During the second and first centuries, as the power of the kings of Syria grew steadily weaker, the pirates had established themselves strongly on the south coast of Asia Minor; from there they were molesting sea traffic and even raiding the shores of the province of Asia. In 67 B.C. Pompey, in a brilliant campaign of less than three months, exterminated them so thoroughly that they were never again a serious menace.

But the Roman republic was now entering on a period of internal dissension and civil war which it proved unable to survive. Pompey, Caesar, Brutus, Antony, Octavian and others played their several parts; under the ultimate victor Octavian, who then took the title Augustus, the republic was converted into the empire (27 B.C.).

For the province of Asia the change was wholly to the good. In the first place, for 300 years the country was entirely free from war. Under the *pax Romana* the cities were able to develop their economy in peace, and most of them prospered greatly. Wealth increased and populations multiplied, till some of the larger cities had something like a quarter of a million inhabitants. The standard of living under the first- and second-century emperors was higher than it has ever been since until quite recent times. The system of administration remained superficially unchanged. A new governor arrived from Rome each year, and not all governors were good; but it was now more possible to obtain redress for injustice. The cities united in a kind of federation called the Commonalty of Asia, so that complaints could be made with authoritative backing, and were indeed frequently successful.

The Commonalty, in fact, conducted all kinds of relations with the imperial government. Important among these was the official worship of the emperor. Augustus himself was reluctant to be deified; but worship of the kings had long been the custom in the east, and the provincials thought of the emperor as they had thought of the kings. They asked permission to establish his cult, and Augustus assented on condition that it be joined with that of the deified Rome, which had long been in existence. Later this was succeeded by a cult of Augustus alone—that is, of the reigning emperor, for all the emperors took the title Augustus. This imperial cult, in fact, played an important part in holding the empire together; it gave the inhabitants of the various provinces a sense of partnership with each other and with Rome, and of belonging to a unified whole.

Another measure tending to the same effect was the grant of Roman citizenship to prominent provincials who had deserved well of their city or of the empire. This privilege was highly prized and extended normally to the recipient's descendants. A climax was reached in A.D. 212, when the emperor, Caracalla, granted the citizenship to all inhabitants of the empire, male and female, except slaves.

By the middle of the first century A.D. the whole of Asia Minor was incorporated in the Roman empire in the form of provinces. Most of these were governed by a legate appointed by the emperor himself; Asia and Bithynia were attached to the Senate, but here also the emperor held the ultimate control. For the first 200 years of our era provincial administration was almost uniformly good; only in the third century did a decline set in. The population continued much as it had always been—mainly Greek in the old Greek cities, mainly Anatolian in the inland parts, with the communities of Roman merchants and bankers spreading gradually to the remoter places. For official purposes the normal language was Greek, though the old Anatolian languages continued to be spoken, and nearly all inscriptions are in Greek; Latin was officially used only in the military colonies which the emperors planted for purposes of security, and even in these Greek inscriptions are also common.

The long continuance of the *pax Romana* brought the cities great wealth and prosperity; on the other hand, it robbed them of the stimulus of armed conflict. Where once the support or the hostility of Ephesus or Smyrna could make or mar the fortunes of a Hellenistic king, the cities were now reduced to striving merely for titles and honours: 'First and greatest metropolis of Asia', 'Four times temple-warden of the emperors', such are the phrases proudly repeated in the official inscriptions. These titles were granted personally by the emperor, and rivalry for them was intense.

Athletic competitions had always been an important feature of Greek life, ever since the foundation of the Olympic games in the eighth century B.C., and they were not less so under the Roman empire. The great festivals of classical Greece continued to be celebrated, and victory at them was still held in the highest esteem; but now every large city, and many of the smaller ones as well, held their own festivals, in most cases once every four years, as also did the provincial Commonalties in the name of the whole province. They included competitions not only in athletics but in music and drama. Sport was by this time highly professionalised; every summer crowds of pot-hunters moved from place to place collecting money-prizes and honours; for those who stood no chance at Olympia or Rome or the Commonalty of Asia, there were plenty of obscurer meetings where victories could be won. Successful athletes were well treated in their home town, for in this field too inter-city rivalry was very keen. The bloodier sports favoured by the Romans had comparatively little appeal for the Greeks; in Asia Minor theatres and stadia are thick on the ground, but amphitheatres on the Roman model are on the whole a rarity.

As their wealth grew, so did the cities beautify themselves. Everywhere, in place of the small but handsome Hellenistic buildings, bigger and better structures of Roman type were erected. Temples, theatres, markets and every kind of public building were constructed, frequently at the private expense of individual citizens; for the richer men were eager to vie with one another in conspicuous service to their city. Except where excavation has revealed the earlier remains, nearly every ancient building which the traveller sees today dates from the Roman imperial age.

The second century, under the 'good' emperors from Trajan to Marcus Aurelius, was the golden age. The third century saw a definite deterioration. In the half-century following the death of Severus Alexander in 235 no fewer than twenty emperors assumed the purple, many of them barbarians, mostly elected by the army, incapable of ruling an empire, and destined for a short reign and a violent death. The incessant wars in which they were engaged on the frontiers of the empire, though far from the soil of Asia, impoverished this and every other province by the constant passage of armies and the severe drain on the imperial finances. The depopulation which normally follows impoverishment was accentuated by the appalling plague which raged over the whole Roman world for fifteen years in the middle of the century; Gibbon estimates that close on half the human race may have been exterminated. And from 258 to 262 Asia Minor suffered from the repeated incursions of the Goths, whose raids extended at one time as far as the Maeander. This was the first time since the days of Mithridates that a foreign army was seen in the province of Asia.

The following centuries brought a variety of fortunes under good emperors and bad; all was not gloom, but the general tendency was to a steady decline. During the long peace, defence being no longer a consideration, the inhabitants of most of the old hilltop cities had moved for convenience to the plain below; in Asia, Pergamum is an obvious example. Some of them continued in this situation throughout antiquity and down to our own day; but in many cases, as city life lost its importance, the people preferred to scatter into villages to be near their fields; and almost everywhere the old cities on the hills lay deserted and overgrown, to fall gradually, under the influence of time, weather and earthquakes, into the state of ruin in which we see them now.

The rise of Christianity, and the fascinating story of the struggles of the early Christians with the Roman power, intensely interesting though they are, must be left in the background here. With the adoption by Constantine of Christianity as the official religion of the empire a new era begins which is beyond the scope of the present work.

The sources for the history of Asia Minor are, of course, immensely varied; ancient literary authorities, inscriptions, coins and modern excavations all contribute their share. It may, however, be useful to say a word about one or two of the ancient writers whose names will figure frequently in the following pages.

Herodotus was born early in the fifth century B.C. at Halicarnassus in Caria. He travelled very widely, not only in Greece and Asia Minor, but in Egypt, Persia, Scythia and southern Italy. The subject of his history is the wars of Greece and Persia, but he introduces incidentally a vast amount of information concerning the places and peoples he has occasion to mention. He retails for our benefit much that he had seen himself and much that he was told by others; in the latter case he leaves the reader to believe or not as he will. Herodotus was regarded at one time as a credulous dupe of his informants, but the charge is not justified. Modern investigation has tended to confirm much that was thought incredible, and to prove the reliability of his observation. For variety of interest Herodotus' history is unsurpassed.

Strabo was a native of Amaseia, the modern Amasya, and was educated at Nysa near Tralles, now Aydın. His *Geography*, written in the time of Augustus, gives a brief description of the whole of the ancient world, much of which he had visited in his travels. The notes on each place are naturally short, but the description is enlivened by historical comment and anecdotes. He used reliable sources, and his value as an authority is highly esteemed.

Pliny the elder (A.D. 23–79), in his *Natural History*, collected a vast mass of information on all kinds of subjects; he begins with a geographical summary of the known world. This work is an uncritical scissors-and-paste compilation of second-hand matter, and must be used with caution; Pliny sometimes retails information from different sources without noticing that they contradict each other. He nevertheless tells us a great deal that we should not otherwise know.

Pausanias lived in the second century A.D. and wrote an *Itinerary of Greece*, a very full and descriptive guide-book to the southern regions of the country. His work does not cover Asia Minor, but, being a native either of Smyrna or of Magnesia-under-Sipylus, he makes frequent incidental references to that neighbourhood. Pausanias, too, is a valuable and in general highly reliable authority.

★

CHAPTER TWO

Smyrna

SMYRNA IS among the pleasant places of the earth. Its sheltered position at the head of a long gulf, at the seaward end of an easy route from the interior, marks it out to be the site of a flourishing port; when to this are added natural beauty, fertile soil and an excellent climate, it is no matter for wonder that a city of Smyrna has existed from pre-historic times. The annual rainfall is an inch or two higher than that of London, but most of it falls in the first three months of the year; the summers are hot and dry, though seldom unpleasantly so. Summer temperatures are mostly in the low nineties, but the heat is normally tempered by the sea-breeze, called the Imbat, which rises in mid-morning and blows until evening. When the Imbat fails conditions are less pleasant. Summer rain is a rarity.

Immediately behind the town, and now largely covered by its houses, rises the hill known in ancient times as Mt. Pagus; the Turks call it Kadife Kale, the Velvet Castle. The view from the summit is superb. In front is the thirty-mile length of the gulf, half closed at the end by the massive promontory of Kara Burun, the ancient 'rugged Mimas'; to the left are the twin summits of the Two Brothers, clouds upon which are a sure sign of rain; behind to the right is Mt. Sipylus, the Manisa Dağı, with its legends of Tantalus and Niobe; to the east is the Nif Dağı, one of the nineteen mountains which in ancient times bore the name Olympus.

The westward view was in antiquity somewhat different. The present northern shore of the gulf is an alluvial deposit of the River Hermus (Gediz Çayı), which until 1886 flowed into the gulf opposite the Two Brothers. In that year it was diverted into its present channel, which seems, in fact, to be

41

its ancient channel, for Herodotus says that the mouth of the Hermus is close to Phocaea, as it is now. When it changed course to the south is not known, but it is certain that in ancient times the coastline ran much farther to the north. A map of 1717, as Cadoux observes, shows Menemen, now some fourteen miles from the sea, almost on the shore; Chandler in 1764 reckoned the scala of Menemen three hours from the town. The silting process is very visible from Kadife Kale; the navigable channel in the gulf was being rapidly narrowed, and the diversion of the river came none too soon.

The flat-topped hill of Mt. Pagus seems destined by nature to be the acropolis of an ancient city. Nevertheless, it was not here that Smyrna was originally founded. The early Greek settlers in general chose for preference two kinds of site, a hill of moderate height close to the sea or a small peninsula joined to the mainland by a narrow neck. Smyrna offered both of these, and the latter was chosen for the original Aeolian city. Beside the present village of Bayraklı is a low hill now called Tepekule (formerly Hacı Muço); this was in antiquity a peninsula, for here too the shore-line has advanced. On this the Aeolians settled, replacing an earlier native settlement dating back to the third millennium. The site was excavated in 1948–51 by the British School at Athens in collaboration with Ankara University.

Concerning the pre-Aeolian Smyrna various legends were related. One tradition told that this, together with other Aeolian cities, was originally founded by Amazons; it is possible that this is an indistinct reminiscence of the Hittite power.[1] Other tales concerned the family of Tantalus, the legendary king of Phrygia; of these more will be said in the following chapter. Yet another tradition said that the coast from Ephesus to Phocaea was held, before the Aeolians came, by Lelegians; this rather shadowy people is located by Homer in the southern part of the Troad, and in historical times in Caria. But none of these legends has received any confirmation from the excavations at Bayraklı.

Of the history of the early Greek town not very much is known. Herodotus tells us that certain Ionians from Colophon,

[1] See above, p. 19, and below, pp. 104–106.

expelled from their city, were received as refugees in Smyrna; this hospitality they repaid by seizing the city while the inhabitants were outside at a festival. By the ensuing agreement the dispossessed Smyrnaeans were accepted as citizens by the other eleven Aeolian cities, and the Ionians kept Smyrna. This narrative is confirmed by other ancient authorities, and the city's change from Aeolian to Ionian is attested by the sherds found during the excavation. Subsequently Smyrna applied for admission to the Panionic league, but the Ionians stood by their resolve to admit no other members beyond the original twelve. These events date to about 800 B.C.

In the seventh century Smyrna shared in the general prosperity of Ionia, and the city expanded considerably; but the country as a whole was much troubled by the aggressive hostility of the Lydians. The first attacks were made by Gyges early in the century; his attempt upon Smyrna was only partially successful, and he was forced to retreat. But a second attack by Alyattes about the end of the century brought the capture and destruction of the city. The site was left in ruins, and for the next 300 years Smyrna, in Strabo's phrase, 'was inhabited village-fashion'.[1] Throughout the whole of the classical Greek age Smyrna was politically non-existent.

Whether Strabo meant that the city was reduced to the status of a village or that Smyrna was represented during this long period by a group of villages, it is clear from the excavations that the site at Bayraklı was by no means wholly deserted. Later in the sixth century, and again in the fourth, habitation there was reasonably prosperous, though it never again rose to the rank of a city. The Delian Confederacy in the fifth century did not include Smyrna. To this 'village-period' also belong the tombs and fortresses on the hill to the north (below, p. 50).

The re-foundation of Smyrna was due to Alexander. According to the story told by Pausanias, Alexander in 334 B.C. paid a flying visit to Smyrna from Sardis and went hunting on Mt. Pagus; as he rested afterwards under a plane-tree

[1] Strabo himself says 400 years, either by a mere slip or possibly reckoning (wrongly) from Gyges' attack.

beside the sanctuary of the Nemeseis on the hill (the Smyrnaeans worshipped not one Nemesis, but two), the goddesses
appeared to him in sleep and bade him found a city on that
spot, transferring to it the inhabitants of the earlier site. The
Smyrnaeans, in accordance with the usual practice before
founding a city, sent for advice to the oracle of Apollo at
Claros; the god replied:

'Three and four times happy shall those men be hereafter
Who shall dwell on Pagus beyond the sacred Meles.'[1]

Thus encouraged they gladly made the move. Alexander himself had, of course, no time to do more than initiate the work,
and Strabo says that the new Smyrna was founded by
Antigonus and after him Lysimachus; these no doubt saw to
the major part of the building, for Smyrna was not, any more
than Rome, built in a day; but Alexander was generally
regarded as the founder, and the excavations have shown that
the settlement at Bayraklı ceased even during his lifetime.
For a short while the new city bore the name Eurydiceia,
bestowed on it by Lysimachus in honour of his daughter
Eurydice, but after a few years this was abandoned.

Early in the third century Smyrna was at last, on the
recommendation of the Ephesians, accepted into the Panionic
league as a thirteenth member. During the difficult times of
the Hellenistic wars the new Smyrna maintained her status
as a free city—free, that is, to lend her support in troops and
money to whichever of the kings she preferred. She attached
herself first to the Seleucid cause, and was rewarded by
Seleucus II with the title of 'sacred and inviolable'; but as the
power of Pergamum grew she transferred her allegiance to
Attalus I. With the same political acumen the Smyrnaeans
were among the first to recognise in Rome the future mistress
of Asia, and in 195 B.C. they instituted the first temple and
cult of the deified Rome. Their ambassadors were also instru-
mental in bringing the Roman armies into the east against
Antiochus III.

Following the defeat of Antiochus at Magnesia in 190 B.C.

[1] For the Meles see below, pp. 45–7.

the Smyrnaeans lived uneventfully under the Attalids of Pergamum until the formation of the province of Asia. They gave no support to the pretender Aristonicus, and were rewarded by the Romans with the status of 'free city'. When Mithridates arrived Smyrna seems, no doubt unwillingly, to have submitted to him for a time, since Smyrnaean coins exist bearing the king's head; it is probable that this enforced disloyalty to Rome may have cost the city her 'freedom'.

Smyrna shared with the other cities in the miseries of the province under the Roman republic and in its prosperity under the empire. She was especially famous for her beauty. Strabo calls her the most beautiful of all cities, and other authors agree. Modern writers, too, are enthusiastic about the beauty of the site and its surroundings. But this was not what Strabo meant; he was referring not to the works of nature but to the works of man. Unfortunately, of the many fine buildings which adorned the city in antiquity hardly anything now remains. Strabo mentions particularly that the streets were paved with stone—a rarity in Hellenistic cities—but that the architects neglected to install drains, so that in rainy weather the streets were awash with refuse. The modern city has a somewhat similar trouble, as anyone's nose will tell him who walks along the front at Alsancak on a summer afternoon: the sewage is discharged into the bay, but the prevailing Imbat prevents it from getting away to sea.

Another building at Smyrna mentioned by Strabo is the Homereion, which he describes as a rectangular stoa containing a shrine and statue of Homer. Many cities claimed in antiquity to be Homer's birthplace, but by far the strongest claim is that of Smyrna. In particular, Homer is constantly associated with the River Meles, and the Meles was the river of Smyrna. The name of Smyrna does not occur in the *Iliad* or *Odyssey*, but neither does that of any Ionian city except Miletus—and that only as the home of barbarians.

The identity of the Meles has been much disputed. No fewer than six streams flow into the gulf between Bayraklı and Mt. Pagus, but only three of them can reasonably come in question. The most considerable is the Caravan Bridge River (Kemer Çayı or Uzun Dere on the Turkish map), which rises some ten or eleven miles to the south of the present city and flows round the base of Mt. Pagus into the sea about a mile east of Alsancak Point. This has acquired the name Meles in modern times, but is, in fact, the weakest candidate of the three. A detailed description of the Meles is given by Aelius Aristides, a distinguished citizen of Smyrna, orator and pamphleteer and *malade imaginaire*, who lived in the second century A.D. Many of his high-flown and effusive writings have survived, and will often be referred to in the following pages. If to Aristides' account we add the details supplied by other ancient writers, we obtain the following picture of the Meles. It rises at a number of springs close together in the suburbs of the city and immediately forms a circular lake; it is so short that the whole can be embraced in a single view, rising and joining the sea in the same area; it flows in an artificial channel smoothly and almost invisibly; it never varies in volume or appearance winter or summer; it is navigable even at its source; it has a cave at its springs, where Homer is said to have written his epics. In this description not one single item is appropriate to the Caravan Bridge River, which is twelve miles long and varies from a full rushing stream in winter to the merest trickle, or even a dry bed, in summer, and is not navigable in any part. On the other hand, the description applies remarkably well to the stream which reaches the sea a few hundred yards east of the Caravan Bridge River. This rises a little way inland from numerous springs and forms at once a large pool known as Halka Pınar (the Circular Spring), also called the Baths of Diana. From here it flows by an artificial cut to the sea, a distance of 1,300 yards. Being fed wholly by the springs, it varies hardly at all with the seasons, maintaining winter and summer a temperature of 75° Fahrenheit. In the last century Diana's Baths were a popular place of resort on summer evenings; today the springs, and part of the stream, are enclosed in the grounds of the Izmir waterworks, and supply the whole of Izmir and Karşıyaka with water. The Circular Spring is now a square pond, in and around which scores of springs well up, probably over a hundred in all. In a corner of the pond are the foundations of a small building with an apse, lying under water; this has no claim to any real antiquity, but several Ionic column-bases and other cut blocks are lying near.

The water of the pond and stream is beautifully clear, but the stream is fouled on its way to the sea by the discharge from factories. The name 'Diana's Baths' seems not to be ancient, but rather to have been attached to the pool in comparatively recent times in consequence of the discovery close to it of one complete statue and the head of another which were thought to represent Artemis. Halka Pınar is still a charming spot, surrounded by trees; and visitors who ask to see it are always most hospitably welcomed.

This Halka Pınar stream corresponds so admirably to the ancient accounts as to leave (in the writer's opinion) no doubt that this is the Meles described by Aristides and other authors of the Roman imperial age. Some scholars have doubted, however, whether it is also the Meles of the early city of Smyrna—that is, Homer's Meles. Two difficulties have been raised. First, there is no natural cave at Halka Pınar where Homer may have sat to write. Second, a passage in a 'Homeric' hymn to Artemis relates that the goddess, 'having watered her horses in deep-reeded Meles, drove swiftly through Smyrna to Claros rich in vines'. Neither author nor date of this little poem is known; but if it says that Artemis, travelling south, came to the Meles before she reached Smyrna at Bayraklı, then the Meles can only be the stream which comes down from the north and enters the sea close to the Bayraklı site. The goddess must in this case have travelled by the road over the summit of the Yamanlar Hills.[1] We must then suppose that the name Meles was transferred to Halka Pınar when the new city was founded. Colonists often take the old names with them. But such a transference to a river only two miles distant seems most unlikely, and it is far easier to suppose that the hymn in question is, in fact, of late origin and refers to the new Smyrna, in which case no difficulty arises. The 'cave' at the source of the Meles was no doubt an artificial structure which has now disappeared; we may compare the case of the 'cave' at Claros which for so long led searchers for the oracle astray.[2]

[1] Below, p. 96. [2] Below, p. 193.

Smyrna has one other Homeric association: here, according to tradition, was made the famous Pramnian wine, the beverage of heroes. Or at least according to one tradition, for there are rival candidates. Pliny, however, is precise: he says it came from Smyrna, from a spot near the temple of the Mother of the Gods. When we hear of it in Homer it is used not for drinking but for mixing in a kind of posset with cheese, meal and honey. It maintained its reputation in later times, and is described as neither sweet nor thick, but dry and rough and very potent; it was accordingly not popular at Athens, in spite of its aphrodisiac properties. The ancients seem in general to have preferred their wine sweet, and they frequently mixed it with honey; Pliny says that sweet wine, though harder on the digestion, is less intoxicating than dry. If this preference earns them the contempt of modern connoisseurs, this is really no more than they deserve, for there is no doubt that they horribly maltreated their wine. They doctored it not only with honey but with chalk and powdered marble, and they habitually drank it in a weak solution with water. Five parts of water to two of wine was normal; four parts to one was thought watery, and half-and-half very strong. Neat wine drinking was considered quite barbarous; and even in Greece today the popular word for wine means properly 'mixture'. Even more horrific was the common practice of mixing wine with sea-water, which was apparently thought to make it sweeter. The resinated wine familiar nowadays in Greece is not mentioned before Roman times; it seems to have been regarded as medicinal, being (we are told) good for a frigid stomach and causing no hangover. Polite custom required that the water should be poured first and the wine added afterwards. At the same time we hear that at Athens wine already mixed with water was sold in the streets—not dishonestly but for convenience.[1] Altogether one is left wondering what sort of wine the ancients made that called for so much adulteration.

Life at Smyrna proceeded uneventfully under the empire. Apparently unaffected by the great earthquake of A.D. 17,

[1] This *eau rougie* in effect took the place of the lemonade and other soft drinks of modern times.

which caused much damage to her neighbours, in 178 Smyrna
alone suffered from another earthquake that completely
ruined a large part of the city; it was rebuilt with help from
the emperor. The year 155 saw the martyrdom of Polycarp,
bishop of Smyrna, and the year 250 that of Pionius, both in
the stadium at Smyrna. Otherwise, apart from an occasional
visit by the reigning emperor, little or nothing occurred to
mark one year from another.

The excavation at Bayraklı produced historically important
results. It proved beyond doubt that Tepekule is indeed the
site of the old Aeolian Smyrna; it confirmed the tradition that
Smyrna was at first Aeolian and later Ionian, and it confirmed
also the fact and the approximate date of the city's destruction by Alyattes, king of Lydia. The actual buildings unearthed
are, however, somewhat unspectacular, and the visitor to
Tepekule is apt to be disappointed. Apart from the foundations
of a seventh-century temple there is little to be seen. The
small finds, on the other hand, are of first-rate quality, and the
best of them are exhibited in the Archaeological Museum in
the Kültür Park. Especially remarkable are the fragments of
the cult-statue of painted terracotta from the temple, and a
column-capital of such unusual form that it was doubted at
first whether it was a capital or a base. The most interesting
thing on the actual site is the mound of Tepekule itself at the
west end of the site. When examined by the excavators down
to a depth of 50 feet below the summit this mound was
found to consist entirely of ancient debris of the seventh
century. A pile of this size, rising actually higher than the
city wall, cannot be explained as a rubbish-dump; it can, in
fact, be nothing other than the siege-mound raised by Alyattes,
by means of which he achieved the capture of the city. It is
even possible to follow to some extent the course of events
during the siege. A mass of mud brick at one point in the
mound is likely to have come from the upper part of the city
wall, where a temporary breach was effected; at other points
carbonised wood and blackening show that the defenders'
counter-measures, too, were for a time successful.

During the 'village period', from the time of Alyattes to that

AT–D

of Alexander, the site at Bayraklı (as was noted above) was by no means deserted. To this period belong the ruins which are still to be seen on the hill to the north. Foremost among these is the so-called 'Tomb of Tantalus' (pp. 59–61 below). Ascribed by early explorers to the remotest antiquity of Smyrna, this remarkable structure is now believed to date to the sixth century B.C.; it is likely to be the tomb of some governor or grandee installed by the Persians. Lower down the hillside to the north-east is a great necropolis extending for the best part of a mile along the slope; the graves are for the most part of the tumulus type, having a general similarity to the Tomb of Tantalus, but on a much more modest scale. Several scores of these may still be seen.

On the summit of the higher hill to the north-west of the Tomb of Tantalus is a fortified enclosure which was formerly believed to be the acropolis of Old Smyrna. Recent investigation has tended to show, both from the sherds found there and from the style of the construction, that it belongs rather to the fourth century B.C. The complex consists of a heavily walled building, apparently a fortified mansion, with an open courtyard adjoining, and a number of lightly walled buildings which seem to be barns or outhouses. The whole is explained as the residence of some influential landlord or Persian appointee.

New Smyrna on Mt. Pagus was a city very different from the old. As is often the case, however, when a site has been continuously inhabited from ancient times, very little of the Hellenistic and Roman Smyrna survives. And the enormous growth of the city in the last twenty years has hidden much that was previously visible. Of the wall erected by Lysimachus nothing is now to be seen. The castle, Kadife Kale, at present standing on the top of the hill, is medieval; there are said to be fragments of Hellenic masonry under the existing walls, but the present writer has never been able to confirm this. The statement, quoted by Cadoux, that a tower at the south-west corner is of Hellenic work up to a third of its height seems to be pure fantasy. About a quarter of a mile to the west of the castle, close below the modern road, is the long hollow which marks the site of the Stadium, scene of the martyrdom of St. Polycarp; it is now completely built over (Pl. 1).

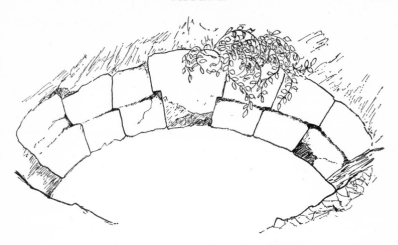

FIG. 3 Smyrna. Joggled Arch in Theatre

Of the theatre a little more remains. A walk up from Bas-mahane station through the old narrow streets and houses which escaped the disastrous fire of 1922 brings the visitor to a large hollow in the hillside at about two-thirds of its height. This hollow, approached by street no. 985 from the principal road up the hill, is also filled with recently built houses, but some traces of the theatre may be seen. On the west side a considerable part of the retaining wall of the cavea is still standing, and just inside it one of the vaulted passages to the seats is well preserved. It runs under house no. 11, and may be approached through the garden, with the owner's permission. This passage, or vomitorium, is interesting because it is roofed with a joggled arch. This form of arch, which gives great strength and security against slipping, is exceedingly rare in antiquity. The existing remains of the theatre at Smyrna belong to a reconstruction following the calamitous earth-quake of A.D. 178, and the joggled arch technique was no doubt adopted as a precaution against further shocks. A substantial portion of the stage-building is also extant, but it is now lost among the houses fronting the road. If this could be excavated, we should have a handsome addition to the antiquities of New Smyrna.

The Agora, or market-place, of the Roman city, called by the Turks Namazgâh, has been repeatedly excavated, and the greater part of it is now cleared. It forms a conspicuous feature of the town as seen from Kadife Kale. The central rectangular space was surrounded, as usual, by colonnaded porticoes, of which many of the columns are standing. On the north side is a large basilica, or hall for the transaction of business; beneath it are very handsome and well-preserved vaults. Statues of Poseidon and Demeter, and a number of inscriptions, came to light during the excavations.

The Baths of Agamemnon lie 10 km. outside the city on the west, half a mile south of the main road to Çeşme.[1] The name is ancient; the story ran that the Greeks under Agamemnon, in the course of the campaign in Asia which ended with the fall of Troy, fought a battle with the native inhabitants in the neighbourhood of Pergamum. The Greek wounded were advised by an oracle to resort for healing to the warm springs near the later city of Smyrna. These springs were said to be forty stades, or something over four miles, from the city; this seems to be an underestimate, but the identification of the spot is not really doubtful. A number of hot sulphurous springs rise in and around a small stream which dries up in summer; the waters, of a temperature up to 160° Fahrenheit, are considered good for rheumatism, sciatica, gallstones and eczema, and a regular thermal establishment is now installed and much patronised by the local residents. Aelius Aristides, too, frequently resorted there, and he tells us that it was on this spot that Asclepius first began to prophesy. Nothing remains of any ancient establishment; the few miserable ruins around the springs are not of any real antiquity (Pl. 4).

[1] On the signpost Agamemnon has become Ağamemnun; in time, no doubt, he will be Memnun Ağa.

★

CHAPTER THREE

Around Smyrna

THE NEIGHBOURHOOD of Smyrna is unusually rich in small
sites and single monuments, some of them of great interest
and high antiquity. Two of them in particular even date back
to the Hittite empire in the second millennium B.C.; they are
the only monuments of that civilisation to be found near the
coast, and almost the only evidence that Hittite control—or
at least influence—extended so far to the west.

The first is a figure carved in high relief on the steep mountainside close above the road at Akpınar, about four miles east
of Manisa. It is a seated female figure and is set in a recess in
the rock a few minutes' steep climb from the road. The arms
are folded on the breast; the feet appear to rest on two humps,
which have been variously understood to represent mountains
or footstools; from their rectangular shape the latter alternative seems the more probable. In a panel on the rock to the
right, outside the niche, some have thought to discern a
hieroglyphic inscription; but this—if indeed it exists—is now
utterly indecipherable. The Turks call this figure *Bereket
Ilâhesi*, the goddess of fertility, or sometimes merely *Taş Suret*,
the stone figure. The whole is badly weather-worn, and the
head in particular is much deformed, apparently by incrusta-
tions of lime. That the monument is of Hittite workmanship
is generally agreed, though full-face figures in high relief are
hardly common in Hittite art. It represents no doubt a female
deity, probably the mother goddess whom the Greeks later
called Cybele (Pl. 3).

The Hittite character of this figure was suggested as long
ago as 1880 by A. H. Sayce; but for a long time both before
and after that date a very different identification was in favour.
According to the ancient legend, Niobe, daughter of Tantalus,

53

was mother of seven sons and seven daughters, and was rash enough to claim superiority over the goddess Leto, who had only two children, Apollo and Artemis. Thereupon Leto's two slew Niobe's fourteen, and Niobe herself was turned into stone on Mt. Sipylus (now the Manisa Dağı), where she continued to weep for her lost children. When scholars first learned of the existence of the Taş Suret they not unnaturally concluded that this was no other than the petrified Niobe. The legend concerning Sipylus is mentioned by Homer and by Sophocles; and if this were our only evidence we might well believe that they had the Taş Suret in mind. That they speak of Niobe as 'on the lonely mountains' and 'on the summit of Sipylus, where the rain and snow never leave her' might be forgiven to poets who, as we are often reminded, are not geographers. But in fact we have much more reliable evidence than this, the accounts of two writers who were both natives of the district. Pausanias is very clear. 'This Niobe', he says, 'I have myself seen when I went up Mt. Sipylus; observed from close by it is just a rocky cliff bearing no resemblance to a woman, mourning or otherwise; but if you stand a little way off you will fancy you see a woman downcast and weeping.' Quintus of Smyrna, a poet who wrote perhaps 200 years after Pausanias, agrees with him entirely: seen from a distance the figure resembles a woman, 'but when you come close it is seen to be just a high rock, a fragment broken off Sipylus'. These authoritative descriptions are quite unsuited to the Taş Suret, of which the exact opposite is true; it is only when the observer comes close that he recognises a carved figure of a woman. Pausanias and Quintus are obviously describing an accidental freak of nature. That scholars were willing, in face of this evidence, to accept the Taş Suret as the phenomenon in question is due to a temptation which constantly besets explorers of the ancient world—namely, before the whole area is thoroughly examined, to identify what is found on the ground with what happens to be mentioned in the fraction of the ancient literature which we possess. In 1938 C. J. Cadoux can still write: 'It is hardly likely that Pausanias' Niobe was a different figure from that known to Homer, or that the latter was other than the Taş Suret; moreover, all efforts to discover a natural

Niobe-rock other than Taş Suret have failed.' This last statement, which is really the heart of the matter, was true when
Cadoux wrote; but it is so no longer. Immediately after
Cadoux's book appeared the true Niobe was found by H. T.
Bossert. It is on the fringe of the town of Manisa on the south-
west, and hardly higher above the plain than the Taş Suret.
From a short distance above the rock presents the appearance
shown in the photograph on Pl. 2, from which the reader
may judge of the resemblance to a weeping woman. That this
is the figure of Niobe described by Pausanias and Quintus
cannot be doubted. As for the Taş Suret, it is not altogether
unmentioned in Greek literature. Pausanias tells us that the
Magnesians of Sipylus possess, 'on the rock of Coddinus', a
statue of the Mother of the Gods which is older than any other;
and they say it was made by Broteas the son of Tantalus. This
can hardly be other than the Taş Suret. After the memory of
the Hittites had passed away, it was natural that tradition
should connect the figure with the house of Tantalus.[1] And
the identification with the Mother of the Gods is highly likely
to be in fact correct.

The other Hittite monument in the neighbourhood of
Smyrna is in the Karabel pass, which leads south from the
Smyrna-Sardis road a little east of Kemalpaşa (formerly Nif)
to Dağkızılca and the country around Torbalı and Tire. At
a point just four miles from the main highway the road passes
under an ornamental arch; immediately beyond this arch,
some 70 feet above the road on the left, is a figure cut in low
relief in a panel on the rock facing south. It is rather over life-
size and represents a warrior holding in his right hand a bow
and in his left a spear, wearing a short tunic and a conical cap.
Between the head and the spear are some partially obliterated
hieroglyphics, not easy to distinguish; the accompanying
sketch shows what the writer believed he could see.[2] This figure
is similar in style and execution to the Hittite monuments of
central Anatolia, and probably portrays a war-god. The Turks
call it Eti Baba, the Hittite Father (Pl. 7).

[1] For Tantalus see below, p. 58 ff.
[2] Below the bird it is possible in some lights to imagine that one sees
the shape of an animal resembling a dog facing left.

FIG. 4 KARABEL.
Hittite inscription

But the Karabel warrior has a particular interest in that he is mentioned by Herodotus. The historian is speaking of Sesostris, king of Egypt in the nineteenth century B.C., and says: 'There are also two figures of this man carved on the rocks in Ionia, on the road by which one goes from the Ephesian country to Phocaea, and on that from Sardis to Smyrna. In either place (*or* on either side) is carved a man four and a half cubits in height, holding a spear in his right hand and a bow in his left . . . and across his chest from shoulder to shoulder is a hieroglyphic inscription saying "By my own shoulders I won this country" '. When the Karabel figure was first discovered by European scholars about 1840, it was at once recognised as one of these carvings of 'Sesostris'; the other remained for some time a mystery, till in 1875 a second figure was found in the same Karabel gorge, about 200 yards from the first. This second figure was cut on a fallen rock (apparently after it fell) and though badly damaged was evidently similar to the other. It has since disappeared, having probably been broken up for road-making in 1927. After this discovery it is virtually certain that Herodotus was referring to these two figures, which stood one on either side of the road leading by the Karabel pass. It is true that this spot is not on the road from Sardis to Smyrna, but four miles to the south of it; and indeed Herodotus' language suggests that he was thinking of two places on two separate roads; but this (in the present writer's opinion) is certainly because Herodotus had not seen the figures himself and had not clearly understood the information he was given. Hence his other inaccuracies in describing them; the mistake about the weapons held in the two hands is particularly characteristic, confusion between the figure's right hand and the spectator's right hand being especially easy in an oral description. Herodotus' informant was trying to say that the two carvings stood on either side of the road from the Ephesian country to Phocaea, close to where that road crossed the one from Sardis to Smyrna, but Herodotus understood him to mean one carving on each of these two roads.

The mistake concerning the identity of the person represented is easily understood. Herodotus attributes to Sesostris extensive conquests, ranging as far as Thrace, which are, in fact, unhistorical; since the Greeks knew nothing of the Hittites it was natural to identify the Karabel figures with the supposed Egyptian conqueror. Sesostris is said to have erected, in the lands he conquered, commemorative stelae which Herodotus claims to have seen himself; since he does not make the same claim in the case of the rock-carvings, it is a fair assumption that his information was at second hand.[1]

The question remains how a road from Ephesian territory to Phocaea came to pass through the Karabel gorge. From Ephesus itself to Phocaea the way would naturally be through Smyrna, but from the Tire valley, which belonged to the territory of Ephesus, the natural route is not so obvious. The choice would be affected by the lowest point at which the Hermus could be forded, for in the fifth century B.C. there was no bridge. This point seems at present to be at Emiralem, and may well have been so in antiquity;[2] in this case, the route may have been over the Karabel pass and then westwards, passing north of Belkahve to join the northward road from Smyrna over the Yamanlar Dağı.[3] If the ford was higher up

---

[1] See also p. 272 below.   [2] Below, p. 96.
[3] Below, p. 96.

the river than Emiralem, the easier route skirting the east
and north sides of Sipylus through Magnesia would no doubt
be chosen.

The region of Mt. Sipylus is closely associated with the early
legends concerning Tantalus and Pelops, in the days before the
Greeks ever set foot in Asia Minor. Some scholars have
thought that the names of Tantalus and Sipylus derive from
the Hittite kings Tudhaliyas and Suppiluliumas; but in the
Greek tradition Tantalus was king of Phrygia and Sipylus
was in very early times reckoned as Phrygian. Tantalus was a
favourite of the gods, and on one occasion invited them to a
banquet; wishing apparently to test their powers of percep-
tion, he cut up the body of his son Pelops, boiled it and served
it at table. The gods duly detected the trick with the exception
of Demeter, who, lost in grief for her daughter Persephone,
absent-mindedly ate a piece of the shoulder. Pelops was restored to life, and Tantalus, either for this or for some other
misconduct, was condemned in Hades to the torture which
has given us the verb to tantalize. Tormented with thirst, and
standing in a lake, he found the waters receding every time
he bent to drink. Pelops was later driven from Sipylus and
crossed the Aegean to the Peloponnese, which took its name
from him.

Pausanias, as a native of the district, has a good deal to say
about these legendary figures. 'There are', he says, 'to this day
indications of Pelops' and Tantalus' residence in my country—
a lake of Tantalus named after him, and a far from incon-
spicuous tomb, and a throne of Pelops on Sipylus, on the
summit (*or* a summit) of the mountain above the sanctuary
of the Plastene Mother.' Elsewhere he notes that he has
himself seen the tomb of Tantalus on Sipylus, that it is well
worth seeing, and that he has noticed white eagles flying
around the lake of Tantalus. Other writers record that there
was once on Sipylus a city called either Tantalis or Sipylus or
Idea, but this was destroyed by an earthquake and its place
occupied by a lake. This last tradition was known to Aristotle
and survives strongly in later authors.

Since the exploration of the country began in modern times,

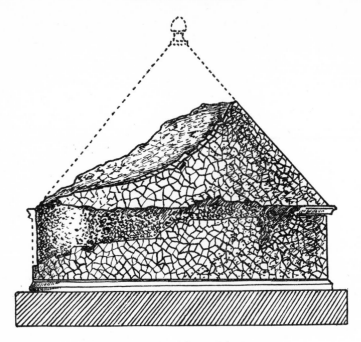

Fig. 5 'Tomb of Tantalus' in 1835

great efforts and many words have been expended in the
attempt to identify these various features on the ground. For
the city and lake of Tantalus no satisfactory results have been
achieved, and the whole problem has been complicated by the
uncertainty whether the Yamanlar Dağı can fairly be reckoned
a part of Sipylus. There is near the summit of the Yamanlar
Dağı a small but deep lake, surrounded by pinewoods and
accessible by a bad road from the Yamanlar sanatorium; it is
called Karagöl. That there was ever a city in this position is
improbable in the extreme; nevertheless it is not unlikely that
this is the 'lake of Tantalus' which went under that name in
Pausanias' time; the eagles that he saw there suggest that it
lay high up.

In the identification of the other items, the tomb of Tantalus, the throne of Pelops and the sanctuary of Mother Plastene,
opinions may be grouped into two schools, the Smyrnaean

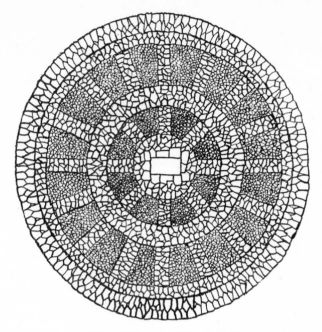

FIG. 6 'Tomb of Tantalus'

which finds them all on the Yamanlar Dağı, and the Magnesian
which finds them all in the vicinity of Manisa.

The founder of the 'Smyrnaean' school was the Frenchman
Texier, who visited Smyrna in 1835. His attention was caught
by a fine circular built tomb on the summit of the rise immediately behind the village of Bayraklı; he at once dubbed it
the Tomb of Tantalus, which name it continues to bear among
the local residents. It stood then some 40 feet high and was
originally about 90 feet; it consisted of a circular drum with
an outer wall of polygonal masonry, surmounted by a conical
superstructure. Nearly in the centre is the grave-chamber, of
regular masonry converging towards the top, leaving a gap
which was covered by a cap-stone. From this chamber internal
walls radiate to the circumference, the spaces between them
being filled with small stones. This superb monument was
deliberately demolished by Texier in order to discover its
mode of construction, an act for which he has never been

forgiven; today all that survives is the lower part of the
drum, the central chamber, and a mass of stones. That this
tomb is worthy to rank as the tomb of Tantalus cannot be
denied, and it is not impossible that it may have done so in
Pausanias' day; that it can really date back to the supposed
time of Tantalus is out of the question. As was noted above,
it belongs evidently with the rest of the necropolis on the
slopes below (Pl. 5).

The other two features, the throne of Pelops and the sanctuary of Mother Plastene, go together; the throne, we are told,
stood above the sanctuary. The 'Smyrnaeans' find them in the
heart of the Yamanlar, in the great hollow on the south side
of the summit. Close above the village of Sancaklı, on a hill
formerly known as Ada Tepe, is a fortified enclosure surrounding two peaks of rock; the southern of these is cut away at one
corner to form a kind of chamber open to the sky.[1] This chamber was identified with the sanctuary of Mother Plastene, and
until recently was called locally the 'hiéron de Cybèle', since
Plastene is certainly a name for Cybele, the Mother of the
Gods. The throne of Pelops was then to be looked for higher
up, and was found in a conspicuous peak of rock between Ada
Tepe and the summit; seen from below this peak bears some
resemblance to a seat with a sloping back. In 1945 the
'chamber' on Ada Tepe was excavated by the present writer
in collaboration with Rüstem Duyuran, then Director of the
Izmir Museum; it proved to be a cistern, and the whole site
is evidently a military outpost. These identifications accordingly fall to the ground, and no others are offered in their place.

The 'Magnesian' school, on the other hand, finds all the
monuments in question within a small area to the east of
Manisa.

About a mile east of the Taş Suret, at the very foot of
Sipylus where the mountain meets the plain, is a rock-cut
tomb of remarkable, if not unique, design. In front is a platform approached by a flight of steps; from it a door leads to
two rock-cut chambers, one behind the other. Both chambers
are quite plain apart from a shallow 'pillow' for the dead man's
head. Above the door the façade slopes backward, following

[1] Below, pp. 65–6.

FIG. 7 'Tomb of St. Charalambos'

the line of the mountain-face; all round it a trench is cut in
the rock, which has the effect of delineating the monument
and of protecting it from the rain-water. This tomb was
formerly known as the tomb of St. Charalambos, but seems
now to have no name. It is undoubtedly very ancient and may
well be Pausanias' tomb of Tantalus.

But the 'Magnesians'' strongest card is the sanctuary of
Mother Plastene. This sanctuary was definitely located, at
least for Roman times, by discoveries made in 1887 at a point
on the plain one hour east of Manisa and some fifteen minutes
from the Taş Suret. Two inscriptions were found actually
naming Mother Plastene. Unless therefore we are prepared to
suppose that the sanctuary was transplanted, any location of
it in the neighbourhood of Smyrna is excluded. And since the
inscriptions are roughly contemporary with Pausanias, the
sanctuary which he mentions as existing in his time can certainly be no other than this. It is likely therefore that Mother
Plastene and the Mother of the Gods, whose statue (the Taş
Suret) was made by Broteas, are one and the same; the sanctuary, for which there was no room on the steep mountainside,
stood a short distance away on the plain.

FIG. 8 'Throne of Pelops'

The throne of Pelops must accordingly be sought on Mt. Sipylus not far from this spot, and a plausible identification is, in fact, forthcoming. Some two-thirds of the way from the Taş Suret to the 'tomb of St. Charalambos' is a great cleft in the mountainside known as Yarıkkaya; on the west side of this, some 900 feet up and accessible at present only by a perilous 'chimney', is an interesting and certainly very ancient site. It is on a steep rock slope some 150 yards in length, in which are cut half a dozen cisterns and the lower parts of a score of houses which were perhaps finished with sun-dried brick. And at the very top, in a steeply sloping rock, is a cutting resembling a large seat. This was perhaps originally an altar, but in view of its shape and size it may well have passed in antiquity under the name of the Throne of Pelops. The rest of the site has been claimed as the city of Tantalus mentioned above, but is distinctly exiguous for the part.

On all counts therefore the 'Magnesians' have the best of the argument.

The other sites in the vicinity of Smyrna are military, connected primarily with the new city founded by the desire of Alexander, and form a strong ring of defensive outposts.

The most important is that on Belkahve. Where the main road from Smyrna to Sardis crosses the pass from the plain of Bornova to that of Turgutlu, directly above the road on the left is a conical hill conspicuous from Smyrna and all parts of the plain. The west face is steep, and the hill is more easily ascended from the south and east. The summit is encircled by a ring-wall whose line may be easily traced, though seldom more than a single course is visible above ground. From the summit two interior walls run down to the ring-wall, forming an inner enclosure. Near the summit is a pit which may have served as a water-tank. At various points on the site more than a dozen rectangular sockets have been cut in the rock; these originally held stelae carrying inscriptions. One of these stelae is in the Izmir Museum; it records the presentation of golden crowns by the defenders of the fort to their commander and his family. An inscription to similar effect is still standing on the site, on a stone in the line of the ring-wall near the north-east corner, so weathered as to be almost illegible. It is probable that all the sockets held inscriptions in similar terms. The two mentioned date from about the end of the second century B.C., and the abundant sherds lying around the summit are of similar date. But the site was occupied in much earlier times than this. On the west side a steep glen leads down the hillside, and this is barred at its lower end by a massive wall nearly 20 feet thick, of very ancient appearance; in the filling of this wall archaic sherds have been found, and it dates no doubt to the time of the early Smyrna at Bayraklı. Indeed, this site, dominating the approach from the east, is such an essential key-point that its possession must always have been indispensable to the occupants of Smyrna.

The Belkahve fortress was supported by two other strong-points, one to the east and one to the west. About six miles south-east of Kemalpaşa, at the north foot of Mahmut Dağı, the ancient Mt. Draco, behind the village of Kızılca, rises a high rock of whitish appearance called Akkaya. On the summit of this are numerous rock-cuttings, and on a smoothed rock-wall on the south side are cut inscriptions of similar date and similar content to those on Belkahve. The summit com-

mands an extensive prospect and overlooks the main highway
to Sardis and the east. The north face is precipitous, but quite
easy to climb; in it is an interesting rock-cut monument whose
purpose is disputed. Rough steps lead up to a double chamber
divided by a central pillar; at the back is a bench. On the
façade, to either side of the pillar, sloping lines have been cut
to suggest a pediment; on the right only one line has been cut.
At the left side is a narrow channel in the sloping rock-face,
apparently intended to carry off rain-water. This monument
has been variously understood as a look-out post or, with
greater probability, as a tomb. The absence of a grave-chamber
and the inadequate provision for a burial have been explained
as due to the tomb being unfinished. Its date is difficult or
impossible to determine (Pl. 6).

Just outside the town of Bornova on the north-west, a few
feet only above the plain, are the ruins of another fort, now
converted into a farmyard. Little remains of the original walls,
those now standing being modern; but the foundations of
seven round towers are still clearly visible. Nothing else remains. If this structure is genuinely ancient (which some
scholars have doubted), it is most naturally explained as a
military installation in support of the greater fortress at
Belkahve. It can hardly be more than a barracks, as its position
is weak in the extreme, being easily commanded from the
slope above.

The northern approaches to Smyrna were similarly defended
by a group of forts, of which the most important is on Ada
Tepe. This site is on a steep hill close above the village of
Sancaklı, to which a road leads in about two and a half hours
from Karşıyaka through the village of Alurca (formerly
Gövdelin). The fort is now known as Sancaklı Kalesi. The hill
rises to two peaks of rock connected by a ridge; that on the
south forms a sheer precipice over 100 feet high, easily visible
from Smyrna and called locally Ölüm Kayası, 'the rock of
death'. The upper part of the hill is enclosed by a ring-wall of
varying style and quality; the best-preserved piece, on the
west, is of polygonal masonry with a strong tendency to
coursing, a style peculiar to the Hellenistic period. On the
summit of the southern peak is a shallow water-trap, and in

the eastern corner of this peak is a rectangular recess some 20 feet by 12 feet, in the floor of which is a cistern of regular masonry. This is the spot which was formerly believed to be the sanctuary of the Plastene Mother.[1] The cistern was fed by a channel leading down from the water-trap above. It is not certain when this fort was originally constructed, but it is clear from the evidence of the sherds that its main occupation was in Hellenistic times. Placed some 1,300 feet above sea-level, about half-way from the coast to the summit of Yaman-lar Daği, it is well situated to command the route over the mountain from the north.

The fort on Ada Tepe, like that at Belkahve, was supported by two subsidiary strongpoints. One of these, now called Çobanpınarı, is on a steep hill immediately above Alurca on the east; it is small and unimpressive. The other is low down, close beside the modern road which leads from Karşıyaka to the sanatorium. Some forty-five minutes walk from Soğuk-kuyu, between the road and a stream, is a hillock crowned by a conspicuous cluster of white rocks. On this hill are numerous cuttings and a deep well sunk into the rock; the site is enclosed by a wall which is now mostly reduced to a pile of rubble. The position is a weak one and, like that at Bornova, it probably served as a barracks.

On the south side Smyrna was defended, so far as is known, by only one fort. This is at Akçakaya, among the mountains some five or six miles to the south-west of the city centre. On the hilltop are remains of a ring-wall, houses and a cistern. This site overlooks, at a distance of about two miles, the main route southward from Smyrna which is followed by the present highroad and railway; it is similar in character to that at Ada Tepe, but has been much damaged by the activities of lime-burners; there is a large disused kiln just below the site. In this connection it may perhaps be observed that the Turks are seldom responsible for the destruction of ancient buildings by lime-burning; the blame is much more often to be laid on the Greeks.

[1] Above, p. 61.

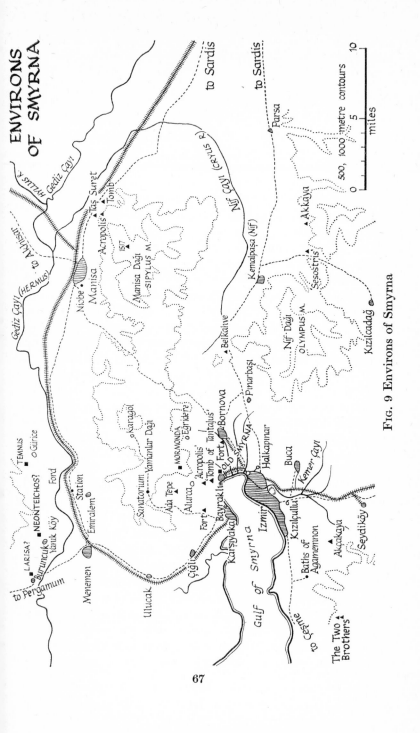

FIG. 9 Environs of Smyrna

67

★

CHAPTER FOUR

Pergamum

OF ALL the cities in this region, the situation of Pergamum is unquestionably the most impressive. The first view of the hill on approaching from the south is not easily forgotten. Smyrna on Mt. Pagus is superbly placed, but for sheer power and majesty the citadel of Pergamum is unrivalled. A royal city indeed. Some 1,300 feet in height, it rises between two streams, tributaries of the Caicus. Steep, almost precipitous, on all sides but one, it forms a type of city site much favoured in antiquity; Athens is a familiar example. Lying back some distance from the sea, however, it was not occupied by the early Greek settlers in the age of the migration, and played no part in the great upsurge of culture in the archaic period. Sherds found in the excavation show that there was a settlement of some sort on the hill at least by the eighth century B.C., but this was not a Greek city. Its distance from the coast is also the reason why it was not included in the Athenian maritime confederacy in the fifth century.

Pergamum makes a first fleeting appearance in history in 399 B.C.—the year of Socrates' condemnation in Athens. At that time the Spartans, fresh from their resounding defeat of the Athenians in the Peloponnesian War, were disputing with the Persians possession of the west coast. Xenophon, safely returned from his adventures in the interior of the Persian empire, decided to offer his services to the Spartan commander, and Pergamum was the scene of their meeting. The town was held by the descendants of a Greek who had betrayed his city to the Persians at the time of Darius' invasion in 490 B.C., and had been rewarded by the Great King for his treachery by the gift of land in this neighbourhood. His family, though nominally Persian subjects, were in effect independent rulers of their

domain, and readily entertained the Greek forces fighting
against Persia.

After this incident nothing is heard of Pergamum until after
the death of Alexander. When Lysimachus came into control
of western Asia Minor and found himself in possession of a
vast treasure from the spoils of conquest, he deposited a part
of this treasure at Pergamum; the sum is said to have been
9,000 talents, or something like £10,000,000 sterling at the
present day. To guard this treasury he appointed a certain
Paphlagonian by the name of Philetaerus. When Lysimachus
was killed in battle in 281 B.C. the country came largely under
the hand of Antiochus, king of Syria; Philetaerus, however,
remained in control of Pergamum and the treasure, and no
serious effort was made to dislodge him.

From this point begins the emergence of Pergamum as a
power in the Hellenistic world. Philetaerus lived until 263 B.C.,
and devoted his energies to establishing his position. His
wealth can hardly be called ill-gotten, as Lysimachus left no
heir to claim it, and Philetaerus' title to it was as good as
another's; and he used it sensibly. By means of handsome
dedications and gifts of money in time of need he won the
favour of the neighbouring cities and kept on good terms with
Antiochus; at the same time he embellished his city with
temples and other new buildings.

Eumenes, adopted son and successor of Philetaerus, was
accordingly able to take over a firmly established dynasty.
Eumenes is reckoned the first of the kings of Pergamum,
though, in fact, neither he nor Philetaerus ever formally took
that title. He enlarged the city's territory in the near neighbourhood, but otherwise little is recorded of him. An inscription tells us that the people of Pergamum granted him divine
honours; and all his successors, as was normal for Hellenistic
kings, were worshipped in their lifetime.

Eumenes was succeeded in 241 B.C. by his adopted son
Attalus, whose long reign of forty-four years is a tale of wars
and battles. His fame rests primarily on his great victory over
the Gauls in 230 B.C. These Gauls were a branch of the central
European nation who had migrated eastwards in the previous
century. They were invited into Asia in 279 B.C. by Nicomedes,

king of Bithynia, who needed mercenaries for his private purposes, and were permitted by him to settle in the district of Asia Minor which from that time bore the name Galatia. Once established, they made themselves a nuisance to all and sundry. Many of the Greek cities suffered from their attacks, for they were a wild and warlike people, and immunity from their attentions could only be had by the payment of tribute. Both Philetaerus and Eumenes had found it advisable to pay this Danegeld, but Attalus felt himself strong enough to refuse. Deprived of this source of income, the Gauls advanced to collect it for themselves. In the ensuing battle Attalus was victorious, and the Gauls were driven away from the west coast. As with many famous victories, legends grew up around this battle. It is said that Attalus' soldiers were terrified at the prospect of a contest with the formidable barbarians; however, when sacrifice was made before the battle the priest announced that the words 'Victory for the King' had become miraculously written on the victim's entrails. Encouraged by this evidence of divine favour, they fought heroically against great odds. It transpired later that Attalus had written the words backwards on his own hand in ink, and while examining the victim had imprinted them on the liver.

After this outstanding achievement Attalus adopted the titles of King and Saviour. A large part of his reign was occupied, with very varying success, in contesting western Asia Minor with the kings of Syria. At one time he was the most powerful monarch in the east, but by the end of his reign his kingdom was no larger than at the beginning. Towards the end of the third century the Romans began to occupy themselves in Greece, and Attalus became their ally. In this capacity he was associated with the first advent of Romans into Asia. An oracle had advised them to transport the Mother of the Gods from Asia to Rome; having no standing in Asia, they applied for help to Attalus, who received the envoys kindly and handed over to them the sacred stone which was believed to represent the Great Mother.

Though Attalus bequeathed to his successor Eumenes II no larger territory than he had himself inherited, he had made Pergamum a force to be reckoned with, and he had earned the goodwill of the Romans. It was Eumenes who benefited from this. When the Romans became reluctantly embroiled with Antiochus the Great of Syria, and finally defeated him in the crucial battle of Magnesia in 190 B.C., faced with the problem of disposing of his possessions in Asia Minor they handed over most of them to Eumenes. At this point the kingdom of Pergamum reached the height of its power and prosperity; it was a power gained by favour of the Romans, and due to their unwillingness to encumber themselves with territory in the east. Eumenes now controlled the whole of the west coastal region as far south as the Maeander, and the centre of the peninsula as far east as the modern town of Konya.

Eumenes, like Pericles at Athens, used the wealth of which he found himself master for the beautification of his capital. The city had hitherto occupied only the upper part of the hill, above the present car park; Eumenes extended it far down the slope, and enclosed the whole with a new wall. This work involved artificial terracing on a vast scale. At this time were constructed not only the lower agora and the great gymnasium, but also, in the older part of the city, the famous library and the altar of Zeus.

All the rulers of Pergamum were enthusiastic patrons of culture in all its forms. In art, sculpture held pride of place, and an individual Pergamene style developed, of which the Dying Gaul and the friezes of the altar of Zeus are well-known examples. The Attalids made generous donations to the philosophical schools at Athens, and collected at their own court many of the most distinguished poets, philosophers, scientists and scholars of the day. Of the famous library more will be said below. In this way Pergamum gained a reputation rivalling that of Athens or Alexandria.

Eumenes was not left by his neighbours to enjoy his new prosperity in peace, but was obliged to defend his territory not only against the Gauls but against Pharnaces, king of Pontus, and Prusias, king of Bithynia; the latter was assisted by Rome's old enemy Hannibal. Having reason also to fear attack from Perseus, king of Macedonia, he aided the Romans in their campaign against him; Pergamene troops took part in the decisive battle of Pydna in 168 B.C., which put an end to the kingdom of Macedonia. Towards the end of his reign, however, a certain coolness arose between Eumenes and the Romans, whose favour was conferred rather on the king's brother, Attalus. Long troubled by ill health, Eumenes died in 159 B.C.

Attalus II, already over 60 when he succeeded his brother, made it his firm policy to do nothing without consulting the Romans. His reign of twenty-one years was mostly occupied by a succession of wars. His most troublesome antagonist was Prusias of Bithynia, who at one moment advanced to the outskirts of Pergamum itself; we are told that he offered sacrifice one day at the Asclepieum and the next day carried off the statue of Asclepius. This war was ended by Roman intervention in 154 B.C. Eight years later at Corinth the troops of Attalus assisted the Romans in the campaign which finally extinguished the freedom of Greece. On his death in 138 he was succeeded by his nephew of the same name.

Attalus III, during his short reign of five years, showed himself utterly unlike his predecessors. He was, we are told, cruel and suspicious, hated by the people; he seldom left his palace, but devoted himself to the study of strange sciences; the cultivation of medicinal and poisonous plants was apparently his particular hobby, and these he tested upon condemned criminals. Zoology, husbandry and metal-working also occupied his attention; his book on agriculture is quoted as an authority by Roman writers on the subject. This portrait of the last king of Pergamum, as drawn by the literary authorities, is to some extent belied by the inscriptions, which show that he did at times take the field, and even won a victory over some unnamed enemy. His crowning eccentricity came last of all. When he died of disease in 133 B.C. it was found that in his will he had bequeathed his kingdom to Rome. For this startling and unprecedented act various motives have been suggested; but however the king's mind may have worked, his famous bequest was really no more than a logical conclusion to the trend of events. Roman influence during the last three reigns had been growing steadily stronger; the annexation, however unwillingly, by Rome of western Asia Minor was, sooner or later, inevitable, and Attalus did no more than hasten it.

The Romans, however, were not permitted to enter peaceably into their inheritance. A certain Aristonicus, reputed to be a bastard son of Eumenes II, at once disputed their claim. Collecting a large army of mercenaries, slaves and other assorted elements, he defied the Romans with considerable success for three years, and even defeated the consul who was sent against him. In 130, however, he was in his turn defeated and taken captive to Rome.

The kingdom of the Attalids was thereupon dismembered. The outlying portions were attached to the principates or provinces which seemed most appropriate, while the core of the kingdom was converted into the Roman province of Asia. The province thus formed comprised the western coastal area, that is the regions of Mysia, Lydia, Ionia, Caria and part of Phrygia, and so included all the district dealt with in the present work.

Pergamum itself was left as a free city, in accordance with Attalus' will. But freedom, within a Roman province, no longer meant what it used to mean. When Mithridates, king of Pontus, invaded the province in 88 B.C. as the self-professed liberator of the Greek cities from Roman oppression, Pergamum joined him readily enough, and served for a time as his headquarters; the massacre of the Italians was carried out there with particular unscrupulousness, and even the sanctuary of the temples was not respected. This was the city's last attempt to play a part independent of Rome, and from that time forward the political history of Pergamum is that of the province of Asia.

The city of the Attalids is still not completely excavated, and of the surviving buildings none is standing to its original height; nevertheless it is not hard to imagine how the city must have looked. It is built on a series of terraces, each artificially constructed. The great wall of Eumenes II is best seen at the extreme summit of the hill, where it stands to an impressive height in regular courses of ashlar masonry.

Not far from the top of the hill are the ruins of the famous Pergamene library. This stood close behind the temple of Athena, and the association is not fortuitous, since Athena was a patroness of learning. The library comprised a group of at least five rooms, probably more; of these only the easternmost is now recognisable as having contained books, most of the others not being preserved to a sufficient height. Round three sides of this room runs a kind of stone bench, some 3 feet high and wide, now almost flush with the ground; between this and the walls is a space of some 18 inches. In the fourth wall is the door (not now recognisable), and in the middle of the wall opposite, where the stone bench is widened to receive it, stood a statue of Athena. A row of holes in the walls held staples or hooks to which the wooden bookshelves were fastened. The shelves stood in the space between the walls and the bench, which accordingly covered the lower part of them. The purpose of the stone bench was to keep the public away from the books while enabling the library attendants to reach them. So at least the excavators explain the unusual features of this interesting room.

Books in the classical period consisted of a long strip of papyrus about a foot wide, rolled around a stick. The reader held the roll in both hands, unrolling with one hand and rolling up with the other as he proceeded. Though reasonably convenient for reading a work through, this was highly inconvenient for other purposes—as, for example, finding a reference. No doubt this explains in part why quotations by one ancient author from another are so often inaccurate. For the introduction of the paged book, or codex as it was called, we are indebted to the kings of Pergamum.

Book-collecting was with the Attalids almost a mania. Eumenes II and his successor in particular combed the kingdom for works of all kinds, which they transported, with or without payment, to the capital. The physician Galen, himself a Pergamene, says that manuscripts were forged to satisfy the king's desire for books and more books; and we hear that at Scepsis in the Troad the owners of the precious library of Aristotle, loth to surrender it, were constrained to hide it underground, where the moths and damp got at it, thus accounting for the defective state of the text of Aristotle's works. The results of this collecting-fever were impressive; the Pergamene library is said to have totalled 200,000 volumes.

If this is anywhere near correct, we must suppose a considerable annexe; the capacity of the room described above has been estimated at some 17,000 volumes.

The only rival to a library of this size was that at Alexandria in Egypt, and the rivalry seems in fact to have been keen. Egypt was the principal, almost the only, source of papyrus; and the Roman writer Varro tells us that Ptolemy, jealous of the growing Pergamene collection, prohibited its export. Thereupon the king of Pergamum, unable any longer to have manuscripts copied on papyrus, resorted for this purpose to the use of skins, as the Ionians had done long before. From this 'Pergamene paper' comes our own word parchment. Skins, being much thicker and heavier than papyrus, were less suitable for rolled volumes, and it was found preferable to make them into paged books. This new type of book, though more expensive, soon found general favour; for several hundred years both kinds continued simultaneously, but the much greater convenience of the codex led eventually to the abandonment of the papyrus roll. With the development of paper in modern times it has become possible to secure the advantages of both types.

The rivalry between the two great libraries was finally extinguished when the Pergamene collection was presented by Antony, who did not own it, to Cleopatra, who had other things to do than read it. It was taken to Alexandria, where it survived, somewhat diminished, till the seventh century. Then the Caliph Omar, or his significantly named lieutenant, Amr ibn el-Ass, reasoning that if a book was inconsistent with the Koran it was impious, and if consistent, unnecessary, ordered the entire library to be destroyed.

A little lower down the hill stood an equally famous monument, the altar of Zeus. Only the foundation is now to be seen on the spot, but enough fragments were found to permit an almost complete restoration. The foundation, some 120 by 112 feet, comprises a vast criss-cross of walls resembling, as a modern writer expresses it, a huge waffle-iron. On this was erected a solid platform, or podium, nearly 20 feet high. Round three sides of the platform ran a wall, the fourth or west side being largely occupied by a broad flight of steps. In front of

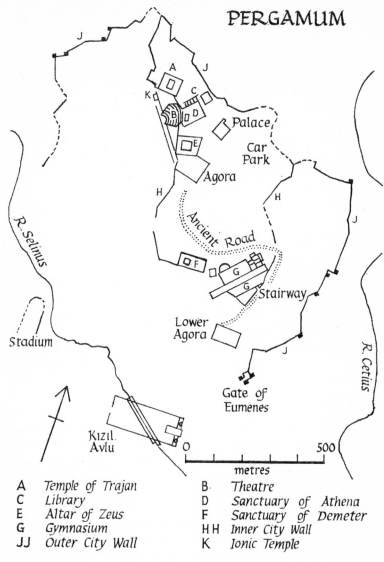

PERGAMUM

Palace

Car Park

Agora

Ancient Road

R. Selinus

R. Cetius

Stairway

Lower Agora

Stadium

Gate of Eumenes

Kızıl Avlu

O   500

metres

A	Temple of Trajan	B	Theatre
C	Library	D	Sanctuary of Athena
E	Altar of Zeus	F	Sanctuary of Demeter
G	Gymnasium	H H	Inner City Wall
JJ	Outer City Wall	K	Ionic Temple

FIG. 10 Plan of Pergamum

the wall, on the inner side, stood a colonnade, and in the centre
of the court thus formed was the altar itself. The outer wall
of the podium was decorated with the famous frieze representing the battle of the Gods and Giants; the blocks composing
this were found built into a late wall close by, and are now
preserved in the Pergamum Museum in Berlin. The strife of
gods and giants symbolises the defence of civilisation by the
kings of Pergamum against the barbarian Gauls. A second
frieze adorned the wall of the colonnade; this depicted the
adventures of the mythical hero Telephus, ruler of this region
at the time of the Trojan War, and later adopted as an ancestor
by the kings of Pergamum. This altar, and in particular the
friezes, constitute the masterpiece of Pergamene, and perhaps
of all Hellenistic art (Pl. 10).

The suggestion has been made that this altar of Zeus is the
throne of Satan mentioned in Revelation in the letter to the
church at Pergamum: 'I know where thou dwellest, where
Satan's throne is.' But the suggestion is hardly probable.
Satan in the Apocalypse, the enemy of Christianity, is represented not so much by the old pagan Greek religion as by the
Roman power, which by that time had taken a firm stand
against the Christians, and by the custom of emperor-worship.
If the throne of Satan really refers to a particular building at
Pergamum, the temple of Rome and Augustus is the most
likely; but more probably the words mean simply 'where is
the central seat of the Roman authority'.

Close to the altar of Zeus is the Greek theatre, the most
spectacular thing to be seen at Pergamum today. It is built
into the steep hillside and faces south-west. The normal shape
of the auditorium in a Greek theatre was rather more than a
semicircle, in a Roman theatre an exact semicircle; but at
Pergamum, owing to the nature of the ground, it is much less
than a semicircle. For this it makes up to some extent by its
exceptional height; it has seventy-eight rows of seats, divided
by two diazomata into three horizontal sections (Pl. 13, 14).

Immediately at the foot of the theatre stretches a long
narrow terrace, so close indeed that the scene-building stood
actually on the terrace. In the oldest form of the theatre, in the
early days of the Attalid kingdom, the scene-building was a

temporary structure of wood, erected for the performances and removed when the theatre was not in use. The purpose of this arrangement was evidently to avoid obstructing the long sweep of the terrace. The post-holes which form a conspicuous feature of the theatre today were used in erecting this wooden building; at other times they were closed with cap-stones. At this period it is probable that there was no stage, the performances taking place on the level of the orchestra. Some time about the middle of the second century B.C. the wooden scene-building was replaced by a permanent stone structure with a stage, covering up the old postholes without destroying them; later, in Roman times, this was rebuilt and enlarged. Of these stone buildings very little now remains.

The handsome Ionic temple at the north end of the theatre-terrace is comparatively well preserved. The walls are standing to a certain height, and the flight of steps in front is still in place. Of the columns and the ornamentation considerable fragments survive. The existing structure is a rebuilding of Roman date, but the original temple goes back to the second century B.C. To what deity it was dedicated is uncertain, since of the dedicatory inscription only five fragmentary letters have been found. Asclepius, Zeus and the deified kings of Pergamum have been proposed; but the proximity of the temple to the theatre suggests rather Dionysus, in whose honour theatrical performances took place. The building was at some period severely damaged by fire, and was eventually rededicated to the Roman emperor Caracalla. Fragments of this second dedication were found during the excavations. The letters of the alphabet carved on the steps on the west side are masons' marks indicating the positions in which the blocks should be placed; they were originally hidden from sight by the blocks above them. The altar of the temple stands in the normal position in front, at the foot of the steps; at its south-east corner is a curious conical stone, now almost buried, with a deep hole in the surface; this may have held a post to which the victim was tied.

Among the buildings lower down the hillside is the precinct of Demeter. It is entered at the east end by a propylon dating from the time of Eumenes II, from which steps lead down into the sanctuary. The columns of the propylon are unusual; they have the rare 'leaf capital', a type found elsewhere only in archaic times, and never common; the shafts are flat, fluted at the bottom only, and the usual base mouldings are lacking. Towards the west end of the precinct is the temple of Demeter, with the altar in front of it; temple and altar date from the reign of Philetaerus, in whose time they were outside the citadel. The dedicatory inscription may still be read. Along the north side of the sanctuary runs a long building of which the western part is a stoa, while the eastern part comprises nine rows of stone seats affording space for about a thousand people. Similar seats are found in the Hall of Initiation in the sanctuary of Demeter at Eleusis in Attica, and served for the initiates to watch the celebration of the mysteries; there can be no doubt that the same was the case at Pergamum (Pl. 15).

The Eleusinian mysteries formed an important element in the so-called Orphic religion, which competed strongly in classical times with the official Olympian cult. Its tenets were largely concerned with the after-life. To many people the traditional conception of Hades, the cold and cheerless abode of the spirits of the dead, seemed unsatisfactory, and it was felt that by means of ritual acts combined with purity of mind and body it might be possible to secure a better lot after death. The ritual cult came to be associated especially with Demeter, whose name means probably Mother Earth, and initiation was essential. No one was excluded who was not under a curse or pollution; not only free men, but women and slaves were readily admitted. The details of the ceremonies were kept secret from all but initiates, and the mysteries still remain mysterious; but ritual purification played an important part, and we know that certain 'acts' were performed and certain sacred objects displayed. It is unlikely that any precise dogma was taught, for dogma in general was a negligible element in Greek religion.

Across the path from the precinct of Demeter is the great gymnasium, one of the finest specimens of its kind to be found in the Greek world. It comprises three sections, each on a separate terrace. These were assigned respectively, though not exclusively, to the 'young men', youths and boys—'young men' meaning those from 19 years of age upwards to an uncertain maximum of at least 30. The uppermost terrace, that of the young men, is by far the largest of the three. Its main feature is an open rectangular court surrounded on three sides by a colonnade; this is the palaestra, used for wrestling and for athletic exercise generally. Along its north side are three good-sized rooms. The westernmost of these has the form of a small theatre—that is, a lecture-theatre, not for dramatic performances, as is clear from the absence of any stage. The gymnasium in an ancient city served not only for physical training but also as a school and university, and it was common practice to invite distinguished orators from other cities to give lectures. Such a visitor would easily fill the thousand seats in the lecture-theatre at Pergamum.

The next room to the east is the largest of the three. It was the ceremonial hall, used for receptions, prize-givings and similar official functions. Next again on the east is a room which, from an inscription found in it, was apparently used for worship of the emperor in Roman times, a kind of college chapel. On the east side of the palaestra is an extensive bathing establishment of the normal Roman type. The water for this and other purposes was brought in pipes from the mountains to the north and carried up under pressure to the citadel; this system was first installed by Eumenes II in the second century B.C., and is the most impressive of its kind before the great aqueducts of the Roman period. The smaller rooms around the palaestra were used as classrooms, dressing-rooms and the like. One of them still contains wash-basins. Along the south side of this upper terrace runs a long, narrow, originally underground building of uncertain purpose, but probably not used for athletics.

The middle terrace is less extensive than the upper and has fewer features. Towards the east end, in the middle, are the foundations of a temple which is likely to have been dedicated to one or both of the gods who in all parts of the Greek world presided over the activities of the gymnasium, namely Heracles and Hermes. Along the north edge of this terrace is a long narrow building lying just below the similar structure on the south side of the upper terrace. This building was in two

1   Smyrna. View of the town from Kadife Kale.

2   Magnesia ad Sipylum. The true Niobe.

3   Magnesia ad Sipylum. Taş Suret—False Niobe.

4   Smyrna. Baths of Agamemnon; the modern installation.

5   Smyrna. Tomb of Tantalus.

6. Akhera Tomb or Lock-cut post?   7. 'Eti Baba' Hittite figure in the Karabel gorge.

8   Pergamum. The Asclepieum.

9   Pergamum. Round building in the Asclepieum.

10   Pergamum. Altar of Zeus.

11   Pergamum. Kızıl Avlu.

12   Pergamum. Kızıl Avlu; double River Channel.

13   Pergamum. Theatre.

14 Pergamum. Theatre.

15   Pergamum. Sanctuary of Demeter.

16   Myrina. The site, with Öteki Tepe in the background.

17   Hierapolis. Tumulus graves in the Necropolis.

18   Elaea. Ancient Quay.

19   Pitane. The Venetian Castle.

20   Phocaea. Taş Kule; tomb on the Eski Foça road.

21   Teos. Ancient Quay with mooring-stone.

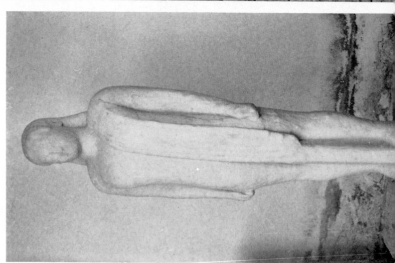

22   Pitane. Archaic Statue now in the Museum at Bergama.   23   Larisa. City Wall.

24   Teos. View from the Theatre.

25   Teos. Curiously-cut blocks in the quarry.

26   Teos. Re-erecting columns of the Temple of Dionysus, 1964.

27   Lebedus. Inscribed stone from the Gymnasium.

storeys. The ground floor comprises a long passage with small rooms at its east end; over this, on the upper floor, was a covered stadium, or xystus, used for indoor training during the winter. The stadium proper, where the games were celebrated in the summer, lay in the lower city to the west, between the river and the amphitheatre, but nothing remains of it beyond the mere outline of the elongated hollow.

The lowest terrace is smaller still and consists merely of an open triangular space. It contains no buildings, and served apparently as a simple playground for the boys. Near its east end is the handsome covered stairway, well preserved, which led up to the middle terrace. The ancient road up the hill passes the foot of this staircase. Since neither the lower nor the middle terrace contains classrooms, the boys and youths must have received their education in the rooms on the upper terrace, and the three terraces together form a single great gymnasium.

The lower part of the ancient city is now largely covered by the town of Bergama. In the town itself the most impressive remnant of antiquity is the so-called Kızıl Avlu, or Red Courtyard, a monument of Roman grandeur remarkable equally for its layout and its vast size. The central point of the complex is the great hall, or temple, originally in three storeys, which still stands almost complete; on either side of this is a round tower, also well preserved, with a colonnaded court in front. Of the colonnade hardly anything survives, but in the middle of each court is a long, narrow bathing-pool fed by pipes for hot and cold water. In front of the whole stretches the huge courtyard, over 200 yards long and now largely built over. The far wall containing the gateway may still be seen among the houses across the main street. Not the least remarkable feature is that this courtyard is built over the River Selinus, which flows obliquely across it in a double-vaulted tunnel which still serves its ancient purpose (Pl. 11, 12).

That this whole colossal structure is a sanctuary is beyond doubt, but no conclusive evidence has appeared to show to what god it belonged. The three separate buildings indicate perhaps a plurality of deities, and certain Egyptian features in the statues found in that on the south have suggested the

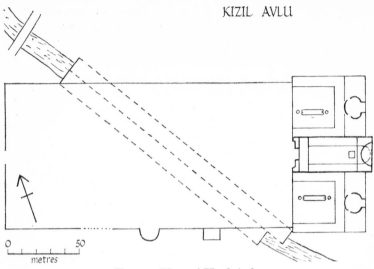

FIG. 11 Plan of Kızıl Avlu

Egyptian triad of Isis, Sarapis and Hermocrates. The monument dates probably to the second century A.D. In later times
a church was installed in the central hall; the present raised
floor belongs to this.

THE ASCLEPIEUM

To many visitors the sanctuary of Asclepius is among the most
attractive features of Pergamum. It is outside the city on the
south-west, and has been admirably excavated by the German
archaeologists; at the time of writing the excavations have
been resumed and are still in progress. Here, more than in
most places, the visitor can feel himself in intimate contact
with antiquity (Pl. 8).

Medicine in the Greek world, like so many aspects of civic
life—public assemblies, drama, sport and others—was under
divine patronage; to the ancient Greek, religion was a constant
part of his daily existence. Most, if not all, gods had powers of
healing, but the god of medicine *par excellence* was Asclepius.
In the *Iliad* Asclepius is not a god at all, but the human
physician whose sons Podaleirius and Machaon served as

medical officers to the army at Troy. It was hardly before the
fifth century that he became accepted into the Olympic
pantheon. Once accepted, his cult grew rapidly in popularity,
and in later times we know of over 200 sanctuaries of Asclepius
in all parts of the world. Of these the greatest and most famous
was at Epidaurus in the Peloponnese, and it was from here,
apparently in the fourth century, that the cult was introduced
to Pergamum by a grateful patient. Under the Roman empire
the Pergamene Asclepieum ranked in importance as second
only to the Epidaurian. Our chronic invalid friend Aristides
was naturally a frequent visitor there; several of his pamphlets
are directly concerned with it, and in the course of narrating
the wonderful cures which Asclepius performed in his case he
gives us a good deal of information about it.

The healing art as practised at Pergamum and in other
Asclepieia was a curious mixture of the supernatural and the
practical. Incubation was the main feature: the patient slept
in the sanctuary and either awoke cured or, if he was not so
fortunate, related his dreams to the priests, who prescribed
accordingly a less spectacular and more mundane course of
treatment. Unless the dreams were very precise—as Aristides'
often were—their interpretation rested with the priests,
who thus performed the functions of physicians; but secular
doctors were frequently in attendance also to help with their
advice. Galen, the most famous physician of antiquity after
Hippocrates, was born at Pergamum and practised in the
Asclepieum, thereby contributing largely to its fame. In fact,
the treatment prescribed appears on the whole to have been
very sensible and a credit to the profession, at least if we remember the very limited knowledge of medicine available in
ancient times. It consisted in the main of three elements, diet,
hot and cold baths, and exercise. A characteristic case is that
of a man of Mylasa, a dyspeptic, who came for treatment to
Asclepius at Epidaurus; he was put on a diet of bread and
cheese with parsley and lettuce, and milk mixed with honey,
and told to go barefoot, to take a run every day, to coat himself
with mud, and, rather oddly, to anoint himself with wine
before entering a hot bath. The treatment was successful and
his grateful dedication survives as a testimonial.

Coating with mud was employed also at Pergamum. Aristides tells us graphically how at the god's command, one bitter winter's night, he smeared himself with mud and ran three times round the temples, finishing by washing off the mud at the sacred fountain. The cold was so severe that no clothes could keep it out, and of two friends who volunteered to keep him company one turned back at once, while the other was seized by a spasm and had to be carried to the baths to be thawed out. Aristides' own constitution must have been exceptionally strong, despite his constant illness, if we may believe the cures which were worked upon him. On one occasion, after forty days of frost, Asclepius bade him rise from bed, put on only a linen shirt, and wash at the fountain outside. The difficulty was to find any water, as everything was frozen, and the water froze as it issued from the spout. Nevertheless he carried out orders, and felt the cold less than anyone. Another time in mid-winter, when he was in Smyrna, the god appeared in a dream and commanded him to go down and bathe in the river that flows outside the city. The cold this time was such that the pebbles at the river's edge were frozen together into a solid mass, yet after plunging into the deepest part of the stream and swimming and splashing for some time, he felt on emerging a warm glow which lasted the rest of the day. The astonished spectators could not refrain from crying aloud, 'Great is Asclepius!'

Aristides himself was much impressed by the apparently paradoxical nature of these cures; but he must have been a familiar figure at Pergamum, and the priests no doubt realised better than he did himself how much his constitution would stand and how largely imaginary his ailments were. Other forms of treatment that seemed to him paradoxical were the drinking of hemlock juice or of chalk and water, and the relief of constipation by prolonged abstinence from food. A story is told of the sophist Hermocrates of Phocaea that he once gave a recital before the emperor, who was so pleased that he asked him to choose his reward. Hermocrates replied that he was under orders from Asclepius of Pergamum to diet on partridge smoked in frankincense; frankincense being hard to come by in his country, he would ask the emperor for a generous supply. Aristides tells us that Asclepius once in a dream taught a boxer tricks for overcoming a formidable antagonist.

But many of the cures attributed to Asclepius are frankly miraculous. At Epidaurus there stood in the sanctuary in the fourth century B.C. marble stelae inscribed with records of cures effected there, and some of these have survived. One woman, we read, had been pregnant for five years; she slept in the sanctuary, and on emerging in the morning at once gave birth to a five-year-old son. Another woman came to Epidaurus in the hope of offspring, and, when asked by Asclepius in a vision what she desired, replied that she wished to conceive a child. Asked if she had any further desire, she said no, she wished for nothing else in the world. Afterwards she became pregnant, and remained so for three years. On coming again to the god for relief, it was pointed out to her that although specially asked she had said nothing about giving birth. This theme of the ill-expressed wish was popular in antiquity, as in the tales of Midas and his golden touch, and Tithonus who received eternal life without eternal youth. But perhaps the most pleasing case at Epidaurus is that of a certain Pandarus. Having evidently once been a slave, he bore tattoo-marks on his forehead, and came to Asclepius praying to be rid of them. During the night the god tied a bandage round his head, bidding him remove it in the morning and dedicate it in the temple. Next morning it was found that the marks had transferred themselves to the bandage. Shortly afterwards a friend of Pandarus named Echedorus, who was similarly tattooed, came to the god for a similar purpose, bringing with him a sum of money given him by the grateful Pandarus, with instructions to make a dedication to the god on his behalf. Dishonestly he neglected this duty, and when the god appeared to him during the night and asked if he had not received money from Pandarus he denied it. In response to his request for the removal of his tattoo-marks the god took the bandage which Pandarus had dedicated and tied it round Echedorus' head, bidding him in the morning remove it and look at his reflection in the sacred pool. When he did so the bandage was found to be clean and Echedorus' forehead to be carrying Pandarus' marks in addition to his own.

These records were compiled and published by the priests, and so have not the authenticity of dedications made by cured patients themselves. Nevertheless, if anyone is disposed to regard them as mythical, let him beware. This was done by a certain man who came to Epidaurus with a withered hand. Reading these cures as he walked round the sanctuary he scoffed at them and declared them impossible. To convince him Asclepius cured his hand, but condemned him to bear for life the name of Doubter, and his case was inscribed on the next stele to be erected.

Such then was the cult of Asclepius, half Droitwich and half Lourdes. But however its results were achieved, whether by auto-suggestion or faith-healing or by rational medical treatment, there is no doubt of its immense popularity; and one reason for this was certainly the intimate personal contact with the deity which it seemed to afford. The Asclepieum was not merely a spa, still less a hospital, but a public religious sanctuary, open to all, whether sick or well, citizens or foreigners. Aristides tells us more than once that the distinctly undignified treatment prescribed for him by the god was carried out in front of numerous spectators, and afforded much entertainment.

Naturally, not all patients could be cured overnight, nor in a matter of days, and prolonged visits were often necessary. Indeed, a year seems to have been quite normal. It is not clear where such patients stayed. For really serious cases accommodation on the spot would be desirable, but the excavations have not revealed any buildings clearly designed for this purpose. Patients who could not be moved were perhaps permitted to remain in the incubation-rooms. Against the danger of boredom in less severe cases good provision was made; the sanctuary contains both a theatre and a library. But, in fact, boredom is not likely to have been a real problem. Day by day the sanctuary was full of patients and visitors; we may imagine the learned men, doctors like Galen and others, each accompanied by a group of listeners, strolling up and down, the priests benevolently accessible to all and sundry, and the patients conversing among themselves. In a slave-owning society leisure was abundant and the Greeks knew how to use it; no Greek was ever bored so long as he had someone to argue with.

The ruins of the Asclepieum as they now stand revealed by the excavation date in the main to a great rebuilding in the second century A.D. All that remains from earlier times is the original kernel of the sanctuary, the sacred well, and the foundations of temple and incubation-rooms to the west and south of it.[1] Most of what we see today was erected in the lifetime of Aelius Aristides; but as it happens the buildings he mentions are mostly those which have not survived.

A visit to the sanctuary begins, as it began in antiquity, at the entrance-gate or Propylon. A sacred way from the city led obliquely to a courtyard in front of the gate; a good stretch of this road has lately been uncovered. Immediately to the right, or north, is the library. This is a single square room with niches round the walls. The middle niche on the east side held a statue of the emperor, Hadrian, to whom the library was dedicated as a patron of learning; the others held books. Light for reading was supplied by a line of windows above the niches. There is no reason to suppose that this was a medical library; rather it was a collection of classical works for the use of patients. The statue, and perhaps the whole building, was dedicated by a lady named Flavia Melitine.

Adjoining the Propylon on the other side is the circular temple of Zeus-Asclepius, the main temple of the existing precinct. Only the lowest courses remain, but the excellence of the masonry is remarkable. At the back on the east was an external staircase apparently giving access to the roof for purposes of repair. In front was a flight of steps symmetrically balancing the steps which led down from the Propylon. The identification of Asclepius with Zeus was considered noteworthy by Aristides; the power of Asclepius, he explains, is great, manifold and all-embracing, comparable with that of Zeus himself. It was in this temple that Aristides dedicated a tripod in commemoration of a choral entertainment he had organised in the god's honour; each of its three legs carried a golden image, one of Asclepius, one of Hygieia, and one of

[1] The latest excavations are revealing more of the earlier buildings, but their full publication is still awaited.

Telesphorus. It stood under the god's right hand. Hygieia, Health, and Telesphorus, the Accomplisher, of whom more will be said later, were minor deities associated with Asclepius.

On the north, west and south the sanctuary was surrounded by porticoes, or stoae. These are a constant feature of Greek civic architecture, affording shelter from the sun in summer and from the rain in winter. The best preserved is that on the north, where the columns have been re-erected after the excavation. The order is Ionic, but the ten columns at the end nearest to the library were overthrown by an earthquake, and were, surprisingly enough, replaced by columns with square bases and Composite capitals—that is capitals combining the Ionic volute with the Corinthian acanthus-leaves.

At the west end of this portico is a small theatre. It has the semicircular shape typical of Roman theatres. The auditorium is divided by staircases into five wedge-shaped sections, and horizontally by a gallery, or diazoma. A 'royal box' occupies three rows of the middle section. The stage-building stood originally three storeys high, with a stage in front about one metre high. An inscription records that the theatre was dedicated to Asclepius and Athena Hygieia. Its seating capacity is about 3,500; since the patients in residence at any one time can never have approached this number, it is evident that the general public must also have been admitted.

The west portico was similar to that on the north, but nothing remains of it. Half-way down its length a door and steps lead up to a building which has not yet been excavated.[1]

The south portico, or at least the stoa itself, is also completely destroyed. The ground being lower on this side, a basement was necessary, and this still survives. It has a row of piers down the middle which helped to support the floor of the stoa, while the basement itself was used as a store-room. At the corner where the west and south porticoes join is an interesting specimen of an ancient latrine. The larger room, used by the men, was splendidly furnished with about thirty marble seats; in the middle of the ceiling was a light and air vent with handsome Corinthian pillars at its four corners. These sumptuous

[1] Just before going to press news arrives that a start has been made on this building.

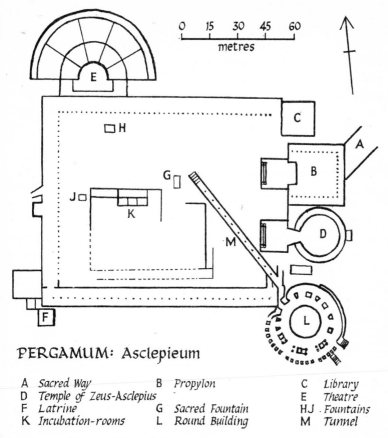

PERGAMUM: Asclepieum

A	Sacred Way	B	Propylon	C	Library
D	Temple of Zeus-Asclepius			E	Theatre
F	Latrine	G	Sacred Fountain	HJ	Fountains
K	Incubation-rooms	L	Round Building	M	Tunnel

FIG. 12 Plan of the Asclepieum at Pergamum

latrines are characteristic of the period. Though affording perhaps less privacy than we should consider desirable today, they are beautifully built and excellently equipped. The ladies' room, on the other hand, is smaller and much less magnificent.

The central point both of the sanctuary and of the cult is the Sacred Well. It was housed in a simple building and fed by a pipe from a spring. The water was not entered by the patients, but was drawn in vessels either for bathing or more especially for drinking. Aristides is enthusiastic over the virtues of this water, and devotes a pamphlet to its praises. The well, he says, is always full, cool in summer and warm in winter; eyes are cured by bathing with it, chest diseases, asthma and foot troubles by drinking it; in one case even a dumb man who drank of it recovered his speech. It is not, like some sacred waters—Delos, for example—sacred because no one is allowed to touch it, but sacred in the sense that with the god's help it benefits all who use it.

There were two other fountains in the sanctuary, both of which also played a part in the cure of the sick. One of these (H on the plan) is close to the theatre; it had a marble basin, unroofed, and was probably used by patients who were ordered the cold bath treatment. The other (J on the plan) is in the middle of the west side; this is a rock-cut basin and was originally roofed over. In winter and wet weather mud collects around this spot; the excavators suggest that the patients coated themselves with this mud, which they subsequently washed off in the basin. If this was the only purpose of this basin, the mud-cure must have been much employed, since the steps leading down to it are deeply worn.

Close to the Sacred Well on the south-west are the incubation-rooms. Only foundations survive, and it is not possible to reconstruct the detail of the rooms. The process of incubation involved a strict ritual, some items of which we learn from a mutilated inscription. The suppliant must wash before entering and must wear white clothes, but without girdle or rings; and he must make sacrifice. At Pergamum this was apparently a white sheep garlanded with olive-branches; at Athens, Aristophanes speaks of sacrificial cakes.

In 1958 the German excavators recommenced work upon this central part of the sanctuary. The trenches which they sank remain open, but it is not easy for the visitor to make much sense of them. They produced, in fact, more than one surprise. Under the Hellenistic incubation-rooms there were found walls running obliquely to the otherwise universal north-south orientation; from their style they can hardly be later than the early fourth century B.C. These, together with certain archaic figurines and a very early sherd found close by, suggest that the installation of the Asclepieum in the fourth century was not the first occupation of the site. The excavators suspect that there may have been here a cult of some female deity, for a number of terracotta figurines of a seated woman have come to light in the neighbourhood. These are of later date, so that the early cult (if indeed it existed) must have continued alongside that of Asclepius. But this question is not yet satisfactorily cleared up.

A further surprising discovery was that of a number of simple graves in and around the incubation-chambers. Some still contained the skeletons, and one of these was found to show a severe swelling of the thigh-bone. It is tempting to suppose that these graves are those of patients who let the sanctuary down by dying under treatment and were hastily, perhaps even secretly, buried on the spot.

On the rocky ground to the north of the incubation-rooms stood three small temples, of which only faint traces remain. They were those of Asclepius the Saviour, Hygieia his wife, and Apollo of the Fair Offspring, his father. These are the temples round which Aristides ran three times clad only in a coat of mud. In or adjoining the temple of Hygieia was a shrine of Telesphorus, a boy-deity associated with Asclepius first at Pergamum, then in other parts of the world. He played an active part in the healing cult: Aristides mentions that Telesphorus, that is the priest of Telesphorus, once gave him a balsam with which to anoint himself. On another occasion Aristides was told in a dream that in order to save the whole of his body he must cut off a part of it and dedicate it to Telesphorus; since, however, this would be unduly painful, the priest decided it would be sufficient if he dedicated the ring which he wore on his finger; this would have the same effect as sacrificing the finger itself. There is a convincing air of truth about this story.

In the south-east corner of the sanctuary is a second round building which, after the theatre, is the best preserved on the site. It was in two storeys. On the upper or main floor was a circular room with six large round niches and a wooden roof, but this is now destroyed. The surviving structure is the lower or basement floor. Round a central core of masonry runs a gallery, divided into two by a ring of solid piers placed at intervals. At the foot of some of the piers are set stone basins for washing or bathing. On the south-east are the remains of two staircases leading to the upper floor (Pl. 9).

This building is not mentioned by any ancient writer, and its purpose is not known with certainty. It can hardly have formed part of the original design of the great rebuilding, whose symmetry it destroys. It has somehow acquired the name of Temple of Telesphorus, but this is certainly wrong; as was mentioned above, the shrine of Telesphorus stood elsewhere in the sanctuary. It is not even sure that it was a temple at all. That it had a place in the healing process is hardly doubtful, both in view of the bathing-troughs installed in the basement and because it is linked to the Sacred Well by a long underground tunnel. This tunnel is excellently preserved, with steps at either end; it is lit by a row of holes in the roof. The excavators suggest that it may have served either for the use of the personnel of the sanctuary or as a cool place for patients in summer; but perhaps more likely it afforded a convenient passage for patients, especially in bad weather, from the round building to the heart of the sanctuary around the Sacred Well. We may reasonably suppose that the round building, or at least its basement storey, was intended to meet the need for a place of resort for resident patients in hot or rainy weather. A stone-paved terrace adjoining it on the south would be convenient for invalids to take the sun and air without mingling with the throng of people in the main sanctuary. The guardian who conducts visitors round the site will tell you that the patient was sent to walk alone down the dark and fearsome tunnel, while from each of the holes in the roof a priest-doctor whispered to him, 'Don't be afraid; you are going to be cured.' For this interesting conception there is unfortunately no authority at all.

On two occasions, both during the Mithridatic War, the Pergamene Asclepieum makes a momentary appearance in history. When the king ordered the massacre of all Roman residents in Asia, those in Pergamum ran for asylum to the sanctuary, but were ruthlessly shot down as they clung to the god's statues. A little later the swashbuckling Roman commander Fimbria, unable by reason of his crimes to return to

Rome, made his way to the precinct of Asclepius and fell on his sword. Even this he bungled, and was obliged to call on his slave to finish the job.

Towards the end of the third century the sanctuary suffered severely from an earthquake. This disaster, and the rising tide of Christianity, were more than it could resist, and it never really recovered. And yet two hundred years later it was still reckoned as one of the wonders of the world. The list of these wonders had, of course, by that time been greatly extended beyond the original seven; nevertheless, the inclusion of the Asclepieum is a handsome testimony to the splendour it once possessed.

On the open ground between the Acropolis and the Asclepieum are the rather scanty remains of the amphitheatre, the only example of its kind in the area covered by this book. The amphitheatre, as its name implies, is a double theatre, that is a circular, or more often oval, building with an arena in the middle and tiers of seats all round. At Pergamum it is built in the valley of a small stream which flows under the arena; of the vast brick structures which supported the seats some rather shapeless masses are standing, but nothing else survives. Amphitheatres were used for the more savage entertainments favoured by the Romans, especially gladiatorial contests and fights between wild animals or between animals and men. In these a good deal of blood was expected to be shed. For the spectators' delectation bears, lions, panthers and more exotic creatures such as crocodiles were imported from the ends of the earth. On occasion the arena was flooded with water for the performance of mimic sea-fights and other shows; for this purpose the stream at Pergamum was obviously convenient. These sanguinary entertainments did not naturally appeal to the Greeks, but under Roman influence it was inevitable that the taste should be acquired, and in the Greek cities under the empire many theatres and stadia were, in fact, made to serve the purpose of amphitheatres.

The network of trenches on the high ground near the amphitheatre was dug recently by the Germans in an unsuccessful search for the site of the Nicephorium, an important

Pergamene sanctuary where a great festival with games was regularly celebrated. Instead, numerous private and one or two public buildings came to light, but there is little to hold the visitor's attention.

Just outside the town of Bergama on the south, to the east of the main road and nearly opposite the side-road which leads to the Asclepieum, is a large tumulus known as Maltepe. The mound, over 500 feet in diameter, was originally surrounded by a wall, of which only the filling remains in a few places. On the north side, but not in the diameter of the circle, a passage over 70 yards long leads into the tumulus; it is lined with handsome ashlar masonry and roofed with a vault. It debouches into a cross-passage running right and left, out of which open three grave-chambers; in these fragments of sarcophagi were found. This part also is handsomely built and vaulted, but is, of course, dark. The method of construction was to erect the masonry first, then to heap the tumulus over it; on the summit stood a monument, but the architectural fragments recovered by the excavators were not enough to indicate its nature. So grandiose a structure was for long believed to be the tomb of a Pergamene king; but, in fact, the lime mortar used in all parts shows conclusively that it must be of Roman date, probably of the second or third century A.D. It carries no inscription, and there is nothing to show what rich and distinguished family was buried in it.

A short half-mile to the south-east is another large tumulus called Yığma Tepe. In this case the ring-wall is preserved, and the fine quality of the masonry suggests that this is indeed the tomb of a king. A tunnel driven into it in 1909 failed, however, to find the grave-chamber.

★

CHAPTER FIVE

Aeolis

THE SMYRNA-PERGAMUM ROAD

OUR FRIEND Aelius Aristides on one occasion made a journey by carriage from Smyrna to Pergamum. He followed the direct main road, whose course was not very different from that of the modern highway. It may therefore be of interest to accompany him along the way. His narrative is lively and detailed; its main purpose is to show the wonderful effect of Asclepius' advice upon his health.

One summer, he says, *my stomach gave me a lot of trouble. I suffered from thirst night and day, sweated abundantly and felt as weak as a rag; when I needed to get up it took two or three men to haul me out of bed. The god gave me a sign to leave Smyrna, where I was at the time, so I decided to start at once on the road to Pergamum. By the time the carriages were ready it was midday and very hot; I therefore preferred to send my servants ahead with the baggage and myself to pass the heat of the afternoon in the suburb. My intention was to spend the first night at Myrina, but beguiled by the charm of the place, and having also some business to transact, we delayed a good while in the suburb, so that we did not reach the inn on the near side of the Hermus till just about sunset.*

Where the 'suburb' lay which Aristides found so seductive he does not say; but since it was presumably on the side of the city towards the Pergamum road it is tempting to conjecture that it was by the springs of the Meles at Halkapınar. There is hardly a pleasanter spot in Smyrna today in which to spend a hot afternoon.

Between here and the River Hermus Aristides names no landmark, and this part of his journey is the only part in

which his route is at all doubtful. In the second century A.D.
the main highroad from Smyrna to the north certainly went,
as it does now, round the west end of the Yamanlar Dağı; a
milestone found near Ulucak leaves no doubt of this, and
Aristides himself on another occasion describes a walk he took
in this direction, looking across, as he says, to the city on his
left—evidently from a spot between Bayrakli and Karşıyaka.
But the matter is complicated by the question of the crossing
of the Hermus. As was said above, the river now runs, exactly
or approximately, in its ancient course, but in Aristides' time
there was no bridge and carriages had to ford the stream. The
question is, what was the lowest point at which this could be
done? At present, according to enquiries made by Professor
J. M. Cook and the present writer, there is a good ford, usable
for carriages for most of the year, close to Emiralem railway
station, but none is recognised below this. Near the new girder
bridge the stream appears normally quite unfordable. If
similar conditions prevailed in antiquity, which is likely
enough, the high road must have made a considerable detour
into the Manisa gorge, and many travellers no doubt preferred
the alternative route from Smyrna direct over the Yamanlar
Dağı. This is much shorter, but involves quite a stiff climb,
nor is it certain that it was ever suitable for wheeled traffic.
The English excavators of Old Smyrna found traces of an old
carriage road, 8 to 10 feet wide, running up from the neighbourhood of Bayrakli to the village of Eğridere, and from there
apparently (though this was not actually verified) over the
crest of the Yamanlar and down by the lake of Karagöl to
the river near Emiralem. It is probable also that a second road
led up the west side of the Yamanlar valley, along the line of
the present road to the Sanatorium; the small fort beside this
road mentioned above[1] suggests that this route was in use.
However, it is doubtful whether either of these would, in fact,
be any quicker for a horse-drawn vehicle, and we shall probably
be safe in picturing Aristides proceeding by the low road
through Ulucak and Menemen.

For most of the way to Menemen this road must have run
beside the sea. It was originally constructed in 129 B.C., when

[1] P. 66.

the province of Asia was formed, and was repaired in A.D. 75 and again in 103, so Aristides should have found it in reasonably good condition. Menemen is not apparently an ancient site, and indeed none is known along this stretch of the road. In the first century A.D. a ferry plied along the coast; and Chandler in 1764 found a busy trade by sea between Smyrna and the scala of Menemen.

At sunset, then, Aristides arrives at the inn by the Hermus crossing, probably not far from Emiralem. The distance from Smyrna is about twenty-four miles.

I was in some doubt what to do, but when I went inside and saw how intolerably disgusting the rooms were, I decided to push on, especially as my servants were not available, having gone on ahead. By the time we had crossed the river it was quite dark, with a light cool breeze, so that I felt refreshed and cheered; and when late in the evening we came to Larisa I was quite happy to find that we had still not overtaken our train, that the inn was no better than the last, and that there was nothing for it but to persevere with the journey.

Larisa is a common name on the ancient map. There were at least ten places so called, three of them on the west coast of Asia Minor, in the Troad, in Aeolis and in Ionia. The one in question here was one of the original twelve cities of the Aeolian League, and earlier still, before the coming of the Greeks, had been the principal town of the region. It may indeed have the honour of being one of the very few towns on the west coast named by Homer. In the *Iliad*, among the Trojan allies, we read of the 'warlike Pelasgians who dwelt around fertile Larisa'; their leader, Hippothous, was killed at Troy, 'far from fertile Larisa'. Since Larisa in the Troad is comparatively close to Troy, some ancient critics believed that our Larisa must be meant, and some modern scholars agree with them. In any case, the existence of a Larisa in this region in the second millennium is not disputed.

The Pelasgians were not merely the occupants of the district of Larisa. The name was given by the Greeks to their own predecessors in many parts of the world, not only in Asia but in Greece itself and the Aegean islands. At Larisa legend

AT—G

preserved the name of one of the Pelasgian rulers, Piasus; this man, it was said, fell in love with his own daughter and offered her violence. But the lady had her revenge: catching him one day bending over a cask of wine, she whipped up his heels and drowned him in the liquor.

When the Aeolian Greeks arrived not long after the Trojan War and wished to settle in the country, they found themselves opposed by the Pelasgians; for these, though somewhat weakened by their sufferings at Troy, were still firmly in control of Larisa. The Greeks therefore, as Strabo tells us, built themselves a base some three or four miles from Larisa and called it Neonteichos, the New Fort. Operating from here they eventually reduced Larisa, after which they founded the city of Cyme and peopled it with the inhabitants of the region. Both to Cyme and to Larisa they gave the epithet Phriconis, after Mt. Phrikion in their native land in Greece. Shortly afterwards the various Greek colonies in Aeolis, including Smyrna, united into an Aeolian League. As in the Ionian League, there were originally twelve members, but, as related above, Smyrna soon passed into the hands of the Ionians.

During the following centuries the Aeolians, unlike the Ionians, lived more or less untroubled, offering no resistance to the Lydian and Persian conquerors. Larisa makes one or two appearances in history. In 546 B.C. Cyrus, after defeating Croesus, settled some Egyptian allies of the Lydian king in the city, which thus acquired the name of 'Egyptian Larisa'. In the Delian Confederacy it is doubtful if Larisa was ever effectively included. She was assessed for tribute at an unknown sum, but there is no evidence that she ever actually paid. The city seems indeed to have been less whole-heartedly Greek than most, and in 399 B.C. she was one of the few to resist the Spartan general, Thibron, when he came to defend the Greek cities against the Persians—and the only one to resist successfully. Thibron attempted to cut off the city's water-supply, but the citizens defended it vigorously and he was forced to withdraw (Appendix II).

When Alexander arrived the whole of Aeolis submitted quietly to him; and when the Attalid kingdom of Pergamum

was established Aeolis formed a more or less permanent part
of it. But at some time during the Hellenistic period the
existence of Larisa as an independent city came to an end.
Perhaps it succumbed to the invading Gauls in 279 B.C. and
never recovered; at all events Strabo calls it deserted and
Pliny speaks of it as having once existed. Nevertheless, it is
clear from Aristides' narrative that a place of some sort still
survived in the second century A.D. and possessed an inn,
though of poor quality. We should picture Larisa at this date
as a village or small town dependent upon Cyme.

Between the Hermus crossing and Cyme, Aristides mentions only one place, Larisa, whereas (if the crossing was near
Emiralem) there are two ancient city sites close above the
road, at Yanık Köy and Buruncuk respectively. Of these, that
at Buruncuk has been confidently claimed as Larisa, and was
excavated as such by German archaeologists in 1902 and
again in 1932–4. Yanık Köy then remains to represent
Neonteichos, from which Larisa was originally attacked and
captured. These locations agree closely with the distances
given by Strabo, namely Cyme-Larisa seventy stades or eight
miles, and Larisa-Neonteichos thirty stades or three and a half
miles.

Recently, however, this view has been called in question.
Professor Cook is now disposed to believe that Larisa was at
Yanık Köy, while Buruncuk probably represents Cyllene, an
obscure Aeolian town of which very little is heard. The
problem cannot be fully discussed here, but it is remarkable
that the excavations at Buruncuk produced no evidence in
favour of Larisa—no inscriptions at all, not a single coin of
Larisa, and no Greek sherds earlier than 800 B.C. Yanık Köy
has never been excavated, so that no comparison in these
respects can be made. Professor Cook points out that Strabo's
distances in this region are habitually underestimated, and
calls attention to a passage in an ancient *Life of Homer* of
uncertain authorship and date and of no historical value, but
evidently written by a man familiar with this country. This
says that the poet, travelling from Smyrna to Cyme, crossed
the Hermus plain to Neonteichos, and from there to Cyme by
way of Larisa. Though at first sight this seems to support the

generally accepted view, in fact it creates a difficulty; for the writer adds: 'because this way it was easiest for him'. Now, Homer was blind, and the plain implication is that for a sighted man there was a shorter but more difficult road which the poet preferred to avoid; but from Yanık Köy to Cyme the road leads straight by Buruncuk and no alternative short cut is possible. On the other hand, if Yanık Köy is Larisa, where is Neonteichos? The site to the east above Gürice is securely identified with Temnus, and no other seems to be discoverable. Aristides' narrative is unfortunately of little help, owing not only to the uncertainty concerning the exact position of the Hermus crossing, but still more to the vagueness of the Greek expressions of time. He crossed the river soon after sunset, say about eight o'clock; but what is meant by 'late in the evening'? If nine o'clock, then Larisa is Yanık Köy; if ten o'clock, it is at Buruncuk. The problem must be left for the present unresolved; meanwhile the ruins at Buruncuk, though spurned by Freya Stark, deserve perhaps an hour or so of the traveller's time.

The hill, some 300 feet high, rises directly above the village and may be ascended on the north side by the ancient road, much of whose paving remains; it led up to the main gate of the city. The acropolis was first fortified about 500 B.C. Before that the town was defended by a wall dating from before the Greek conquest; it enclosed a considerable area, larger than that of the contemporary Troy or Mycenae. Early in the fourth century the whole of the fortification was reconstructed; an extension to the acropolis was built (F on the plan) and the town walls were renewed. The line of the wall L,L may be traced, except where the hill has recently been quarried away, but hardly a stone remains in place; K,K is rather better preserved, though nowhere more than a single course is visible. Remains of all three building-periods may be seen in the north-west wall of the acropolis, showing a mixture of polygonal and ashlar masonry still several metres in height (Pl. 23).

The interior of the acropolis was covered with closely packed buildings, of which only the foundations survive. Chief among them are the two temples B and C and the palace J. One of the

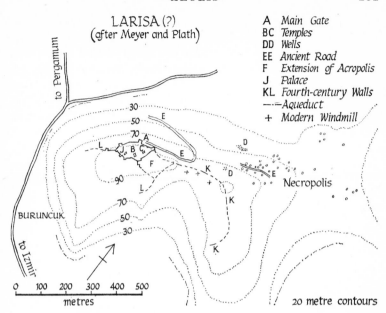

A   Main Gate
BC   Temples
DD   Wells
EE   Ancient Road
F   Extension of Acropolis
J   Palace
KL   Fourth-century Walls
—·—Aqueduct
+   Modern Windmill

Fig. 13 Plan of Larisa (?) after Meyer and Plath

temples, probably B, was surely that of Athena, the principal
deity of the city. The palace, several times rebuilt, was the
residence of the Greek tyrants in early days and later of the
Persian governor.

East of the citadel, beyond the hill with the ruins of three
modern windmills, is the main part of the necropolis. About
a hundred tombs have been recognised, strewn over the lower
slope of the windmill hill and on the saddle between it and the
next hill. They were mostly of tumulus type, with a low ring-
wall of one or two courses of polygonal masonry surmounted
by a conical mound of earth; a tall stone was probably set on
the summit. Tombs of this kind, though much later in date,
may be seen in the necropolis at Hierapolis (Pl. 17). The grave
itself, placed generally near the middle, was constructed of
stone slabs set on edge; some tumuli contained two graves. A
remarkable feature is the manner in which many of the tumuli
have been later enlarged by the addition of one or more seg-
ments of circles of varying size; in one case the tomb has been

enlarged in this way no less than four times. A few of the tombs are rectangular, divided in some cases into partitions. The whole necropolis is dated by the sherds found in it to the sixth century B.C. All the bodies were buried; no sign of cremation has been observed. Today it is still quite easy to recognise a number of these tombs by a ring of polygonal blocks, and in one or two cases the upright slabs of the grave are still in place.

A supply of water was ensured in the first place by the two groups of wells, D, D, both dating from very early times. They are still full of water, and were in use by the villagers until quite recently. The larger group is called Yirmikuyu, and contains in fact twenty wells, all within the space of some 30 yards. About 500 B.C. this source of water was supplemented by a great aqueduct or water-channel which descended from the mountain and encircled the city on the east, south and west. Most of the remnants of this which were noted by the excavators have now been obliterated. Inside the citadel rain-water was collected in numerous cisterns (Appendix II).

On the next hill to the north-east, rather less than 600 feet high, are the ruins of a fort of roughly triangular shape; the masonry, not very well preserved, is polygonal and apparently of early date. Below it on the east and south-east are extensive traces of ancient settlement. The excavators suggest that this fort was built by the Greek settlers when they were attacking Larisa, and that after the capture it was incorporated as a suburb of the city.

The site at Yanik Köy lies directly above the village, an easy half-hour's climb. It is conspicuous from afar by the curious circular rock which forms the citadel. Never having been excavated, it offers little to the visitor beyond a pleasant excursion and a fine view. On the slope towards the village are a number of pieces of handsome polygonal wall, mostly terrace walls; and a long stretch of the city wall, also polygonal, is preserved on the south side of the hill. On the summit is a rock-cut stairway and a little to the north-east some remains of ashlar masonry. The surface sherds range in date from the sixth century B.C. to Byzantine times, the majority being of the fourth and third centuries. The ancient paved

Fig. 14 Yanık Köy

way may be followed from below the village for a considerable
way up the hill.

*At midnight or a little later we reached Cyme, where we found
everything shut. Still undismayed, I urged my companions to
make a further effort and to carry on for the rest of the way to
Myrina, pointing out that it was not far to go and that it was much
better not to abandon our original intention. When we left the
city gates there was a damp chill in the air and I felt distinctly
cold.*

Cyme was in Greek and Roman times the most important
town of this region; Strabo calls it 'the biggest and best of the
Aeolian cities'. Tradition recorded, as was mentioned above,
that Cyme was founded by the Greek settlers after the capture

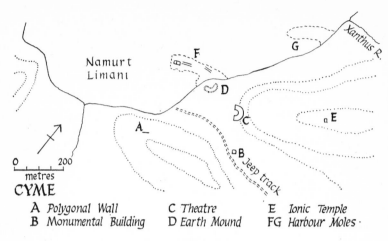

CYME

A *Polygonal Wall*	C *Theatre*	E *Ionic Temple*
B *Monumental Building*	D *Earth Mound*	FG *Harbour Moles* ·

FIG. 15 Plan of Cyme

of Larisa and the subjugation of the Pelasgians. It served as a centre for the settlement of numerous small towns, many of which did not survive into classical times. The city was said to have received its name, like Smyrna, Myrina and others, from an Amazon, by name Cyme; some scholars have seen in these traditions an echo of the Hittite invasion of these parts which has left its traces in the Taş Suret and Karabel figures.[1] Like the Aeolian cities in general, and unlike the Ionians, Cyme was more land- than sea-minded; Strabo says that the citizens acquired a name for stupidity because it was not until 300 years after the foundation that they thought of raising revenue by farming out their harbour-dues—as if it took them all that time to realise that they lived on the sea-coast.

Stupid or not, the Cymaeans flourished, and were not negligible even at sea. Aristagoras, tyrant of Cyme, led a contingent of his own ships to assist the Persian king Darius in his invasion of Scythia in 512 B.C.;[2] and when Xerxes invaded Greece in 480 Sandoces, the Persian governor of Cyme, contributed fifteen ships to his fleet. No other Aeolian city was represented on either of these campaigns. In the

[1] Above, pp. 19, 53–5.
[2] Below, pp. 222–3.

Delian Confederacy, Cyme paid a tribute of nine talents, not only far more than any other Aeolian town, but more than was paid by Ephesus, Miletus or any of the biggest cities of Ionia.

The Cymaeans were also not entirely without an answer to the cultural brilliance of Ionia. The epic poet Hesiod, rival of Homer, who lived and wrote in Greece, tells us that his father had emigrated from Cyme, so that if not the poet himself, at least his family was of Cymaean stock. No other Aeolian city could claim as much. The fourth-century historian Ephorus was also a native of Cyme. Strabo says that it was a joke against him that, having no great Cymaean achievements to record in his history, but not wishing his own city to remain without a mention, he wrote: 'About this time the Cymaeans were doing nothing.' So, with the rest of Aeolis, they continued to do under the Hellenistic kings and in the province of Asia, living quietly and leaving little mark on the course of history.

The location of Cyme at Namurt Limanı is abundantly proved by inscriptions and coins found on the spot; but the ruins are scanty in the extreme. Here, as in so many cases on the coast, the ancient stones have no doubt been removed by sea for use in the building of Izmir, Istanbul and other cities; the fortifications are said to have been destroyed by the Turkish conqueror Mehmet in the fifteenth century.

The site includes two hills, a northern and a southern, of which the latter carried the main habitation. Some small-scale excavations were carried out by French scholars in 1924, but the remains which they brought to light are not now easily discoverable. At A there is, or was, to be seen a short stretch of polygonal wall of early date. At B, close beside the modern track, are the ruins of a monumental building; two parallel rows of unfluted columns are visible. At E, towards the summit of the northern hill, the excavators unearthed a small Ionic temple dedicated to the Egyptian goddess Isis; this is now hard to find among the dense bushes. Of the theatre at the foot of the northern hill nothing remains but the semi-circle of the cavea in the hillside.

Two streams enter the sea close to the city. That on the south has converted the valley into a marsh; that on the north is identified with the River Xanthus which appears on coins of the city. Between their mouths are the ruins of two harbour-moles now under water. The southern, F, is the better preserved and much of its masonry survives. Investigations made recently by German scholars have shown that the sea-level has risen rather more than 5 feet since classical antiquity.

Nothing more remains of the biggest and best of the Aeolian cities. The place is now quite deserted apart from one or two isolated houses.

About cock-crow we reached Myrina, and there we found our men outside one of the inns, still not unpacked because, as they said, they too had found nothing open. In the porch of the inn was a pallet-bed; we spent some time carrying this up and down, but could find no comfortable place to put it. Knocking at the door was useless, as no-one answered it. At long last we managed to get into the house of an acquaintance; but by bad luck the porter's fire was out, so that I went in in complete darkness, led by the hand, seeing nothing and myself invisible. By the time a fire had been procured and I was preparing to enjoy a drink in front of it, the morning star was rising and dawn had begun to break. Pride rebelled against going to bed in daylight, so I decided to make a further effort and go on to the temple of Apollo at Gryneum, where it was my habit to offer sacrifice on my journeys up and down the road.

Myrina is a city without a history. Legend told of Myrina, a great queen of the Amazons, who led her victorious armies not only over Asia Minor but to many parts of the world; of the cities she founded one was called after her, and others, such as Cyme, Pitane and Gryneum, after her lieutenants. Of the Greek settlement nothing is recorded. Myrina appears in the Delian Confederacy with a tribute of one talent, well above normal for the Aeolian cities other than Cyme. Here and there in the historians we find a casual mention of Myrina, but in most cases it is doubtful if these refer to our city at all, for there was a second Myrina on the island of Lemnos.

The great earthquake of A.D. 17 destroyed twelve cities in a single night, of which Myrina was one. The Emperor Tiberius was generous with his help and the twelve cities were rebuilt,

Myrina apparently under the new name of Sebastopolis, or Emperor's City; this name was in use in Pliny's time, but the old name afterwards revived. The twelve cities in gratitude erected in Rome a colossal statue of Tiberius, with twelve figures on the base representing themselves. A copy of this monument was found at Puteoli near Naples; the figure representing Myrina is shown not as an Amazon, as might have been expected, but as a priestess of the Gryneian Apollo. In the course of time Gryneum had lost its independence and become incorporated in Myrina, and such importance as Myrina had was mostly due to her possession of this famous sanctuary.

A second destruction by earthquake in A.D. 106 was followed by a second rebuilding; but as the influence of the pagan sanctuaries waned before the rise of Christianity, Myrina sank into utter obscurity, relieved only by the reputation of her oysters.

Like Cyme, Myrina offers little to the traveller in the way of standing ruins. The charm of the site itself is delightfully conveyed by Freya Stark in her description of her visit; she notes that even the few ancient stones that were to be seen were being broken up and carried off for building. But her visit was hurried, and there is, in fact, a certain amount for the energetic traveller to discover (Pl. 16).

The site lies at the mouth of the Güzelhisar River, the ancient Titnaeus or Pythicus. It is reached by a very bad track which turns off the main road half a mile north of the river; the distance is a mile and a half. The city occupied two hills, formerly known as Epano Tepe and Kato Tepe, but now called merely Birki Tepe and Öteki Tepe ('the One Hill' and 'the Other Hill'). Birki Tepe formed the acropolis, and was defended by a polygonal wall, of which two pieces were noted by the French excavators, but they are not now easy to find. On the other hand, a piece of Byzantine wall, E, is conspicuous to the visitor arriving from the east. On the west slope is a hollow, C, which probably held the theatre. There is nothing to be seen on the summit, nor on the Other Hill, though the latter is terraced and was evidently occupied in antiquity.

At F is a small landing-stage, of which the seaward side is formed by the remains of an ancient quay. Several of the blocks project into the sea and are pierced by round holes for the purpose of mooring vessels. Similar blocks are also to be seen at Teos.[1]

On the north slope of Birki Tepe and the hill facing it on the north between 4,000 and 5,000 tombs were excavated in 1880–82; of these the great majority were hitherto unopened. Most are simple rectangular graves, taking a single occupant, sunk into the chalky rock; sometimes two or three are superposed. There is no rule about orientation. A few are circular, and a few are smaller cavities holding a cinerary urn; but cremation is exceptional and inhumation is the normal practice. Over many of the graves stood a tombstone inscribed merely with the name of the dead person and his or her father; in other cases a slip of bronze in the grave itself gave the same information. These inscriptions date the necropolis as a whole to the late Hellenistic period, approximately the last two centuries B.C.

The tombs varied greatly in the richness of their contents. Some were almost or quite empty apart from the corpse itself, others contained a variety of objects deposited at the time of burial. Many of these were deliberately broken, seemingly with the purpose of discouraging tomb-robbers.[2] These objects fall into several categories. First, nearly every grave was found to contain one or more coins. The original custom was to place an obol (say a penny) in the dead man's mouth to pay his fare in Charon's ferry over the Styx into the underworld; at Myrina the coins used are all bronze of small value, though not actually obol-pieces. Inflation had been at work in the interval and Charon's prices had gone up with the rest. These coins are nearly all of Myrina itself, and date from Alexander to Tiberius. Next in importance are the plates for the dead man's food and the bottles for his drink. These are in many cases token offerings only; some of the clay bottles are merely an inch or two high and quite solid. Third come the objects used habitually in life—lamps, mirrors, needles, perfume-boxes and

---

[1] Below, p. 142.

[2] So say the excavators; but the breakage may well have had a ritual purpose, as was certainly the case in other countries, e.g. Central America and Egypt; see for example L. Cottrell, *Lost Cities*, p. 186. We may compare the custom of breaking the glass after drinking a toast.

AEOLIS   109

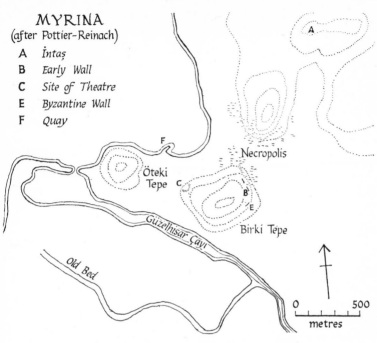

MYRINA
(after Pottier-Reinach)
A   İntaş
B   Early Wall
C   Site of Theatre
E   Byzantine Wall
F   Quay

FIG. 16 Plan of Myrina (after Pottier-Reinach)

many others. Jewellery, however, is scarce. Finally come the
famous terracotta figurines, of which a thousand or so were
found by the excavators and entitle Myrina to rank with
Tanagra. They include all kinds of figures, men, women,
children, gods and animals; Eros and Aphrodite are especially
popular. There are also grotesque and comic figures, and
tragic and comic masks. The purpose of these figurines has
been much disputed, but it seems that often they have no
particular significance, being merely favourite possessions of
the dead during life.

Of all these graves nothing whatever is to be seen now, the
ground having long since been ploughed over.

Some half a mile to the north-east of the acropolis, in a
conspicuous yellow outcrop near the top of the second hill in
that direction, is a rock-cut chamber-tomb known as İntaş.
The main chamber has a vaulted roof, and from it ten vaulted

niches some 6 feet deep open off. There are numerous other rock-cut tombs of more modest character in the neighbouring hills, which the local shepherd-boys will readily point out.

FIG. 17 Gryneum

On reaching Gryneum I made my sacrifice and occupied myself in my customary way; then proceeding to Elaea I put up there for the night, and on the following day arrived in Pergamum.

Strabo observes that Apollo was held in especial honour all down this coast; and of all his seats of worship in these parts the oracular sanctuary of Gryneum was the most famous.

Gryneum was one of the original twelve Aeolian cities, but nothing is recorded of its foundation by the Greeks. Tradition spoke of an earlier town named after the Amazon Gryne, who followed Queen Myrina on her campaigns and had the honour, or misfortune, to be violated by Apollo. The city first appears in history in the fifth century as a member of the Athenian maritime confederacy, in which she paid the modest sum of one-sixth of a talent, later raised to one-third. By the end of the century Athens, defeated by Sparta in the Peloponnesian War, had lost control of this region to the Persians, and about 405 B.C. we hear that the Persian satrap was drawing revenues of fifty talents a year from Gryneum. The figure is astonishingly high in view of the city's humble assessment in the Delian League, and is likely to be wrong.

The country was still in Persian hands in 335 B.C., when the Macedonian general Parmenio, sent ahead to prepare the way for Alexander's crossing into Asia, captured Gryneum by assault and enslaved the inhabitants. This event did not put an end to the city's independent existence, for the rare coins of Gryneum date from the third century; but at some time during the Hellenistic period it became a dependency of Myrina, noted henceforth mainly for the sanctuary of Apollo.

Of this sanctuary we have short descriptions in the writers of the Roman period. Strabo mentions the ancient oracle of Apollo and a costly temple of white marble. Pausanias speaks of a most beautiful grove of Apollo with trees, some cultivated for their fruit, others such as give no fruit but are pleasing to the sight or smell. These are still represented today by the olives and by the great expanses of pink oleanders which adorn the site. Pliny, who says there is now nothing but a harbour where Gryneum once existed, clearly does less than justice to the place.

We read in Virgil that it was Gryneian Apollo who urged Aeneas, after the fall of Troy, to go to Italy, where he became the legendary ancestor of the Romans. Apart from this somewhat unhistorical case, despite the fame of the oracle not a single response of Apollo at Gryneum was known until the present writer found at Caunus in Caria an inscription recording a consultation by the Caunians in the second century B.C. The Caunians ask to what gods they should sacrifice in order to obtain fruitful harvests. Of Apollo's reply in hexameter verse only the beginning is preserved; it is involved in suitable oracular obscurity, but advises that honour be paid to Apollo and Zeus.

Pliny mentions the oysters of Gryneum along with those of Myrina; and, in fact, both oysters and mussels are frequent on this coast. The coins of Gryneum show on one side the head of Apollo and on the other a mussel, thus commemorating the city's two chief claims to distinction.

The site of Gryneum is marked by the little promontory of Temaşalık Burnu, rather more than half a mile south of the village of Yenişakran. On this headland the temple of Apollo is supposed to have stood, though no very clear traces of it have been found. At present a rectangular mound or platform may be seen on the highest part of the peninsula, which may represent the sacred precinct; a dozen or more unfluted column-drums lie around its perimeter, but nothing more is visible. Even these are not of white marble, so cannot come from the

temple, but they might belong to a surrounding enclosure.
There are no signs of any ancient harbour-works; though
Pliny finds the harbour worth mentioning, it can never, in
fact, have been usable by any but very small boats, as the
Mediterranean Pilot makes clear.

The peninsula is too small to carry a city, even a modest one
like Gryneum, especially if a large part was occupied by the
temple precincts. The main habitation must have been on the
mainland. A few years ago there came to light, close beside the
main road, a cemetery with sarcophagi dating to about 500 B.C.
and a handsome mosaic pavement of late Roman date.
Nothing else, and in particular no acropolis, has yet been
found.

On the little Temaşalık Burnu, then, we may picture
Aristides making his sacrifice and occupying himself 'in his
customary way'. What this may have been he does not say,
but if we imagine him chatting with the priests, telling them
the news from Smyrna and the condition of his stomach, we
may not be far from the mark.

Elaea differs in several respects from the other cities of
Aeolis. It has the distinction of being apparently the earliest
Greek foundation on this coast; tradition said that it was
settled at the time of the Trojan War by Menestheus, leader
of the contingent from Athens, a hundred years or more before
the Aeolian migration from Greece. For this or some other
reason it was not included among the twelve members of the
Aeolian League, and in classical times was a place of little
account; its assessment in the Delian Confederacy was very low,
no more than one-sixth of a talent. The city's importance
began in the Hellenistic period, when most of the Aeolian
towns were sinking into obscurity, and was connected with the
rise of the Pergamene kingdom. Being situated at the nearest
point on the coast to the capital, it was made into a port and
naval station by the Attalid kings, and in this capacity it is
mentioned from time to time by the historians. With the
conversion of the kingdom of Pergamum into the province of
Asia this importance was largely lost. Elaea furnished a bed
for Aristides in the second century, and was still existing in

early Byzantine times. Oysters are not mentioned here, but Galen of Pergamum speaks of a thyme-covered hill not far away which produced the most excellent honey. Elaea means 'olive', an obviously appropriate name which is repeated today in the village of Zeytindağ some three miles to the north-east.

Little more remains at Elaea than at Gryneum, and the site has never been excavated. It is reached by a rough road turning off the highway at the coffee-house of Kazıkbağları, rather more than four miles north of Gryneum.

The principal surviving remnant of antiquity is the harbour wall D, now called Taş Liman. Still solidly preserved, this runs out for some 200 yards into a melancholy waste of mud-flats. It is constructed of large blocks laid horizontally and secured with metal clamps; the clamps themselves are gone, but the holes remain. The other walls of the harbour and quay are not now in evidence (Pl. 18).

The acropolis A is a low hill barely 60 feet high. Nothing remains standing on it, but ancient marbles are frequently turned up by the plough; a number of these are collected at the coffee-house. Sherds are abundant all over the hill; lamps, tiles and sometimes coins may be picked up. Those who enjoy searching for fragments of antiquity will find here a happy hunting-ground.

The line of the city wall B,B is traceable in places, especially between the acropolis and the main road, as a ridge in the ground, but nothing appears above the surface except a few stray blocks. German scholars sixty years ago were able to determine its thickness as 11 feet, and to date it to 234 B.C. by an inscription on one of the blocks. Of the gate H the position is identifiable in a dip between two hills close above the road, but the gate itself is not visible.

The necropolis seems to have been in the neighbourhood of N; here at least were found two inscribed funeral stelae which are at the time of writing in a private house near the café at Kazıkbağları.

No sign of a theatre or stadium has been found, and apart from the wells G,G nothing more is at present to be seen of ancient Elaea.

AT–H

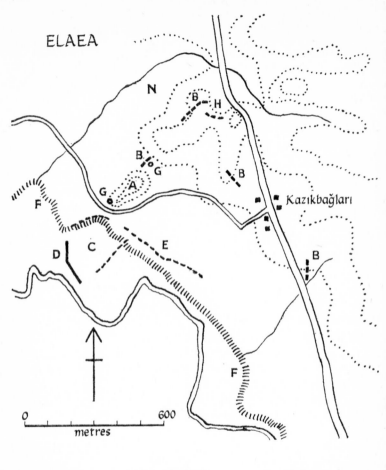

ELAEA

Kazıkbağları

A	Acropolis	B	City Wall	
D	Harbour Mole	E	Quay	
G	Well	H	Gate	

C Harbour
F Ancient Coastline
N Necropolis

FIG. 18 Plan of Elaea

At Pergamum we take leave of Aristides, cured of his disorder by the mere effort of the journey. On the way back to Smyrna we may turn aside to look at one or two sites which lay off his road.

A little to the north of Elaea a road leads westward to

Çandarlı, site of the ancient Pitane, on its tongue-like peninsula. The excursion is worth while if only for the fine Venetian
castle which stands in the town. Pitane was the northernmost
of the members of the Aeolian League, but no Greek foundation-legend survives. The town itself was far older than the
Aeolian colonisation; pottery has been found there dating back
to the third millennium. The Greek settlement was not unopposed, for we hear that the native people, called as at
Larisa 'Pelasgians', succeeded in recapturing the city, which
was only recovered with the help of the men of Erythrae.

In later times Pitane was noted for its vicissitudes of
fortune, so that the expression 'I'm a regular Pitane' became
proverbial of one who had experienced the ups and downs of
fate. These varied fortunes were related by the fifth-century
historian Hellanicus of Mitylene just across the water; but his
works are lost, and apart from the incident mentioned above
we know nothing of the early history of Pitane. The city was
included in the Delian League with the same modest assessment as Elaea and Gryneum.

Despite this evidence of comparative poverty, however,
Pitane had an extensive territory, and at least in the third
century was not destitute of funds. She was able to purchase
from King Antiochus I a piece of land on the gulf of Adramyttium to the north at a price of 380 talents; to this sum Philetaerus of Pergamum, anxious to secure good relations with his
neighbours, contributed perhaps forty talents out of the
9,000 of which he had possessed himself. Soon afterwards
Pitane, together with most of Aeolis, was incorporated in the
Pergamene kingdom. The city appears again for a moment in
history when Mithridates, hard pressed by Fimbria, fled there
and was besieged; but he escaped easily enough by sea to
Mitylene.

Pitane produced one famous citizen, the philosopher
Arcesilaus, who in the third century became head of the
Platonic Academy at Athens. He was noted for his readiness
to plead both sides of a question and for reserving judgment—
so much so, it is said, that he could never bring himself to
write a book.

Otherwise, the city's chief claim to fame was her bricks.

The soil being volcanic and lighter than an equal volume of water, the bricks when dried would not sink. This statement of Strabo's, repeated by Pliny, does not seem to have been verified in modern times; indeed, the ancient pottery found there is remarkable for its fine hard clay, and nothing is known at Çandarlı of any floating bricks.

Little now remains of ancient Pitane; the ruins have been thoroughly plundered for the building of Çandarlı. The peninsula was fortified by a wall of irregular masonry 8 feet thick, running round close above the sea; some very battered remnants may be seen here and there on the west side. Strabo refers to the city's two harbours; that on the west is formed by a mole now under water, running out to a tower on an islet. No such harbour-works are visible on the east, but this side being protected against the prevailing wind it is probable that none were needed.

Of the city's public buildings nothing survives, but the site of the theatre is recognisable about half-way down the east side of the peninsula; and a partly artificial terrace near the southern point seems to mark the position of a stadium. The Venetian castle is said to stand on ancient Greek masonry visible here and there (Pl. 19).

In 1958 an archaic statue of Ionian type was found by the villagers near the base of the isthmus, and is now in the Bergama museum. It is a life-size figure of a young man, naked apart from a mantle thrown over his left shoulder, 5 feet 4 inches in height. The very low relief of the features (which are, however, somewhat rubbed away), and the rigid upright posture, are typically archaic. The statue is dated to the latter part of the sixth century B.C. (Pl. 22).

This discovery led to an excavation by Turkish archaeologists in the following year, and a necropolis, dating in the main to the sixth century B.C., was brought to light. The custom here was to cremate the dead body and put it into a plain urn, of which the mouth was closed by a stone more or less carefully shaped for the purpose. The urns were either stood upright or laid on their side, according to their shape, but here again no rule is observable with regard to the orientation. In some cases a number of urns were enclosed by a circle

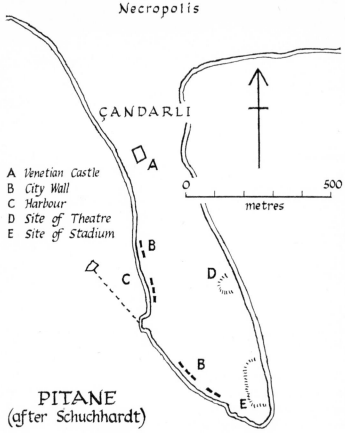

FIG. 19 Plan of Pitane (after Schuchhardt)

of rough stones some 10 to 15 feet in diameter, forming a family burying-place. Many handsome vases were found buried with the dead in the urns; these, too, are in the museum at Bergama. Of these burials nothing is now to be seen on the spot.

Some two and a half miles north of Buruncuk a road turns off westward to Eski Foça, the site of ancient Phocaea. Though situated fairly in the Aeolian country, Phocaea was always Ionian; Smyrna, on the other hand, being at first Aeolian, to

Fig. 20 Phocaea

this extent Ionia and Aeolis originally overlapped. The harbour
at Eski Foça is one of the best on this coast, and Phocaea was
at all times a place of some consequence.

In the history of Greek colonisation in Asia, Phocaea was a
late foundation, subsequent not only to the occupation of
Aeolis but also to the establishment of the Ionian League;
this would bring it down to the eighth century B.C. The
tradition was that the colonists came from Phocis in central
Greece under the leadership of two Athenians; the land being
already apportioned among the Greek settlers, they obtained
a site for their city by agreement with the men of Cyme—
further evidence of the un-sea-mindedness of the Cymaeans,
for the harbour they gave away is far superior to their own.
The Phocaeans applied for membership of the Panionium, and
were told that they must first take kings from the descendants
of the sons of Codrus who played so large a part in the colonisation of Ionia. They accordingly took three from Erythrae and
Teos and were admitted to the league. It is likely, however,
that this tradition is false and was invented at a later date to

explain the name Phocaea by a supposed connection with Phocis. Modern scholars think it more probable that the city was a secondary foundation from Erythrae and Teos, and received its name from the humpy, seal-like appearance of the off-lying islets; for *phoce* is the Greek word for a seal. The coins of Phocaea, and especially the earlier issues, commonly bear the image of a seal (Pl. 60).[1]

Profiting from its fine site and the enterprise of its citizens, the city quickly rose to a place of eminence. The Phocaeans, like the Ionians in general, were great mariners, and their adventurous spirit led them to the west, where they were the first to explore the Adriatic and the western Mediterranean, even as far as Tartessus near Cadiz. Hereabouts they founded a number of colonies, of which the most famous was Massalia, the modern Marseilles. In this connection a curious little tale was told. The Phocaean adventurers arrived hoping to establish a city, and found the country in the possession of a local chieftain by the name of Nannus. This man was on the point of marrying his daughter off, and invited the Greek leader to attend the ceremony. The custom was for the girl to enter the room where the suitors were assembled and to offer to the man of her choice a cup of wine and water. She, however, 'whether by chance or for some other reason' (one wonders which), gave the cup to the Phocaean visitor. Nannus, seeing in this erratic behaviour the hand of the gods, made the best of the situation; he accepted his Greek son-in-law and gave him the land on which to found Massalia. The colonists were afterwards able to be of service to their mother-city.

When at Tartessus the Phocaeans struck up a friendship with the king of that country, who urged them to leave Ionia and settle where they liked in his dominions. Their refusal gave him so little offence that, on learning from them that the Persians were then growing dangerous, he gave them a sum of money to fortify their city. 'He gave with no niggard hand, for [says Herodotus] the wall they built was not a few stades in length and all of large stones carefully fitted.' Of this wall nothing remains today.

[1] We may compare the islands at Erythrae known as 'The Horses' (below, p. 157).

In due course (544 B.C.) the Persians arrived and laid siege to the town. Their commander Harpagus offered remarkably easy terms, merely demanding that the inhabitants should demolish one breastwork of their wall and consecrate a single house to the Persian king. The Phocaeans asked for one day to think it over. Harpagus replied that he knew very well what they had in mind to do, but would nevertheless grant the delay. While he withdrew his army the citizens hastily put on board their wives, children and movable property, together with most of the statues and offerings from the temples, and sailed away to Chios. Next day the Persians marched into an empty city. From Chios, where they found themselves unwelcome, the Phocaeans set sail for the island of Corsica, where they had a colony called Alalia; but on leaving they put back into Phocaea and slaughtered the garrison left there by the Persians. Thereupon they swore mighty oaths to stick together on their migration, and threw a lump of iron into the sea, vowing never to return till it should reappear. No sooner had they left, however, than more than half of them, overcome by longing for their familiar haunts, broke their oaths and sailed back to the city. How they made their peace with the Persians for the murdered garrison we do not hear, but Phocaea was permitted to exist. The others meanwhile made their way to Corsica, and from there after a time to Rhegium, and finally to Elea in the south of Italy. The city they founded there became rapidly one of the greatest of western Greece, and developed in the fifth century the Eleatic school of philosophy; the best known of its professors is probably Zeno, whose notorious paradox of Achilles and the Tortoise, and his other puzzles concerning motion, were famous in antiquity and are still none too easy to explain away (Appendix III).

The loss of half its population had the natural result of reducing the prosperity and commercial activity of Phocaea; for several decades the coinage appears to have ceased. By the end of the sixth century, however, the city had so far recovered that she could venture to take part in the Ionian revolt against the Persians, though her modest contribution of three ships to the Ionian fleet at Lade in 494 is evidence of her continuing weakness. So in the Delian League her tribute is assessed at only two to three talents, less than one-third of that of her neighbour Cyme. During the fifth century Phocaea issued an abundant coinage of electrum, an alloy of gold and silver, but this money seems to have had a bad reputation, perhaps because the gold content was too low.

In the fourth and third centuries little is heard of Phocaea. Later, when the Romans came to Asia in their war with Antiochus III of Syria, the Phocaeans were reluctant to see in them the future masters of the country and preferred to take the king's part. The Romans accordingly invested the city in 190 B.C. The fine wall admired by Herodotus, now over 300 years old, was not proof against the Roman battering rams, and was breached in two places; the citizens, however, repelled the first assault and continued to resist with such fury as to provoke the Roman commander Aemilius to remark that by fighting on they seemed more determined than the Romans to ensure the city's destruction. When reasonable terms were offered, and no help was forthcoming from Antiochus, the Phocaeans at length opened their gates, on condition that they should suffer no hostile treatment. But Aemilius proved unable to contain his men; his commands were disregarded and the city plundered by the Roman soldiery. Afterwards he restored it to its owners, together with its territory and its independence.

Sixty years later the Phocaeans were guilty of a second error. When Aristonicus contested the Roman inheritance of the kingdom of Attalus, they made the mistake of supporting him. The Romans this time were less forbearing, and Phocaea was condemned to destruction by the Senate. The Massaliotes, however, came to the rescue of their mother-city; they interceded with the Senate and secured a pardon for the offenders. In the Mithridatic War nothing is heard of the Phocaeans, and it may be presumed that they had learned their lesson.

The site of Phocaea at Eski Foça has never been in doubt. It is amply proved by the survival of the name, by the Phocaean coins found on the spot, and in particular by the description given by Livy in narrating the events of 190 B.C. 'The city', he says, 'is of oblong shape and situated at the head of a bay. The wall encloses a space of two and a half

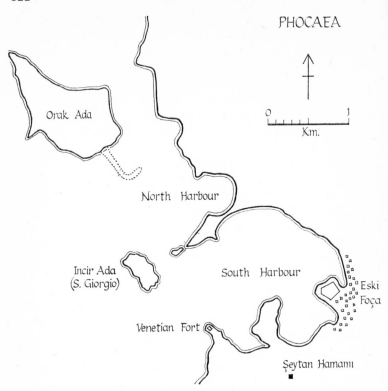

FIG. 21 Plan of Phocaea

miles, then runs in from either side to form a kind of wedge, which the natives call Lampter. There is at this point a width of twelve hundred paces. Next, a tongue of land a mile long runs out and divides the bay approximately in the middle; where it joins the narrow entrance it forms on either hand a very safe port. That on the south is called Naustathmos because it will shelter a vast number of ships; the other is close by Lampter.'

There can be no doubt that this account refers to Eski Foça, of which it has often been called an exact description. Nevertheless it is not easy to relate all the details to the actual terrain. Livy's text is no doubt taken from his Greek authority; he does not write from personal knowledge. Lampter must be the little peninsula on which the modern town stands, and the tongue of land a mile long must be the spit running out towards the island of San Giorgio (now Incir Ada), though, in fact, it is little over half that length. This spit runs out from a spot

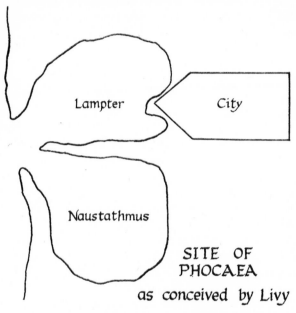

Fig. 22 Site of Phocaea as conceived by Livy

twelve hundred paces across the harbour from Lampter, which is approximately correct. The two harbours are then the present harbour (Naustathmos) and that beyond the spit which the Admiralty Chart calls the North Harbour. So far, so good; the difficulty lies in Livy's last few words. How can the other, i.e. northern harbour, be said to be close by Lampter when Lampter is at the very heart of the southern harbour? This difficulty is so severe as to wreck the whole description, and some have even been led to identify the two harbours with the little bays immediately north and south of the Lampter peninsula. Since Lampter means a lamp or beacon, we might then suppose that a beacon or lighthouse stood on the north side of this peninsula, so that the northern harbour might be said to be 'hard by the beacon'. But we are not really any better off; the tongue of land a mile long will not fit in at all. Livy's account is certainly faulty; he seems to have imagined that the spit was to the south of Lampter, with the harbour of Naustathmos beyond it, somewhat as in the adjoining sketch; his description will then hang together.

Hardly anything remains of classical Phocaea. That the ancient city stood in part on the small peninsula which is the centre of the modern town was proved by the excavations undertaken in 1913 and 1920 by the French archaeologist Sartiaux, but his discoveries were limited to sherds and other small finds. A further investigation by Turkish archaeologists, begun in 1953, located a temple (probably that of Athena) on a rocky platform near the tip of the peninsula; but in general the ancient remains lie deeply buried under the modern buildings.

The surviving monuments consist principally of two tombs. Outside the town on the south-west, a short distance up the hillside, not easy to find without a guide, is a rock-cut chamber tomb known as Şeytan Hamamı, the Devil's Bath. The arched entrance is approached by a passage cut in the rock, with a recess on right and left just in front of the door. Inside are two plain chambers, one behind the other, connected by a second arched doorway. Each chamber contains two rectangular graves let into the floor on either side. The whole tomb is very neatly carved and well repays a visit.

The other monument, called by the Turks Taş Kule, stands five miles to the east of the town, close beside the road where it crosses a stream. It consists of a tomb entirely cut out of an outcrop of rock, and still stands nearly 20 feet high. Its appearance has been compared to that of a small country church with a square tower. The main cube is about 28 feet long by 19 feet wide; upon this base, at its east end, are four steps leading up to a smaller cube on which there stood originally some further object which is now broken away—perhaps a stepped pyramid surmounted by a phallus-stone, but this is uncertain. Otherwise the monument is quite plain except on its eastern face, which is decorated with a false door divided into four panels.

The burial-chamber is in the interior of the cubical base. The entrance is on the north side and leads to a small ante-

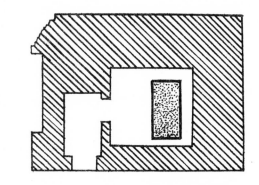

FIG. 23 Phocaea Road. Taş Kule

chamber which opens on the right into the grave-chamber itself. Both these rooms are plain, with flat roofs; in the floor of the inner room is the actual grave, a simple rectangular trough.

There are numerous cuttings in the rocks around the tomb and in the bed of the stream close by. These latter may have been used for washing clothes, in the manner of Nausicaa—as indeed the present writer has actually seen them being used.

Nothing whatever is known about this remarkable tomb. No expert who has seen it doubts its great antiquity, and its general style is reminiscent of the early monuments in Phrygia, dating to the time of the Old Kingdom in the eighth century B.C. This was a time of good relations between the Phrygians and the Greeks, when King Midas was the first barbarian to make an offering at Delphi. Later, when the Lydians and then the Persians intervened, Phrygian influence in Ionia is hardly to be expected. There seems no reason why this tomb should not date back to this early period; it may indeed be earlier than Phocaea itself (Pl. 20).

A little farther down the coast is the site of Leucae, at a spot now called Üç Tepeler, the Three Hills. A curious story is told concerning the origin of this city. Diodorus says that it was founded in the fourth century, not long after the King's Peace, by a Persian officer Tachos, and that after his death Clazomenae and Cyme quarrelled for the possession of it. After some indecisive fighting they agreed to consult the oracle at Delphi, and the god decreed that Leucae should belong to whichever of the two peoples should first make sacrifice there —the conditions being that each party should march from its own city at dawn on an appointed day. Leucae being by land much nearer to Cyme than to Clazomenae, the Cymaeans expected to win easily, but the Clazomenians were equal to the occasion. After agreeing on a day for the sacrifice they sent a party of colonists across the gulf of Smyrna and founded a city close to Leucae; by starting from this they comfortably forestalled the Cymaeans. Since the new foundation could fairly be called 'their city', the Clazomenians were recognised as masters of Leucae, and to commemorate their ingenuity they established there an annual festival by the name of the Festival of Forestalment.

This story, though it lacks corroboration, is perhaps less suspect than it might seem. Tachos was at the time engineering a rebellion against the Persian king, and Leucae was no doubt founded as a base for his operations; but in the event the rebellion fizzled out and nothing was done. The subsequent contest for possession of the place may also be historical; at least, the Festival of Forestalment must be an historical fact, and there is nothing to prove that the explanation given is not the true one.

The town itself was never of any great consequence. In the latter part of the fourth century it was sufficiently independent to strike its own coins, bearing the type of a swan; this is the normal type of the coins of Clazomenae. It makes one momentary appearance in history when, after Attalus III had bequeathed his kingdom to Rome, the pretender Aristonicus persuaded the men of Leucae to support his cause and used the town as a base. What penalty, if any, the inhabitants were made to pay to the Romans we do not know.

The site of Leucae lies on the great expanse of alluvial land created by the Hermus River. This region has for many years been a prohibited zone, and it is not normally possible to visit it, at least without special permission. The coastline has, of course, advanced since antiquity. When founded, Leucae was on an island; by Pliny's time this had become a headland, and it is now some way from the shore.

★

Westward from Smyrna

CLAZOMENAE

FOR TWENTY miles west of Smyrna the south coast of the gulf offers nothing in the way of a harbour. The present Izmir–Çeşme highroad, once past the Baths of Agamemnon, follows the coast below the Two Brothers, and in the neighbourhood of Kızılbahçe (formerly Kilisman) enters the territory of ancient Clazomenae. The city itself is six miles farther on, situated on a small island joined to the mainland by a causeway. This island carries a quarantine station, and is also occupied by a hospital specialising in diseases of the bone; visitors desiring to wander over the island may therefore be somewhat coolly welcomed, and a letter of introduction from the Kaymakam of Urla is a useful precaution.

Clazomenae, like Phocaea, was a comparatively late foundation in the Ionian settlement of the coast. Pausanias observes that the sites of these two cities were uninhabited until the Greeks came. In the case of Clazomenae this is not strictly true, for pre-Greek sherds have been found on the little hill just to the east of the scala of Urla (A on the plan); this, however, was not the spot chosen by the Ionians. Pausanias tells how a group of the Greek settlers, later comers than the rest, took a leader from Colophon and founded a city under Mt. Ida in the Troad; this they soon abandoned and settled for a while on the territory of Colophon, then finally occupied the land which became their permanent home, and built a city called Clazomenae on the mainland. The move to the island came later, 'through fear of the Persians'.

That Clazomenae was originally on the mainland, not the island, is certain from other evidence as well. Strabo notes a

128

place called Chytrion on the mainland, 'where the Clazomenians were once settled'; there will be more to say of this
place later. Over a wide area several miles long and broad
there have been found large numbers (certainly over a hundred) of the distinctive painted terracotta sarcophagi which
are peculiar to Clazomenae. One or two specimens of these
may be seen in the Izmir Museum, but most of those which
were taken to Izmir were destroyed in the great fire of 1922.
These sarcophagi date in general to the sixth century B.C.,
and none appears to have been found on the island. The exact
site of this early Clazomenae has been determined with great
probability by Professor J. M. Cook. About a mile to the
south-west of the hill A, in a small enclosed valley (B on the
plan), he found much pottery of sixth century and earlier date
clearly indicating habitation at that time; no remains of
buildings are now visible here, but some eighty Clazomenian
sarcophagi were unearthed in the immediate neighbourhood
by the Greek excavator G. P. Oikonomos in 1921–2. The
acropolis of this early city must have been the hill C, on which
stands an isolated house; it is low for the purpose, but no more
so than, for example, the acropolis of Elaea. We should nevertheless have expected a rather stronger site; for about 600
B.C. the Lydian king Alyattes, fresh from his capture of
Smyrna, invaded Clazomenae and was severely defeated. This
seems to argue either very strong walls, of which no trace
survives, or great valour on the part of the citizens.

From here the Clazomenians moved to the island 'for fear
of the Persians'. This would naturally suggest a move at the
time of the Persians' first descent to the coast after the fall of
Croesus in 546 B.C.; since, however, the pottery on the archaic
site continues till the end of the sixth century, it appears that
the move must have been rather in connection with the ill-
fated Ionian Revolt of 500–494. At this time there was no
causeway; and throughout the fifth century Clazomenae continued to be strictly an island-city. In the Delian League her
normal tribute was one and a half talents, a sum which puts
her little above the level of the humblest in Ionia; but during
the Peloponnesian War it was suddenly raised, first to six
talents, then to no less than fifteen. Moreover, it appears that

AT–I

these amounts were, in fact, paid. It is not known what the reason may have been for this startling increase; the Athenians needed money for the war, but this in itself would not enable the Clazomenians actually to pay, and no cause is known why the city's fortunes should have taken such a turn for the better. However this may be, a few years later Clazomenae was easily persuaded by the Spartans to revolt from Athens; the citizens crossed to the mainland and fortified a small place called Polichna as a refuge. Shortly afterwards the Athenians attacked and captured Polichna and moved the Clazomenians back to their island; Clazomenae rejoined the Athenian alliance, and a subsequent Spartan assault was unsuccessful.

FIG. 24 Clazomenae

By the terms of the King's Peace in 386 B.C., when peace was made between the Greeks and Persians, it was laid down that 'the Great King deems it right that the cities in Asia should belong to him, and of the islands Cyprus and Clazomenae' (an oddly assorted pair). From this we should naturally infer that the causeway was still not in existence; and, in fact, we have the testimony of two ancient writers that the idea of the causeway was due to Alexander the Great more than fifty years later. Pliny says that, Clazomenae being an island, Alexander ordered it to be joined to the mainland across a space of two stades. Pausanias says that Alexander intended to make Clazomenae into a peninsula by means of a mole from the mainland to the island. This explicit evidence has, however, been called in question in recent years—in the writer's opinion, mistakenly. The problem may be set forth briefly.

In the years before the King's Peace, Clazomenae was disturbed by internal dissensions, apparently of long standing, to which we have three separate items of testimony. An Athenian decree of 387 B.C., preserved on stone, permits the Clazomenians to decide 'whether they will or will not make a truce with those at Chyton, and also what to do with the hostages they hold from among those at Chyton', and refers to 'those who fled and those who remained'. Aristotle, writing about 330 B.C., observes that faction in cities sometimes arises owing to the nature of the ground, when the physical conditions are not suited to a single city, and two separate cities would be more appropriate, 'as for example at Clazomenae between those at Chytron [*sic*] and those on the island'. Evidently the men of Chyt(r)on on the mainland found it difficult to get on with their fellow citizens on the island, and when a split occurred on the island, probably between democrats and oligarchs, one of the parties had withdrawn thither expecting to find sympathy, and no doubt widening the breach between the two parts of the city, so that hostilities resulted. It is no doubt to these events that Ephorus refers in a fragment of his history dealing with this same period: 'those from Clazomenae settled in a place on the mainland called Chyton'. This place is presumably the same as Strabo's Chytrion, where the Clazomenians used to live.

The place in question has given rise to much controversy. First, which is the true form of the name, Chyton, Chytron or Chytrion? The presence or absence of the 'r' affects the meaning of the word. In a question of this kind preference is naturally given to the inscription, which is an original document, over the literary passages, which are liable to the hazards of corruption. Suppose, then, that Chyton is right. This word is used in literature of earth heaped up into a mound or dyke, and some scholars have seen in it an allusion to the causeway; they accordingly place Chyton at or near the landward end of the causeway. In further support of this view they point to the words of Pliny, who appears to say that Clazomenae was at one time called something like Chytoporia; this would mean 'the passage by the dyke', which could hardly be other than the causeway. But the reading is uncertain, and the passage is corrupt in other respects too. These considerations are not, in the present writer's opinion, sufficient to displace

the definite statement of two authorities that the causeway
was due to Alexander. Moreover, as Professor Cook rightly
points out, Aristotle ascribes the trouble at Clazomenae to
the nature of the ground being unsuitable for a single city;
this would naturally imply not only some distance between
the two parts but also a difference in their situation liable to
give rise to an incompatibility of outlook. Clazomenae being
an island city, Chyton should be looked for inland, not by the
shore at the end of the causeway. Remembering Strabo's
Chytrion, 'where the Clazomenians used to live', we might
suppose that the place in question was simply the original city
(B on the plan), which may well have continued to exist as a
deme of the island city; but Professor Cook prefers a site still
farther inland, on the plain to the south-west of Urla. Here
he found sufficient sherds to indicate settled habitation, though
again no traces of buildings are to be seen. We can then easily
understand that the men living here, occupied mainly with
agriculture, found it hard to achieve sympathy with the
maritime preoccupations of the islanders. If this is right, as
appears probable, we are not obliged to choose between the
various forms of the name; if Chyton is the true form, the
reference may be to some other dyke or mound not now
identifiable. When Strabo says the Clazomenians were formerly
settled at Chytrion, he need not mean that this was the
original site of the city; he may mean merely that it was no
longer inhabited in his own day. This problem is of a kind that
frequently faces those who are concerned with the topography
of the ancient world; its solution, or probable solution, is one
of the many services that Professor Cook has rendered in this
branch of science.

Clazomenae was not backward in the field of learning; two
of her citizens at least were distinguished philosophers.
Anaxagoras, born about 500 B.C., was reckoned the last of
the Ionian Physicists. These men, the fathers of Greek
philosophy, sought to discover the basic elements of matter,
the material of which the world is composed; more will be said
of them below.[1] Whereas his predecessors had looked for a
single basic element, such as water, air or fire, Anaxagoras

[1] See p. 221.

broke new ground by admitting that the elements of all substances existed from the beginning, and were sorted and
arranged to form the substances we know by a controlling
principle which he called Mind. By thus introducing an in-
telligent rather than a mechanical causation he paved the way
for the yet more enlightened views of Plato and Aristotle.
Anaxagoras taught at Athens for thirty years, counting
Pericles and Euripides among his pupils; but some of his views,
for example that the sun was a mass of red-hot stone, were too
much for the conservative Athenians, and he was prosecuted
for impiety. This could be a capital offence, as was later shown
in the case of Socrates, and Anaxagoras was only saved by the
personal intervention of Pericles. He was obliged to withdraw
from Athens and ended his days at Lampsacus on the Dardanelles.

The second Clazomenian philosopher was the sophist Scopelianus, who lived more than 500 years later in the time of
Domitian. His name is hardly known now, but he was a man
of distinction in his day. He lived and taught in Smyrna, and
when the Clazomenians urged him to return and adorn his
native city he declined to do so, on the elegant plea that the
nightingale will not sing in a cage. He had personal reasons,
too, for not wanting to live in Clazomenae, for he had quarrelled with his father. The old man desired to take a second
wife out of matrimony, and took his son's disapproval in bad
part. The lady declared that Scopelianus was in love with her
himself, and a rascally slave joined in with a tale that he had
bribed him to poison his father's food. Shortly after, when the
old man died, it was found that he had left all his property to
the slave.

In A.D. 92 Domitian issued his notorious edict that all vines
in Ionia should be destroyed and no new ones planted. In this
the emperor was credited in antiquity with prohibitionist
motives, but it is no doubt more probable that he wished to
encourage the cultivation of corn. Viticulture being, then as
now, a main industry in the region of Smyrna, there was
consternation in the province, and Scopelianus was chosen to
lead an appeal at Rome. Such was his success that he brought
back from the emperor not only permission to plant vines but

penalties against those who failed to do so. This was certainly
something of a triumph, for Domitian cannot have been an
easy man to plead with.

The island, now again under its old name in the form
Klazümen, has a little more to show in the way of ancient
remains than the mainland sites, but still not very much. The
famous causeway still exists, close beside its modern successor.
Chandler in 1764 rode across it on horseback, and had some
difficulty in getting back when the Imbat got up in the afternoon. It is doubtful whether this could be done today; normally only a few of the blocks are visible above water. Chandler
estimated its width as 30 feet; the length of the modern causeway (slightly longer than the ancient) is 700 yards, so that
Pliny's 'two stades' is a distinct underestimate.

The harbour was in the bay at the waist of the island on the
west. On the north side of this bay at J are clear remains of
harbour-works, now nearly submerged, containing good
squared blocks and apparently ancient. At the northern tip
of the island there are also remains of a quay, now almost
flush with the water, and the sea is full of blocks fallen from
it; just above the waterline are two small intercommunicating
basins, one of which has been used as a kiln. On the shore at
this point is a short stretch of the city wall, in ashlar masonry
of smallish blocks; the rest of the wall has disappeared. After
the construction of the causeway, that, too, would afford a
convenient landing-stage, on east or west according to the
wind.

On the north slope of the northern hill was the theatre, of
medium size, but virtually nothing remains of it beyond the
hollow in the hillside. When the writer was there in 1946
numerous well-squared blocks had recently been dug out, but
these have since been removed. On top of the hill above the
theatre, at the highest point on the island, is a corner of the
foundation of a rectangular building, neatly cut in the rock.
Of the building itself nothing survives; in this situation it is
likely to have been a temple.

Quite close to the shore, at F, is a cave containing a well.
As its name Ayazma implies, this has in the past been regarded
as a holy place. The steps leading down to it are not ancient,

A Pre-Greek Site
B Archaic Greek Site
C Acropolis (Archaic)
D Theatre
E Quay
F Ayazma
G Temple ?
H Angle of City Wall
J Mole

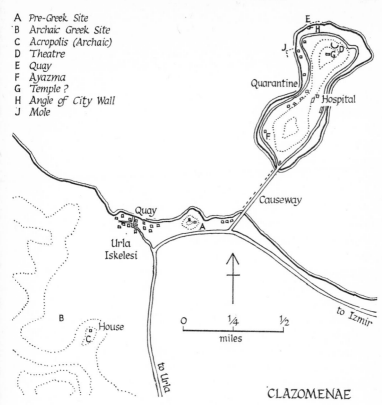

FIG. 25 Plan of Clazomenae

but the masonry over the entrance is good and regular. The
cave is said to consist of four communicating chambers; these
were cleared out some twenty years ago, but in the process the
roof fell in, and only one chamber and part of another are now
visible. This one contains the well; its roof, only about 5 feet
high, is of rock and is supported by two rock-cut pillars. There
are several niches in the walls. The well is about 5 feet deep;
the water, though not salt, is unfit for drinking. Pausanias,
speaking of the various noteworthy features of Ionia, says that
the Clazomenians possess a cave which they call the 'Cave of
Pyrrhus' mother'; Pyrrhus was a shepherd, and there was a
tale told about him—but he does not tell us what the tale was.

Whether this may be the cave just described we cannot know; at least no other remarkable cave seems to have been noticed on Clazomenian territory.

TEOS

'There is', says Freya Stark, 'a welcome about the approach to Teos. . . . It is where I should live, if I had the choice of all the cities of Ionia.' The present writer well remembers his own welcome in 1946; within ten minutes of his arrival in Sığacık he found himself presented with a quantity of ancient vases, lamps, figurines and knucklebones, together with a bag of some seventy coins, all of which had recently been found among the ruins of Teos. Knucklebones are the neck vertebrae of a sheep or other animal, and were used as dice; there are four surfaces on which they may rest, scoring respectively one, three, four and six. Loaded dice were by no means unknown; Aristotle speaks of 'leaded dice', and, in fact, one of the 1946 collection has a lump of lead let into one side. Another has scratched upon it 'Herostratus loves B.Z.'—a little cryptic, but perhaps it brought him luck.

The traveller today can hardly hope to be quite so fortunate in his reception. In 1946 Teos had only just ceased to be a forbidden zone, and strangers were a rarity; now they are commonplace, for the headland of Teos has been converted into a N.A.T.O. bathing-beach, and a tarmac road leads all the way from Smyrna. But the villagers are as friendly as ever, and Sığacık is a delightful spot.[1] The houses are built in and around a Genoese fortress occupying the position of an ancient landing-stage. In the ruins of Teos a party from Ankara University has recently undertaken an excavation, still in progress at the time of writing.

According to tradition Teos was founded by Minyans from Orchomenus in Boeotia; Ionians and Athenians led by two of the numerous sons of Codrus came later. The city prospered from the beginning and led a number of colonies overseas, though most of these remained obscure. About 600 B.C. Thales of Miletus proposed that the twelve Ionian cities should

[1] The name is now written Sığacak on the signposts.

establish a common political assembly at Teos, as being centrally situated. The idea was a good one, for the Panionium was religious only, and the lack of a common policy was the Ionians' great weakness, as was to be proved in the time of danger; but the proposal was not adopted. When the Persians came and Teos fell with the rest, the citizens, 'unable to endure the Persian arrogance', set sail in a body for Thrace, and there founded the city of Abdera. This, though the best known of the Teian colonies, was not a great credit to them, for its inhabitants were later noted for their stupidity, and Abderite became proverbial for a simpleton. Many of the colonists, in fact, soon returned to the mother-city, and at the battle of Lade in 494 B.C. were already able to muster seventeen ships.

The early prosperity was quickly regained, and in the Delian Confederacy Teos was assessed at six talents, a figure which places her among the richest of the Ionian cities. Her wealth came surely from sea-borne commerce; Smyrna was at this time reduced to village status, and Teos must have taken a large share of the trade that would otherwise have gone there. Indeed, when Hamilton visited Sığacık in 1836 he expressed surprise that its harbour was not even then more used in preference to Smyrna, to avoid the long beat up the gulf and the much more difficult return journey against the prevailing Imbat.

In the year 304 B.C. the whole of Ionia was shaken by an earthquake. Perhaps in consequence of this Antigonus proposed to transfer to Teos all the population of Lebedus and to fuse the two cities into one. His elaborate plans for this 'synoecism' are preserved in a long inscription found at Seferihisar; but they were never put into action, for Antigonus lost Teos to Lysimachus in 302 and was himself killed in battle in the following year. Lysimachus had other ideas; he needed men to fill the new city of Ephesus which he had just founded, and he transplanted thither a number of the citizens both of Teos and of Lebedus.

The principal deity of Teos was Dionysus, and the great sanctity of this god led, about the end of the third century, to a notable accession of dignity for the city. Teos was chosen as the residence of the Asiatic branch of the Artists of Dionysus,

and her territory was recognised as sacred and inviolable.
These Artists were a professional guild of actors and musicians
which supplied paid performers at the dramatic and musical
festivals held all over the Greek world. In addition to the
centre at Teos there were local branches at many other cities
to serve the surrounding country and to compete for the prizes
given in the contests for tragedy, comedy, music, singing and
the rest. Drama being always under the patronage of Dionysus, his Artists were a religious as well as a professional body,
and enjoyed certain privileges universally recognised, notably
freedom from taxation and safe conduct for their person
wherever they went. Each branch had its own organisation
and was largely independent of the city to which it was attached; relations between Artists and city were regulated by
agreement in each case. But the artistic temperament is
notoriously difficult. Indispensable as they certainly were, the
Artists seem to have been overconscious of their own importance, and they had a bad reputation as troublesome cus-
tomers. Philostratus calls them 'a very arrogant class of men
and hard to keep in order', and one of the Aristotelian Problems is devoted to the question 'Why are the Artists of Dionysus in general bad men?' The suggested answer is that too
much of their time is occupied in loose living, and that their
arts are practised not for art's sake but in order to earn a
livelihood, leaving little or no time for the acquisition of
wisdom.

The history of the guild in Ionia does nothing to contradict
this judgment. At first all was well; the Teians bought a piece
of land of the value of one talent and presented it to the
Artists with compliments and prayers for their well-being. But
before long quarrels broke out and became frequent; about
the middle of the second century the Artists were obliged to
move to Ephesus. They seem to have been no more popular
there, and Attalus II of Pergamum transferred them to
Myonnesus. Whereupon the Teians complained to the Romans
of this accession of strength to a town on their frontier, and the
Artists were moved on once more, this time to Lebedus. Here
at last they found themselves welcome, for Lebedus was
meagrely populated and glad of any addition to its manpower.

Mark Antony moved them again to Priene, but this was only a temporary measure for the benefit of Cleopatra, and they were soon back in Lebedus.

In 190 B.C. there occurred an incident which has an especial interest owing to the topographical detail with which it is described by Livy. Antiochus III and the Romans were at that time contesting possession of the coast, and the Teians had collected considerable supplies, including five thousand jars of wine, which were destined for the king's forces. Learning of this, the Roman admiral put quickly into Teos, anchoring in the northern harbour behind the city, and began to plunder the Teian territory. When the Teians complained of this conduct he gave them the choice of surrendering to him the provisions collected for Antiochus or being treated as an enemy. After deliberation they decided to do as he wished. Meanwhile the king's fleet lay a few miles to the south at the island of Macris (now Doğanbey Adasi). Its commander, hearing of the Roman activities, conceived the design of trapping them in the harbour; for, says Livy, the entrance is so narrowed by projecting headlands that two ships can hardly emerge together. This is certainly an overstatement: the channel is, in fact, scarcely less than half a mile in breadth: nevertheless, the plan of stationing ships at the headlands to attack the Roman vessels as they made their way out against the wind was no bad one and might well have succeeded. Before it could be put into operation, however, the Roman admiral decided that for purposes of taking on board the wine and other provisions it would be more convenient to move the fleet to the southern port close in front of the city. When this was done and the men were ashore collecting the stores (and especially, says Livy, the wine) news was brought that the king's fleet was preparing to put out. Great was the alarm; amid the utmost confusion the men were recalled and hurried on board; Livy compares the scene to a sudden outbreak of fire or the capture of a city. In the subsequent engagement, however, the steadiness of the Roman fighters prevailed, and Antiochus was reduced shortly afterwards to suing, unsuccessfully, for peace. This incident lives again vividly for the visitor to Teos. It constitutes in effect the last appearance of Teos in history,

for with the establishment of the Roman province she disap-
pears from the current of events.

As notable citizens of Teos, Strabo can name two men.
One is, of course, the lyric poet Anacreon, the first, it is said,
after Sappho the Lesbian to make love the theme of his poetry.
This charming hedonist, whose statue in Athens showed a man
singing in his cups, was Teos' only contribution to the early
culture of Ionia. The second, Apellicon, was not a great man
at all, and is remarkable only for the part he played in the
curious history of Aristotle's library. On his death Aristotle
bequeathed his books, the only library hitherto collected, to
his successor Theophrastus, who in turn left them to his pupil
Neleus; this man carried them to Scepsis in the Troad, where
they passed to his descendants, unscholarly men who neglected
to look after them, and to avoid surrendering them to the
library of Pergamum[1] hid them away in a damp place underground where they suffered badly. Consequently, when the
books were sold about 100 B.C. at a high price to Apellicon of
Teos, he found the texts defective in many places. Being a
bibliophile rather than a scholar, he copied the texts on to
fresh sheets, filling in the gaps with his own conjectures, and
so published the books full of errors. Apellicon's library was
later carried off by Sulla to Rome, where the texts were re-
edited by a keen Aristotelian scholar named Tyrannion.
Strabo adds that mistakes continued to be common owing to
the rascality of the booksellers, who employed inefficient
copyists and neglected to check the copies.

The site of Teos is in some ways unusual. It is of the peninsula
type, but the acropolis was not on the headland itself but on
a separate hill in the middle of the isthmus, half-way between
the northern and southern harbours, about a mile from each.
The earliest fortifications are on the acropolis hill; some
remnants of polygonal wall survive, but the whole is much
overgrown and little can be made out. The town extends on
the south side, between the acropolis and the harbour, and
was fortified in the third century B.C. with walls of regular
ashlar; the ground being level, the walls run in straight lines at

[1] Above, p. 74.

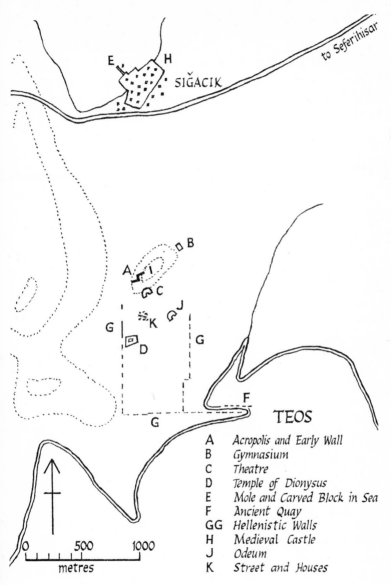

to Seferihisar

SIĞACIK

TEOS

A   Acropolis and Early Wall
B   Gymnasium
C   Theatre
D   Temple of Dionysus
E   Mole and Carved Block in Sea
F   Ancient Quay
GG   Hellenistic Walls
H   Medieval Castle
J   Odeum
K   Street and Houses

0   500   1000

metres

Fig. 26 Plan of Teos

141

right-angles to one another—a highly unusual feature. Little
of them is visible above ground, but a short stretch of the
western wall has been excavated close to the temple of Dionysus and gives a good idea of the masonry.

The south harbour has been much silted up since antiquity
by a small stream which flows into it, but a part of the ancient
quay survives on the inner side of the southern spit; at intervals are projecting blocks pierced to form stone rings to which
boats might tie up. Hamilton reasoned from their position
just above water that there can have been no great change in
the sea-level since ancient times; in fact, however, it has risen
by nearly a fathom,[1] and the rings must have stood well
above the waterline. In the northern harbour, too, there are
remains of a mole or landing-stage running out under water
from beneath the Genoese castle (Pl. 21).

The famous temple of Dionysus, the great deity of the
Teians, stood on the west side of the city just inside the wall.
It was first excavated by the Society of Dilettanti in the
eighteenth century, after which an enterprising Smyrniote set
up business in the sanctuary as a marble quarrier, with the
result that when French scholars dug the site in 1924 little
remained beyond the foundations. The architect was Hermogenes of Priene, who built it early in the second century B.C.;
it was perhaps his first important work. It was evidently a
completely new building, for no traces of an earlier temple
have been found beneath it. The order is Ionic and the plan
is normal, except that the surrounding enclosure is, surprisingly, of trapezoidal shape. In Roman Imperial times the temple
was renovated with a fresh dedication to the emperor, probably
Hadrian; fragments of the inscription have been found.
Dionysus had here the curious epithet Setaneios, which means
normally 'of the present year' with reference to the fruits of
the earth. Dionysus, the Roman Bacchus, was at Teos, it
seems, the god of the new wine. The Turkish excavators have
now begun to re-erect a number of the columns, and between
the temple and the city wall have uncovered part of a paved
street with a water-channel running down the middle. Between the temple and the theatre they have also cleared an

[1] Above, p. 106.

area containing private houses and another narrow street with
a water-channel (Pl. 26).

At the south foot of the acropolis hill is the theatre, an
important building in the home of the Artists of Dionysus.
As it stands the theatre is a reconstruction of a Hellenistic
building. The cavea is poorly preserved, but parts of the
vaulted gallery running under the upper seats still remain.
The stage-building has recently been cleared by the excavators;
it is of Roman type, with a stage about 14 feet from front to
back. A curious feature is that the projecting blocks of the
proscenium are pierced horizontally by pipes; the blocks being
several feet apart, the pipes are not continuous, and it is not
easy to understand their purpose. It has been suggested that
they were intended to improve the acoustics, but this suggestion is perhaps hardly probable. The acoustics of Greek theatres
were always excellent, as any visitor may prove for himself;
and in ancient times they were further assisted by sounding-
vessels placed in the auditorium. It was recommended that
these should be of bronze, thirteen in number, tuned to intervals of a fourth or fifth, and placed upside down in a horizontal
row round the cavea. No such bronze vessels have actually
been found in ancient theatres, but earthenware vases apparently intended for this purpose have occasionally come to
light.

The view from the theatre at Teos has aroused the enthusiastic admiration of modern writers. It embraces the site of
the city, the harbour, and the coast as far as the promontory
of Myonnesus. 'How intensely', says Hamilton, 'the contem-
plation of such a scene must have heightened the enjoyment
of the spectator during a performance of the Agamemnon or
the Medea.' Ximinez, in his *Asia Minor in Ruins*, goes even
further: 'In choosing the position of a theatre the Greeks'
first thought was for the landscape they would have before
them.' This, in the present writer's opinion, is a misconception.
Most Greek theatres have certainly a good view, because they
were built on hillsides, and the Greek and Anatolian scenery
is naturally beautiful. But this view could be enjoyed any
day of the year, and from better viewpoints than the interior
of a theatre; from the lower seats at least the stage-building

would cut off any view at all. Performances in ancient theatres were special occasions, confined to a limited number of days in a year; the spectators assembled to watch a play, and it is unlikely that they gave a thought to the scenery familiar to them all their lives. Indeed, it is doubtful if a view of this kind would have impressed them much. Sea and shore, mountains and blue skies are commonplace in Greek lands; we think them beautiful, but the Greeks preferred a good well-watered arable plainland. The writer once commented to a peasant in Attica on the beauty of the scenery; he smiled at my quaint foreign enthusiasm and replied: 'Too many stones' (Pl. 24).

A handsome addition to the attractions of Teos was made in 1964, when the excavators cleared the Odeum (J). This is a small theatre-like building with eleven rows of seats largely preserved; two tall statue-bases carry inscriptions in honour of distinguished citizens of Teos under the Roman Empire. Odea were used for musical recitals and, in some places at least, for rehearsals of dramatic performances intended for the theatre.

A short distance to the north-east of the acropolis are the ruins of a large building (B on the plan), identified by an inscription found in it as a gymnasium. The inscription is interesting for the information it gives about schooling in the second century B.C. It records a donation by a rich citizen for (among other things) the appointment of staff in the gymnasium. The children, boys and girls, are divided into three classes, to be taught their letters—that is, reading, writing and literature—by three masters drawing salaries from 500 to 600 drachmae per annum, or something like £100 to £120 today. Two physical training instructors draw 500 drachmae each. Such payments are not below average for the time; in a school at Miletus they are respectively forty and thirty drachmae a month. The music master is somewhat better remunerated at 700 drachmae. A drill-sergeant and an instructor in archery and the javelin are to be engaged from outside for two months at a fee of 300 and 250 drachmae respectively. A provision which strikes an echo today is that made for possible overcrowding of classes; if necessary, extra classes are to be held in the Council Chamber. Salaries on this

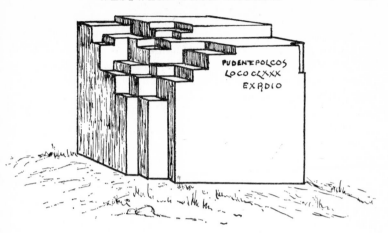

PUDENEPOLCOS
LOCO CLXXX
EXADIO

FIG. 27 Teos. Curiously cut block

scale seem meagre nowadays, but it is only in quite recent
times that the profession of schoolmaster has been held in any
high esteem; the sums mentioned are comparable with those
paid only a few years ago to a Turkish village schoolmaster.

The buildings of Teos were constructed of a hard blue local
limestone of the quality of marble. The quarries from which
it, or some of it, came are to be seen on a small but steep
isolated hill a mile from Seferihisar on the road to Sığacık.
This hill is, in fact, being used as a quarry at the time of
writing. Half a mile to the north-west is a small lake, reached
by a rough road turning right off the main road 500 yards
beyond the hill. Across the road from the lake, in a hollow,
were lying a hundred years ago fifteen or twenty quarried
blocks of marble of huge size, cut into such extraordinary
shapes that Hamilton observed he had never seen anything so
remarkable. Many of them contained 10 or 12 cubic yards of
stone. Most have now been removed, but two or three may still
be seen close to the road, and others are hidden among the
bushes. The style of the cuttings is shown in the accompanying
sketch, but no two were alike in detail. Some carried inscriptions in Latin recording the date (by the Roman consuls of
the year), the place (indicated by a numeral) from which they
were quarried, and the name of the quarry-owner. Hamilton

AT—K

imagined they might be intended as stands for the display of cups, statues and other objects in a temple treasury; but the true explanation is more commonplace. A similar block is still lying half above water in the sea beside the ancient quay at Sığacık, where it evidently fell while being loaded into a boat; these stones were clearly intended for export, and were trimmed in this curious way for reasons of economy, to lose as little material as possible, short of sending out the stone as a mere jagged block. Teian marble was, in fact, well known and highly valued. The consuls named in the inscriptions are those of A.D. 165–6, from which it appears that at that date the quarrying activities for some reason came to a sudden end, and the blocks were left where they were cut. The one now lying, a good deal water-worn, in the sea is of similar dimensions to the rest; it is remarkable that the exporters, with comparatively primitive tackle, preferred to transport and put on board blocks weighing upwards of 30 tons rather than cut them into more manageable sizes. Large blocks were evidently in demand. Remarkable, too, that the stone, instead of being blocked out at the quarry to suit the customer's ultimate purpose, was apparently exported simply as bulk material (Pl. 25).

Pliny surprisingly lists Teos among the islands. On this evidence some scholars have believed that a canal was constructed, probably by Alexander, joining the north and south harbours; but no trace of such a work has ever been seen, nor does Livy's narrative of the events in 190 B.C. favour its existence. It is more likely that we have merely another of Pliny's numerous mistakes.

MYONNESUS

An attractive excursion, though not very easy, is that to Çıfıt Kale, the ancient Myonnesus, or Mouse Island.[1] The island itself is a steep rock 190 feet high and very picturesque, joined to the mainland by an ancient causeway now under water. It lies about a mile north of Doğanbey Point. The approach by land is difficult; from Seferihisar the road is

[1] This name is now transferred to Sıçan Adası, a little east of Lebedus.

FIG. 28 Myonnesus

respectable as far as Doğanbey, after that very rough and
hardly possible to find without a guide. To reach the island it
is also necessary, short of swimming, to cross the causeway;
the water at most seasons comes about up to the knee. It is
easier therefore, if possible, to approach by boat from Sığacık.

Myonnesus makes one or two appearances in history. As
was mentioned above, it was for a short time the seat of the
Artists of Dionysus, till the Teians objected and they were
moved to Lebedus. Some years earlier than this, in 190 B.C.,
Antiochus III of Syria was attempting to hold the coast
against the Roman fleet. The Romans, in search of supplies,
were one day making for Teos when off Myonnesus they caught
sight of a dozen or fifteen vessels which they supposed at first
to be part of the king's fleet. Soon they realised that they were,
in fact, pirate vessels loaded with spoils from a raid on Chios,
and accordingly gave chase; the pirates, however, having
swifter craft and a good start, reached Myonnesus in safety.
Loth to abandon a rich prize, the Roman commander decided
to put in and carry off the vessels from the harbour. This he
did, says Livy, in ignorance of the nature of the place; and the
historian proceeds to give a description of Myonnesus which
could hardly be bettered. 'The hill', he says, 'rises like a
pyramid from a broad base to a sharp point; it is approached
from the mainland by a narrow pathway; on the sea side it is
surrounded by cliffs so eaten away by the waves that in some
places the overhanging rocks project further seaward than the

boats sheltering under them.' The Romans therefore, for fear
of rocks dropped upon them from above, dared not come close,
but abandoned the attempt and went on to Teos. There
followed the events described above (p. 139), ending with the
battle of Myonnesus and the defeat of Antiochus.

From this narrative alone one would naturally infer that
the rock of Myonnesus was nothing more than a pirates'
hide-out, for which it is well enough adapted. Other notices,
however, make it clear that Myonnesus was a proper town, if
not a city. Hecataeus of Miletus about 500 B.C. apparently
called it a city; Artemidorus of Ephesus, on the other hand,
about 100 B.C., called it merely a 'place'. Pliny says it was once
a town, but had perished in his own time. It is in any case
obvious that the Artists of Dionysus cannot have been settled
in a mere pirates' nest. But the habitation, whatever it was,
has almost entirely disappeared.

The rock itself is utterly inadequate to support a town,
having virtually no level ground at all. It is split in the middle
by a great cleft running east and west, only a few feet wide;
on the portion to the north of this is a stretch of fine ancient
wall still 9 or 10 feet high in places. The masonry is of the type
that used to be called 'Cyclopean', with very large blocks of
irregular shape; one block measures almost 8 feet by 4. This
wall has a very archaic appearance, and belongs no doubt to
Hecataeus' 'city'. This is the sole surviving remnant of ancient
Myonnesus; the rest of the hill is covered with ruins, but they
are nearly 2,000 years later, for Myonnesus had a part to play
in Turkish history too. The three cisterns lined with red plaster
at the top of the hill are undatable, but are likely to belong to
this later habitation.

The town, and the seat of the Dionysiac Artists, must have
been on the mainland opposite. Here there is a valley, reasonably fertile and now rather patchily cultivated, which must
represent such territory as Myonnesus possessed; the surface
is thinly strewn with sherds, but no trace of any ancient
building has ever, it seems, been observed. Since the country
is almost deserted for miles around, it is likely that stones have
been removed by sea, but the total absence even of foundations
suggests that Myonnesus never possessed the massive buildings

Fig. 29 Lebedus

which are familiar on the larger sites. The Artists, one would
suppose, can hardly have managed without a theatre; but
none has ever been discovered.

LEBEDUS

Of the twelve Ionian cities two were noticeably humbler than
the rest; these were Myus and Lebedus. Their ruins are among
the scantiest, and both are very rarely visited. Myus was
ruined by the mud and mosquitoes of the Maeander; Lebedus
lived quietly on her peninsula and played no significant part
in history.

The foundation legend is of the familar kind. The country
was originally occupied by Carians, till in the course of the
Ionian migrations another of the sons of Codrus and his
followers drove them out. His name is variously given as
Andraemon or Andropompus; this latter name, 'escorter of
men', is suspiciously appropriate to the leader of a colony, and
may safely be regarded as mythical.

Lebedus is a characteristic example of the peninsula type
of settlement. The peninsula itself is low and rocky, some 300
yards across, joined to the mainland by an isthmus about a
furlong broad. On the mainland opposite is a hill some 200 feet
high which formed the acropolis. The country around, though

thinly populated now, was considered in ancient times to be good fertile land, and it had the special peculiarity of possessing the finest and most abundant thermal springs on the Ionian coast. But the city's position precluded it from ever growing really prosperous. Completely cut off landward by the territories of Colophon and Teos, its wealth could come only from the sea; but it lacked a good harbour and, with the far better favoured Ephesus and Teos to north and south, could attract little in the way of seaborne commerce.

Consequently the early history of Lebedus is a blank. So far as we know she never led a colony overseas, nor did the great age of Ionian civilisation bring forth any Lebedian poet, philosopher or scientist; indeed, Lebedus never in any age produced a famous citizen. To the Ionian fleet at Lade she contributed no ships at all. In the Athenian maritime league in the fifth century (the Delian Confederacy) Lebedus was at first assessed at three talents, but this proved to be altogether more than the city's resources could meet, and the assessment was quickly reduced to one talent. Alone among the cities of Ionia Lebedus struck no coins in the classical Greek period.

In Hellenistic times the city makes two or three appearances, but they hardly show her in any brilliant light. Antigonus' plan for merging Lebedus into Teos has already been mentioned;[1] it seems to have involved the complete abandonment of the site, but was never actually put into execution. Lysimachus, on taking over from Antigonus, is said to have uprooted Lebedus entirely and transferred its population to Ephesus. Despite these attempts to erase it from the map, the city managed to survive; about 266 B.C. it came into the possession of Ptolemy II of Egypt, who carried out some form of refoundation under the new name of Ptolemais. This name continued only for some sixty years.

In the second century Lebedus became the permanent home of the Ionian branch of the Artists of Dionysus. These troublesome associates, expelled in turn from Teos, Ephesus and Myonnesus, were welcomed at Lebedus purely as an accession of manpower; shortage of men had always been a trouble there. There at all events they stayed, except for a brief sojourn at

[1] Above, p. 137.

Priene, and in Strabo's time they were celebrating annually at Lebedus a festival with games in honour of Dionysus. Horace, writing shortly before Strabo, surprisingly refers to Lebedus as a deserted village, but this is clearly an error, or at least an exaggeration; the city, in fact, continued to exist, and struck coins down to the end of the second century A.D.

The peninsula of Lebedus is now known as Kısik; on earlier maps it is called Xingi. Ürkmez village lies a short distance to the north-west. The most pleasant approach is by boat from Sığacık, but the site is also easily accessible by land. Leave Seferihisar by the Doğanbey road, and a quarter of a mile out of the town fork left where a tall iron gateway stands on the right, with a well opposite. The road is dusty but passable for a car. Beyond Lebedus it continues by the Gümüldür gorge to Bulgurca and Cumaovası, so that the round trip from Smyrna to Teos and Lebedus may be made in a long day in either direction.

Lebedus has never been excavated, and the visible ruins are scanty. By far the most striking is the wall around the peninsula, which is still preserved to a height of three or four courses. It is some 7 feet thick, of good regular ashlar constructed in the familiar fashion with an inner and outer face of squared blocks and a filling of rubble. It has four towers and three gates opening directly on the sea; to that on the south-east, which is the best protected from the prevailing Imbat, a rock-cut ramp leads up from the water. No trace is to be seen of any quay or mole either on the peninsula or on the isthmus. The wall does not at present continue across the isthmus, though it presumably did so in antiquity; here as at Myonnesus it is likely that many stones have been removed by sea in modern times, and the villagers of Ürkmez admit to taking them as required for building. Inside the wall are fairly numerous traces of ancient buildings, but only the foundations survive. At the east corner is the foundation of an old church of basilica form with three aisles, of which little can now be made out; a bishop of Lebedus is recorded in the Byzantine lists (Pl. 34).

But the main habitation was certainly on the mainland

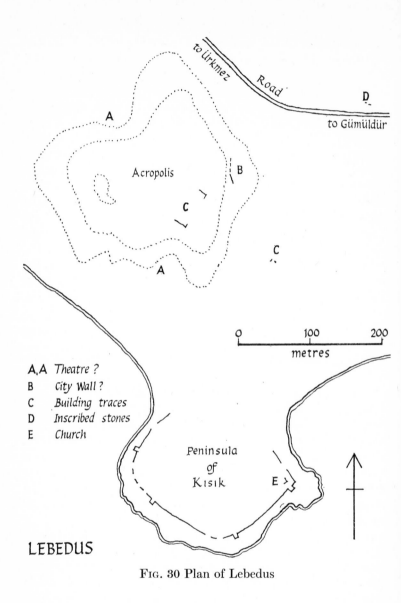

to Ürkmez

Road

to Gümüldür

D

A

Acropolis

B

C

C

A

0   100   200

metres

A,A *Theatre ?*
B   *City Wall ?*
C   *Building traces*
D   *Inscribed stones*
E   *Church*

Peninsula
of
Kısık

E

LEBEDUS

FIG. 30 Plan of Lebedus

opposite. Here the ground is thickly strewn with sherds, and the slopes of the hill carry many vestiges of buildings. Here and there short pieces of wall may be seen, but whether they are terrace walls or belong to a defence wall is not easy to decide. Just below the summit is a broad platform; at the edge of this, on the south and south-east, are foundations of large buildings, or perhaps of a single large building, of uncertain purpose. The permanent seat of the Artists of Dionysus must presumably have possessed a theatre, but as at Myonnesus none has been found. Several hollows in the hillside would afford a suitable site, in particular one which looks towards the peninsula and one on the north-west side, but no clear traces of theatre building are to be seen.

Lying close to the north side of the road, opposite to the isthmus, are two blocks of stone, one of which carries a cross; the other once formed part of the wall of a gymnasium, and on it are roughly cut the names of various students. These were cut by the boys themselves, to reserve the places: 'Eikadios son of Menas, his place' and the like (Pl. 27). This same proceeding may be observed again at Priene.[1]

As was said above, the territory of Lebedus was noted for the abundance of its thermal springs. One of these is at a spot called Karakoç, 17 km. from Seferihisar on the road to Ürkmez, just below the road on the right. The water is good for rheumatism, and varies in temperature from about 104° to 120° F.; the mud baths and hot-water baths are much patronised in summer, even by visitors from as far afield as Ankara. Close beside the modern installations are the ruins of the ancient baths. Other medicinal springs for bathing and for drinking exist on the shore to the west of Lebedus; they are reached by a road forking right about a mile north of Karakoç.

ERYTHRAE

Legend said that a statue of the deified Heracles was launched into the sea on a raft from the Phoenician city of Tyre, though no one could say why. The raft floated to the shores of

---

[1] Below, p. 214.

Ionia and came to land on the headland of Mesate (now Top Burnu) half-way between Chios and Erythrae. The Chians and Erythraeans used every endeavour to bring the statue to their own country, but it could not be persuaded to move, until a blind fisherman of Erythrae had a remarkable vision: it was revealed to him in a dream that the women of Erythrae must cut off their hair, from which the men should plait a rope to draw the raft to their shores. The noble ladies flatly refused to co-operate in so absurd a proceeding; but the Thracian women, both slaves and resident foreigners, readily consented, and with the rope thus made the Erythraeans secured possession of the raft and statue. The fisherman recovered his sight and a sanctuary was built for the statue of Heracles; into it no women were allowed to enter save Thracians. The rope of hair was preserved and could still be seen in the time of Pausanias. Statue and sanctuary, he says, were both of great antiquity, and the statue was more Egyptian than Greek; both are shown on coins of the city (Pl. 60).

Erythrae retains its ancient name in the form Ildır; the intermediate forms Ritri and Litri are recorded. Top Burnu is, in fact, just half-way between here and the town of Chios; but it is not certain that Erythrae was always in this situation. Professor J. M. Cook has recently suggested that the city may have moved its site about the middle of the fourth century B.C. from the small peninsula of Kalem Burnu just to the west of Ilıca. He points out that about that date the signs of habitation, especially sherds, cease at Kalem Burnu and begin at Ildır; and further that a fourth-century inscription found at Ildır provides for the laying-out of a network of streets as if in a newly founded city. A recently discovered archaic deposit of sherds and other objects on the acropolis may, however, prove an obstacle to this theory.

The original foundation is said to have been due to a party from Crete under the leadership of a certain Erythrus, who gave his name, 'Red', to the city; but such 'eponymous' founders are invariably mythical. Later, a son of Codrus named Cnopus collected a band of Ionians from the other cities of Asia and whether by force or by agreement (the accounts differ) introduced them to Erythrae. This early city is de-

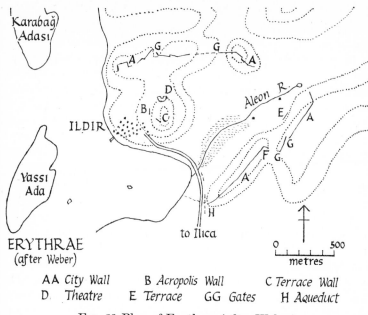

ERYTHRAE
(after Weber)

AA	City Wall	B	Acropolis Wall	C	Terrace Wall
D	Theatre	E	Terrace	GG	Gates	H	Aqueduct

FIG. 31 Plan of Erythrae (after Weber)

scribed as rich and prosperous, but not much is known of its
history. Herodotus says that Erythraeans and Chians spoke
the same dialect of Ionic; but this produced no amity between
them, for in the seventh century Erythrae was at war with
Chians and Milesians combined. Relations between the cities
were, however, constantly changing; a little before this Erythrae had joined with Miletus in founding the colony of
Parium on the Sea of Marmara.

At the battle of Lade in 494 B.C. Erythrae contributed eight
ships to the Ionian fleet, as compared with a hundred from
Chios. In the Delian Confederacy the Erythraean assessment
was seven talents, equal to the highest among the Ionian
cities; in this case no comparison with Chios is possible, for
Chios never paid tribute in money to Athens, but preferred to
contribute ships, of which the number is not known. The
wealth of Erythrae was no doubt due to the same causes as
at Teos.[1]

[1] Above, p. 137.

Fourth-century inscriptions found at Ildır give us tantalizing glimpses of the city's history which our information does not allow us properly to understand. One is a decree in honour of Mausolus, dynast of Caria, who is called a benefactor of Erythrae, but we cannot tell why. Another refers to defacement by certain oligarchs of the statue of a patriot who had slain 'the tyrant'; but again we cannot fill in the details. A third is particularly frustrating: it honours a citizen for providing funds 'for the sending out of soldiers and the demolition of the acropolis'. We should like to know where the soldiers were sent, and why the acropolis required to be demolished, especially if at that time it had only just been built; but we are reduced to conjecture.

Among the city's titles to distinction was the possession of the famous Sibyl named Herophile. Sibyl was a name given to a number of women in antiquity—some said four, others ten—who possessed the power of prophecy. The most famous were the Sibyl of Cumae in Italy, and after her Herophile. This woman, in the course of her inspired utterances, was recorded as speaking of herself in verse in the following terms:

'I am by nature midway between mortal and goddess—
My mother a nymph, my father an eater of fish—
Ida-born from my mother; my native land is red
Marpessus, sacred to my mother, and the river Aidoneus.'

According to this text, therefore, Herophile was born at red-soiled Marpessus in the Troad under Mt. Ida. The Erythraeans, however, strenuously disputed this origin and claimed the Sibyl for themselves. To maintain their claim they resorted to an ingenious piece of 'higher criticism'. In the passage quoted they rejected the last line as spurious, so that the text should read simply 'my native land is Red'—that is, Erythrae,which means red. The term 'Ida-born' they explained as relating not to Mt. Ida at all, but to a poetic word *ida* meaning wooded country. Their own account was that Herophile was born in a cave on Mt. Corycus in the territory of Erythrae, that she travelled widely and lived for 900 years. In the year 1891 the actual seat of the Sibyl was found at Ildır, in the form of a fountain-house containing a number of inscriptions of the second century A.D. In one of these the Sibyl strongly reasserts her Erythraean origin as against the claim of Marpessus. Unfortunately this discovery was involved in a good deal of secrecy, and the spot seems to be no longer identifiable.[1]

The ruins of Erythrae are in general scanty, largely owing to systematic plundering of the stones by contractors in the nineteenth century. The site itself is a fine one; the acropolis, 280 feet high, rises directly from the shore, well isolated from the surrounding hills; the harbour is admirably protected by an off-lying islet, one of the group called in ancient times Hippi, the Horses. The wall-circuit, two and a half miles in length, follows the low ridges to the north and east. The territory thus enclosed is watered by a stream which rises at a spring just inside the city wall on the east; its total length is less than a mile. Its water, however, is bitter and unfit to drink; it is usable for crops, but not good. In its lower course this stream forms a marsh; it has an abundant flow and turns two mills on the way. Its ancient name is not certain; inscriptions speak of a River Aleon, and this is confirmed by Pliny, who notes that it has the unusual property of causing hair to grow on the body. On the other hand, coins of Erythrae show a river-god with the name Axus. If these are two different streams, which of them is the stream just described, and where the other may be, remains uncertain. The water being undrinkable, the city was supplied by earthenware pipes laid on or under the ground; many of these have been found on the site. The aqueduct H is of much later date (Pl. 33).

The circuit of the city wall may be followed for the greater part of its length, a pleasant walk of an hour or so. The wall is a strong one, of beautiful ashlar masonry, from 12 to 17 feet thick, with gates and towers at intervals. At F is a particularly striking piece, where the pale, almost white limestone is diversified by two courses of dark brown stone; the effect is most unusual. The wall ends on the north side at a rocky knoll, forming almost a second acropolis; along the shore no trace of it remains (Pl. 28).

[1] It is described as 'at the east foot of the acropolis hill, close on the left of the road as you approach from the south'—which is hardly intelligible with the line of the road as it now is.

Of the inner citadel wall defending the acropolis very little is now to be seen, except for a few pieces above the village at B; the masonry is similar to that of the outer circuit. At C is a short stretch of polygonal wall which appears to be rather a terrace-wall than a fortification; the masonry is of the 'coursed polygonal' style which dates generally to the early Hellenistic period. Nothing survives on the summit but the ruins of a Greek church.

The theatre is cut into the north slope of the acropolis hill, but its state of preservation is not more than moderate. An excavation was undertaken here in 1963 in the name of the Izmir Museum; it has revealed that the stairways of the cavea are quite well preserved, but of the rows of seats hardly more than the foundations remain. Nothing is visible of the stage-building. The theatre faces north, an arrangement of which Vitruvius approved; a south aspect he regarded as undesirable, not because the sun would be in the spectators' eyes (a point which he does not mention) but as being unhealthy, because the hot air would become imprisoned in the auditorium and dry the moisture from their bodies. In practice Vitruvius' rule was by no means always followed, and Greek theatres, in fact, face in all directions; those of Miletus and Priene face due south, those of Teos and Cyme south-east and south-west. The main consideration seems to have been merely the exist-ence of a suitable concave slope in a convenient position. If anyone really believes that the Greeks' first thought was for the view which the theatre would command, let him consider the theatre at Erythrae, where east, west or south the view is greatly superior. It is not known when the theatre was origin-ally built; a theatre is mentioned in an inscription of the second century B.C. (Pl. 29).

At E on the plan is a stretch of handsome wall supporting a terrace (not easy to find without a guide); its masonry is a mixture of polygonal and ashlar. Ionic architectural fragments found close by, and a number of votive niches in the rock to the south, indicate that a sanctuary stood here; Hamilton thought this might be the famous temple of Heracles, but others have considered the situation, so far from the sea and the oldest part of the city, to be unsuitable. If Erythrae was indeed trans-

ferred from another site in the fourth century, this objection
loses most of its force. But. in fact, we do not know where any
particular temple of Erythrae was situated; the ruins have
been too thoroughly despoiled. We do know that they were
numerous; an inscription records the official sale by the city
authorities of some forty priesthoods.

FIG. 32 Erythrae. Carved blocks

North of the village, not far from the theatre, is a well-
preserved mosaic floor; the building to which it belonged is
destroyed. Other mosaics have been found in various places,
but these are no longer to be seen. A small museum has been
built in the village to house the smaller objects found in the
recent excavation. These include the rather unusually decorated blocks shown in the accompanying sketch.

Erythrae is now less inaccessible than it used to be. A
respectable road has recently been constructed from Ilıca to
Ildır; alternatively, travellers may charter a motor-boat at
modest expense from Ilıca, the journey occupying about an
hour and a half each way.

Ilıca itself is not an ancient town, but represents the site of
the thermal springs for which the territory of Erythrae, like
that of Lebedus, was famous; it is now a popular seaside
resort, much frequented in the summer by the people of
Smyrna. Ildır on the other hand presents a melancholy
spectacle. Most of its houses are empty shells, deserted since
their Greek inhabitants left in the great exchange of populations after the First World War.

★

CHAPTER SEVEN

Ephesus

BEFORE THE last war a visit to Ephesus was something of an adventure. 'Ephesus', says H. V. Morton, writing in 1936, 'stands dignified and alone in its death . . . with no sign of life but a goatherd leaning on a broken sarcophagus or a lonely peasant outlined against a mournful sunset. Few people ever visit it. Ephesus has a weird, haunted look.' In 1939 the road from Smyrna was so bad that the vehicle in which the present writer was travelling was unable to follow its course and finished up in a cornfield. Conditions are different now. A fast highway brings the motorist from Izmir in something over an hour; visitors in the season are numbered by scores or hundreds every day, and are able to refresh themselves at a restaurant installed in a corner of the agora. The Austrian excavations, first begun in 1896, have lately been resumed and are in progress at the time of writing.

Ramsay calls Ephesus the city of change. Its history is varied, and the nature of the ground has changed; and like many other Greek cities—we have already seen the cases of Smyrna and Clazomenae—it did not always stand on its present site.

The foundation legend as told by Athenaeus (VIII, 361) is somewhat picturesque. The founders, he says, being at a loss for a site, consulted the oracle, who told them to choose the spot which a fish and a wild boar should point out. It happened that some fishermen were roasting fish for their lunch near the later harbour, and that one of the fish jumped out of the brazier with a live coal attached and set fire to some shavings; the fire spread to a thicket in which a boar lay hidden; the boar rushed away in alarm and was pursued and finally shot down where the temple of Athena afterwards stood. In memory

160

28   Erythrae. The City-Wall.

29   Erythrae. The newly excavated Theatre.

32   Ephesus. Temple of Hadrian.

33   Erythrae. Source of the Aleon.

34   Lebedus. The Sea-Wall.

35   Ephesus. Theatre.

36   Ephesus. Statue of Ephesian Artemis.

37   Ephesus. Gateway in the newly excavated street.

38   Ephesus. Belevi Mausoleum; Corinthian Capital.

39   Ephesus. The newly restored Basilica of St John on the
      hill above Selçuk.

40   Ephesus. Marble Street and Doric Stoa.

41   Ephesus. Aqueduct in the valley south of the city.

42   Ephesus. Belevi Mausoleum, the Grave-Chamber.

43   Ephesus. Belevi Tumulus.

44   Ephesus. Panaya Kapulu, supposed House of the Virgin Mary.

45   Ephesus. Belevi Mausoleum.

46   Claros. The Oracular Chamber in 1963.

47   Claros. Arm of the Colossal Statue of Apollo.

48   Claros. The newly excavated Temple of Apollo, showing
      the passage leading to the Oracular Chamber.

49   Priene. Front Seat in the Theatre.

50   Priene. Wash-room in the Gymnasium.

51   Priene. The Council Chamber.

of this remarkable fulfilment of the oracle the effigy of a wild
boar stood as late as A.D. 400 beside the main street of the city.

These founders, according to Strabo and Pausanias, were
Ionians led by Androclus, another of the numerous sons of
Codrus, the legendary king of Athens. They found the region
occupied by Carians and Lydians living around a sanctuary of
the great Anatolian mother-goddess; with these they came to
an amicable arrangement, founded a new city and adopted the
native goddess under the name of their own Artemis. This
earliest city of Ephesus occupied the north slope of the theatre-
hill—anciently Mt. Pion, now Panayır Daği—and the land at
its foot, which at that time was on the coast; the sea then came
up past the city as far as the modern Selçuk. In this neighbourhood presumably stood the temple of Athena, but it has not
been located. Of this early city nothing now remains with the
exception of a small piece of polygonal wall high up on the
north slope of the hill.

Here the city remained for the first 400 years or so of its
existence. It had two advantages which gave it a prominent
position among the Greek settlements in Ionia; first, its
harbour, conveniently situated in the middle of the west
coast of Asia Minor, at the mouth of the River Cayster, and
second, the sanctuary of Artemis, a place of pilgrimage from
prehistoric times. By the sixth century Ephesus was in a
prosperous way; perhaps for this reason it was the first object
of attack by the Lydian Croesus. The Ephesians defended
themselves by tying a rope from the temple of Artemis to the
city, a distance of about three-quarters of a mile, so placing
themselves under the goddess's protection; this pious measure
was, however, unavailing. Croesus, never a bitter enemy of the
Greeks, treated the sanctuary well; the sculptured column-
drums which he presented towards its reconstruction may be
seen in the British Museum with his name carved upon them.
The city itself, however, he could not permit to continue
as it was; he destroyed it and transplanted the inhabitants
farther inland, to the level ground south of the temple of
Artemis.

That this was its position through the classical period has
been proved by soundings, but no proper excavation has yet

AT—L

been attempted there. Excavation will, in fact, be difficult, owing particularly to the rise in the water-table since antiquity. This classical city was unwalled and militarily weak, but its harbour and its sanctuary remained; first under the Lydians, then under the Persians, then as a member of the Athenian maritime confederacy, its prosperity continued undiminished. Its normal tribute in the confederacy, six or seven talents, puts it about on a par with Miletus, Teos and Erythrae; the only city on this coast with a considerably higher assessment is Cyme. With the King's Peace in 386 B.C. Ephesus fell back with the rest under Persian dominion until the coming of Alexander.

In the course of this period the great temple of Artemis underwent numerous vicissitudes. The earliest building of which traces have been found seems to date to the eighth century and to have been destroyed by the Cimmerians; it was replaced by another of which the architect's name was Chersiphron. This was still unfinished in the sixth century when Croesus arrived and made his contribution to it. In 356 B.C.—tradition said on the very night when Alexander was born—this temple was set on fire and destroyed by a lunatic named Herostratus, apparently with the object (which, in fact, he has achieved) of perpetuating his memory. The Ephesians at once set to work to raise a still finer structure, under an architect whose name is variously given as Deinocrates or Cheirocrates. The work was still going forward when Alexander reached Ephesus in 334 B.C.; much impressed by what he saw he offered to defray all expenses, past and future, of the building, if he might be permitted to make the dedicatory inscription in his own name. This handsome gesture was courteously declined, on the ground that it was not fitting for a god to make a dedication to another god.

The temple, finished eventually by the Ephesians' own efforts, later ranked as one of the seven wonders of the world. The list of these wonders was not drawn up before Hellenistic times; it included, besides the temple of Artemis, the pyramids of Egypt, the Colossus of Rhodes, the statue of Zeus at Olympia, the hanging gardens of Babylon, the lighthouse at Alexandria and the Mausoleum at Halicarnassus. Later, certain alternatives were admitted, and later still the list was greatly extended beyond the original seven.[1]

After Alexander's death Ephesus came with the rest of Ionia into the power of Lysimachus. The harbour at this time lay between the north end of Panayır Dağı and the mouth of the Cayster away to the north-east, and the silt brought down by the river was already impeding it; the process was observable even in Herodotus' time. Lysimachus, perceiving that the city in its then position was doomed to inevitable decay, undertook a complete rebuilding on a new site. For this great benefit the Ephesians displayed a regrettable lack of gratitude; as always happens, they were reluctant to leave their homes, and the king was obliged to resort to a stratagem. Taking advantage of a heavy downpour of rain, he blocked up the water-channels of the old city and rendered the houses uninhabitable.

The site chosen by Lysimachus was that where the ruins now stand, though of its original buildings hardly anything still survives. It was on an impressive scale, with a circuit-wall not far short of six miles in length. The old harbour was abandoned in favour of a new one in the bay (as it then was) below Mt. Pion on the west. In the wars of the Hellenistic kings Ephesus was not remarkable for the consistency of her allegiance. After Lysimachus' death she supported first the Seleucid kings of Syria, then for a time the Ptolemies of Egypt; she served as headquarters to Antiochus the Great, then after his defeat at Magnesia in 190 B.C. passed into the power of Eumenes of Pergamum. When Aristonicus attempted to dispute the Roman inheritance of the Pergamene kingdom, the Ephesians took the Roman side and with their own forces defeated the pretender in a sea-battle near Cyme. On the other hand, when Mithridates arrived as a professed liberator they readily supported him and joined whole-heartedly in the slaughter of the Roman residents.

As the capital city of the province of Asia, and normal residence of the Roman governor, Ephesus flourished exceedingly. Strabo, writing in the time of Augustus, observed that it was increasing daily in prosperity and was the greatest trading-centre in the whole of Asia west of the Taurus. Its population

[1] Above, p. 93.

under the early empire is estimated at something like a quarter
of a million. In its inscriptions the city calls itself 'first and
greatest metropolis of Asia'. There was, however, one perpetual
menace with which the Ephesians had to contend, namely the
constant silting up of the harbour by the River Cayster. A
misguided attempt to meet this danger had been made by
Attalus II of Pergamum, who tried to deepen the channel for
large merchant-ships by constructing a mole at the harbour
entrance; this, however, had the opposite effect to that intended,
and by the first century of the empire the situation was serious.
In A.D. 61 the proconsul of Asia under Nero had the whole
harbour dredged; and in the next century Hadrian attempted a
different cure by diverting the course of the Cayster. In the
third century, as an inscription tells us, a private citizen made
a donation of 20,000 denarii for the cleaning out of the harbour.
But nothing could permanently avail; the silting continued,
and the port of Ephesus is now a good three miles from
the sea.

The fame of the temple of Artemis continued undiminished.
Among its privileges was that of asylum, which conferred
sanctuary and complete inviolability on any person taking
refuge in the temple. Alexander extended the limits of the
protected area to a distance of one stade all round the temple;
Mithridates determined them by shooting an arrow from the
corner of the temple roof, and was judged to have slightly
exceeded a stade—a shot of some two hundred yards. Mark
Antony, emulating the action of Julius Caesar at Didyma,
doubled this distance, so actually including a part of the city
itself; but this was found to be unsatisfactory, as putting the
city at the mercy of malefactors, and it was rescinded by
Augustus. In A.D. 22 Tiberius instigated a thorough investigation of the claims to asylum maintained by the various Greek
temples, for complaints of abuse were becoming frequent; the
cities were invited to send delegates to Rome to defend their
claims. The Ephesians, relying on the recent edict of Augustus,
had the satisfaction of heading the list of those who were
accepted.

The pre-eminence of the cult of Artemis was without pre-
judice to the cult of the emperors. All the leading cities of the

province were eager to build a temple for the imperial worship; but this could only be done by permission of the emperor himself, and competition was severe. The privilege, which carried with it the title of Neocorus, 'Temple-Warden', was granted to Ephesus four times in all by different emperors; but one of these, Caracalla, 'in his modesty (as he expresses it himself) made over his neocorate to the goddess', so that no new temple was built to him, but the title was granted by virtue of the existing cult of Artemis. Ephesus' proud position as 'four times Temple-Warden' is illustrated on the fourth century coin of the city shown on Pl. 60. Of the four temples and statues represented, that on the top left is of Artemis, the other three are emperors. This exceptional compliment paid to the old Anatolian goddess illustrates the readiness of the Roman government to encourage the long-established institutions of the eastern world.

But the enemy who was finally to humble the proud Ephesian Artemis was already at hand. Christianity took root quickly in Ephesus. St. Paul arrived in A.D. 53 and found a small nucleus of converts. St. John, accompanied or not by the Virgin Mother,[1] was in Ephesus and other cities of Asia certainly by 67 and perhaps a good deal earlier; it may well have been he who founded the churches later visited by St. Paul. St. Paul himself lived in the city for three years; the success of his mission is clearly shown by the story told in the nineteenth chapter of Acts. A certain silversmith, by name Demetrius, made his living by manufacturing silver shrines of Artemis, and he found that Paul's preaching was seriously damaging his business. Calling a meeting of all those engaged in his and similar trades, he pointed out to them the danger not only to their livelihood but also to the dignity of the goddess herself. Roused to anger they created a clamour that quickly spread through the city; the people rushed to the theatre, taking some of Paul's companions with them. Paul himself would have gone too, but was dissuaded. In the theatre uproar prevailed; for more than an hour the people, many of whom had no idea what the matter was, continued to shout, 'Great is Artemis of the Ephesians!' The tumult was

[1] See below, p. 180.

finally quelled by the secretary to the city council, who came out on to the stage with words of severe common sense. 'The greatness of Artemis,' he said, 'is not in dispute, and these men have committed no indictable offence against her; if anyone thinks they have, let him apply to the law courts in the proper way. If this riot continues, we shall be held to account by the Roman authorities, and shall have no defence.' The incident thus passed off, but Paul immediately left Ephesus.

The general decline of the empire in the third century affected Ephesus like other places. Moreover, the silting of the port was rapidly becoming unmanageable; when Justinian in the sixth century founded the great church of St. John, he built it not in the city, but on the hill to the north-east above the present town of Selçuk, which thenceforth became the centre of habitation. The connection with the sea was broken, and the great days of Ephesus were over (Pl. 39).

The modern visitor to Ephesus may begin appropriately with the site of the temple of Artemis. It lies a few yards to the north of the Kuşadası road, and is marked by the mound of the excavators' spoil. It presents a melancholy spectacle. Until a year or two ago all that could be seen was a large pool of water, from which a single block of marble sadly emerged. The Austrian excavators recently drained this pool, and for a time the foundations were partially visible; at the time of writing the former state of affairs again prevails.

The discovery of the famous temple was due to an English engineer, J. T. Wood, who had made it his life's ambition. The position of the temple was quite unknown, except that it was sure to be deeply buried, and for a long time no clue was available. Wood worked at Ephesus from 1863 to 1874, and spent a considerable private fortune in more or less random soundings in various parts of the plain. The clue was at length provided by a long but fragmentary inscription found in the theatre, containing a regulation that whenever a performance or an assembly was held in the theatre the sacred images should be carried there from the temple and afterwards returned. The route prescribed was by the sacred way from the Magnesian Gate. It remained to find the Magnesian

Gate, which would naturally face in the direction of Magnesia, and to follow the sacred way. This Wood successfully did; the street, deep under ground, proved to be quite well preserved, with a marble paving 12 yards wide; it led to the precinct wall, and so to the temple itself, 15 feet below the surface. This discovery ranks as one of the romances of archaeology. Wood, however, did not excavate the temple to its lowest level; this task remained for D. G. Hogarth in 1904, when the fabulous foundation-deposit of objects in gold came to light.

The unimpressive situation of the Artemisium on flat ground outside the city has often been remarked. Leake, however, pointed out that the greater Ionic temples of Asia Minor, almost without exception, are similarly placed; he believed the reason to be that the tall and slender Ionic order shows to better advantage on flat ground, whereas the comparatively squat Doric temple calls for an elevated position. We shall see further examples at Magnesia, Sardis and Didyma; but Claros is an exception.

Artemis of the Ephesians never became a truly Greek goddess, but always retained a large measure of her oriental nature. Her non-Greek character is evident enough from the form of her representation in art (Pl. 36). The feet and legs fused together give the statue the effect of a pillar. The rows of egg-shaped objects across the chest have been understood to be breasts, but the most recent opinion is that they are in fact eggs, the egg being a familiar symbol of fertility. These features are quite unsuited to the virgin huntress of the Greeks. On the other hand, the numerous beasts portrayed on the lower limbs—bulls, lions, sphinxes and others—might be thought to represent the animal world which the Greek Artemis loved and protected; though here again the inclusion of the chimaera gives a definitely eastern touch.

Similarly, the cult of the goddess was served by orders of ministers most of which were utterly strange to any Greek hierarchy—some of them not Greek words at all. At the head was the Priest (or priests, whether one or more is not certain), a eunuch with the title of Megabyxus; this word is Persian, meaning, 'set free by God'.[1] The Megabyxus, as Strabo tells us,

[1] Or perhaps 'given by God'.

was always chosen from abroad, no doubt from the non-Greek nations, and was held in great honour. Assisting him was a numerous body of virgins, compared by Plutarch with the Vestal Virgins at Rome. They were divided into three classes, the Priestess-to-be, or Novice, the Priestess, who performed the actual ritual, and the ex-Priestess, whose function was to instruct the novices. A further order of priests was known as the Essenes. This again is a non-Greek word, used with the meaning 'king'; whether it may be Semitic and have some connection with the Jewish sect of Essenes is not clear. It has been suggested that the Ephesian hierarchy was built up around the bee, the bee being the national symbol of Ephesus, appearing regularly on the city's coins and on the effigies of Artemis. According to one ancient interpretation the word Essen means properly 'king-bee'—that is queen-bee, for the Greeks were in error on this point—and some have thought that the virgin priestesses were called Melissae, 'bees'. It is known that certain priestesses of the Mother Goddess had this title, but there is no actual evidence for it at Ephesus, and this whole theory must be regarded as dubious. The Essenes appear to have acted as intermediaries between the religious and the civic sides of the city's activities; they offered sacrifice to Artemis in the city's name, they assigned new citizens to a particular tribe, and they organised the public banquets that followed the religious ceremonies.

Another college of priests attached to the service of Artemis was the Curetes. In Greek mythology the Curetes were demi-gods associated primarily with Zeus; but a local Ephesian legend told that they assisted Leto in giving birth to Artemis—which event the Ephesians located in the neighbourhood of their city—by scaring away Hera, who was jealously watching to do what mischief she could. This event was celebrated by an annual festival, at which the human college of Curetes held sacrifices and banquets.

Yet another order had the curious name of Acrobatae, or walkers on tiptoe. Why they walked in this way we do not know; all we learn of them is that they were twenty in number and performed sacrifices. These again are peculiar to Ephesus.

Strabo's language suggests that not all the exotic features

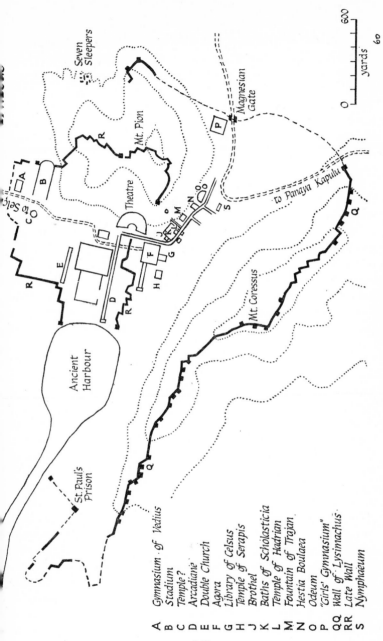

Fig. 33 Plan of Ephesus

A Gymnasium of Vedius
B Stadium
C Temple?
D Arcadiane
E Double Church
F Agora
G Library of Celsus
H Temple of Serapis
J Brothel
K Baths of Scholasticia
L Temple of Hadrian
M Fountain of Trajan
N Hestia Boulaea
o Odeum
P "Girls' Gymnasium"
QQ Wall of Lysimachus
RR Late Wall
S Nymphaeum

169

of the cult of Artemis survived unchanged in his own day. Indeed, it is remarkable that the goddess and her hierarchy resisted the influence of Hellenism so long and so successfully as they did.

The surviving ruins of Ephesus belong almost exclusively to the Roman imperial period. The outstanding exception is the circuit-wall built by Lysimachus. On the low ground it has largely disappeared, but it still stands along the crest of the 1,100-foot mountain, now called Bülbül Dağı, to the south of the city, and provides a recommended excursion for those with half a day to spare. With its towers and postern gates it affords an excellent example of a Hellenistic fortification wall. When it stood complete it contained, by Miltner's calculation, not less than 200,000 cubic metres of stone, exclusive of the towers. Where it descends at its west end to the ancient harbour it contains a very handsome tower set on a low hill, which has, for no good reason, acquired the name of 'St. Paul's Prison'. It is conspicuous from the city. An inscription in the tower identifies the knoll on which it stands as the 'Hill of Astyages'; who Astyages may have been is not known.

The road which diverges to the ruins from the Kuşadasi highway brings the visitor first to the Gymnasium of Vedius, constructed in the second century A.D. as a gift to the city by a rich citizen named Publius Vedius Antoninus. The visitor enters it from the rear. The standing remains are those of the baths which were normally attached to gymnasia in the Roman period; we have seen the case of the upper gymnasium at Pergamum. The palaestra, the open area for gymnastic exercise, lay to the east, with a well-appointed latrine in its south-west corner.

Just to the south is the stadium. In its present form it is not earlier than the third century A.D., and its poor state of preservation is due to plundering of the stones for the Byzantine fortification on the hill above Selçuk. The starting-lines are not preserved, and the most interesting part of the stadium is at the east end, where a circular area has been enclosed to serve as an arena for gladiatorial and similar contests, and rooms are installed for the apparent purpose of housing the wild beasts.[1] As in most Greek cities, there is no amphitheatre at Ephesus; and since the substitute thus produced was certainly no part of the stadium as it was built, it was evidently only at a late date that the need was felt to stage this kind of display.

Directly across the road from the stadium is a low mound on whose summit there once stood an octagonal building, of which only the rock-cut parts remain. It was probably a temple, and has been thought to belong to the early Ionian Ephesus, before the time of Croesus, but there is no real evidence either of its nature or of its date.

Farther to the south is the great theatre, a good example of the so-called Graeco-Roman type, that is to say a theatre of Greek form reconstructed in the Roman fashion. The original building dates from the time of Lysimachus or shortly after; from this period there survive the main core of the scene-building and the general form of the cavea, rather over a semicircle, with its twelve stairways, eleven cunei and two diazomata. A noteworthy feature is that the steepness of the cavea slope increases above each diazoma, thus improving the view of the spectators at the back. The ground floor of the stage-building consists of a long hall running north and south, with eight rooms lying to the west of it; the two end rooms at north and south opened on to a narrow terrace behind the building, the others open into the hall. A passage runs through from the terrace into the orchestra. All of this is preserved. Of the upper storey, which formed a background to the stage, little now survives. The stage itself is calculated to have been 8 feet 6 inches in height and about 10 feet in depth; it sloped from back to front, like a modern stage, with a gradient of about 1:25 (Pl. 35).

In the classical period, as is now generally agreed, the theatre had no stage; the actors in the plays of Euripides or Aristophanes performed on the same level as the chorus in the orchestra, or at most were raised above them only by a low dais or platform. In the Hellenistic period, when the impor-

[1] At the time of writing the cross-wall is almost lost to sight among bushes and tall thistles, and the stadium as a whole is in a poor state of maintenance.

tance of the chorus was much reduced, a high narrow stage
for the actors was introduced, making them more audible
from the upper seats without being less visible from the lower.
This Hellenistic stage is generally some 8 to 10 feet high and
about the same in depth; a good example is preserved at
Priene.[1] In the Roman period all the action took place on the
stage, which was accordingly increased to about double in
depth from front to back; the orchestra, now useless to the
performers, was occupied during the performance by chairs
for the more distinguished spectators.

During the first century A.D., therefore, the theatre at
Ephesus was subjected to an extensive reconstruction to bring
it up to date. The stage, still of the same height, was carried
forward another 10 feet into the orchestra and supported on
the two rows of columns and one row of square pilasters which
are still standing. In the front of the stage-building, behind the
stage, a great façade was erected, rising in three storeys above
the stage and decorated with columns, niches and statues.
The long hall in the ground floor was now roofed over, in place
of its old wooden ceiling, with a stone vault resting on walls
placed against the side walls of the hall; their handsome
blocks were probably taken from a dismantled part of the
Hellenistic theatre. A second row of eight rooms was also
added on the west. The side entrances to the orchestra, called
parodoi, were in the Hellenistic theatre open passages between
stage and cavea; these were blocked by the new constructions,
and fresh covered entrances were built, of which that on the
north side is well preserved. These changes involved a reduc-
tion of the cavea at its two extremities by about 5 feet and the
construction of new retaining walls; an inscription was found
recording the dedication of this huge work to the Emperor
Domitian in A.D. 92.

These massive alterations were begun about A.D. 40 and
completed some seventy years later. They were accordingly in
progress when St. Paul was at Ephesus in the 'fifties. To
visualise the riotous assembly caused by Demetrius the silversmith we should picture the stage-building enveloped in
scaffolding and the astonished workmen looking on during an

[1] Below, pp. 202-5.

unexpected rest-period. We must also imagine the rows of seats extending right down to orchestra level, for the lowest six rows were removed at a later date and the present semi-circular wall constructed.

The acoustics of the theatre are, as always, excellent, and were further improved in ancient times by placing bronze or clay sounding-vessels at various points in the auditorium—a remarkable anticipation of the loud-speakers used today at Wimbledon and elsewhere.[1] The spectators were shaded, at least partially, by a huge awning stretched from side to side of the cavea.

From the hillside above the theatre an excellent view may be had of the greater part of the city. In front, a little to the right, a marble-paved street runs straight for some 600 yards to the ancient harbour, whose shape can be distinguished by the different colour of the grass. There was always a street in this position, but the present paving dates only from about A.D. 400. It is some 35 feet wide and had a stoa on either side. The name of the street is given by an inscription found in it, which says: 'Arcadiane contains in its two stoas, as far as the wild boar, fifty lamps.' The wild boar, as was mentioned above, recalls the foundation legend of the city. The provision for street-lighting is interesting and a great rarity; Antioch had it in the fourth century, but in the first century, even at Rome, the streets, as we learn from Juvenal, were unlighted. The name Arcadiane, given in honour of the Emperor Arcadius (A.D. 395–408), tells us the approximate date. Another inscription found beside this street gives interesting information concerning charges payable to the Record Office. For example, a parsley-vendor's licence, 1 denarius; a salt-vendor's licence, 1 denarius; proclamation of a victor in the games, 6 denarii; registration of birth, 1 denarius—but if the mother is of a prohibited class (such as a priestess or a slave) the charge is 100 denarii. Evidently possession of a birth-certificate in such cases conferred certain privileges and was worth paying for.

From Arcadiane a short walk to the north brings the visitor to the Church of the Virgin Mary, sometimes called the Double Church. The original building was not a church at all

[1] See above, p. 143.

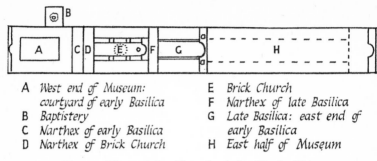

A   *West end of Museum:*   E   *Brick Church*
     courtyard of early Basilica   F   *Narthex of late Basilica*
B   *Baptistery*   G   *Late Basilica: east end of*
C   *Narthex of early Basilica*   *early Basilica*
D   *Narthex of Brick Church*   H   *East half of Museum*

FIG. 34 Plan of the Church of the Virgin Mary

but a secular building of usually elongated form, some 100 feet wide and about eight times as long, with an apse at each end and a row of small rooms along each side. This was the Museum—that is, not what is now understood by a museum, but a Hall of the Muses, used for lectures, disputation and higher education generally. This building was destroyed by fire, and in the third century A.D. the ruins of its western half were converted into a church of basilica form with a court-yard in front on the west (A-G on the plan). In this church, dedicated to the Virgin, was held the stormy third Ecumenical Council of A.D. 431, where the Nestorian heresy was con-demned. On the north side of the courtyard a baptistery was added; this is comparatively well preserved, and has in the floor of its central room a font for baptismal immersion, with steps leading down on each side. The form of this early basilica is not now easy to recognise, owing to later alterations. At an uncertain date a domed church of brickwork (E on the plan) was installed in the western half of the basilica, with a new apse at its east end; and later still, after the destruction of this church, a small basilica G was inserted between it and the east end of the early basilica. The remains of these later chur-ches have almost completely overlaid the church of the Virgin. The courtyard A, however, remains unaltered; a number of inscribed blocks have been re-used in its paving. The eastern half H of the original museum was converted into dwelling-houses.

Below the theatre, at right-angles to Arcadiane, runs a

similar marble-paved street. Wheeled traffic was permitted along it,[1] as is shown by the ruts in the surface. This paving is probably of similar date to that of Arcadiane; but the handsome Doric stoa on its west side was dedicated in the middle of the first century A.D. (Pl. 40).

Beyond this stoa on the right is the Library of Celsus, probably the finest surviving specimen of its kind. Following the rule laid down by the Roman architect Vitruvius, it faces the east, so as to take advantage of the morning light. From the courtyard in front steps led up to a two-storeyed façade with windows in the upper storey and an inscription naming the building as the 'Celsian Library' and recording that Gaius Julius Aquila left 25,000 denarii for its upkeep and for the purchase of books. This Aquila was son of Gaius Julius Celsus Polemaeanus, proconsul of Asia in A.D. 106–7, in whose honour and as whose tomb the library was built. Statues of Celsus stood on the wings of the front steps, with honorific inscriptions in Greek and in Latin which may still be read.

The interior consisted of a single large room 50 feet high, surrounded by galleries, in three storeys; it has a number of features in common with the library at Pergamum. In the middle of the back wall is a semi-circular niche which probably contained a statue of Athena. At the foot of the walls is a platform 3 feet high and rather more broad, which carried columns supporting a gallery above. In the walls are ten rectangular niches which held the books; similar niches, with a narrow gallery in front, no doubt stood in the second and third storeys. Round the exterior of the walls runs a passage 3 feet wide, serving to protect the books from damp. On the north side this passage leads round to the grave-chamber of Celsus, situated directly under the semicircular niche in the back wall. This chamber is generally kept locked, the guardian holding the key. It contains a marble sarcophagus in which is the actual coffin of lead, still unopened. Tombs in ancient times stood normally outside the city; the privilege of burial in the city was a considerable distinction.

From the courtyard in front of the library a three-arched gateway leads through to the agora on the north. This gate,

[1] Or at least along part of it.

built almost entirely of marble, was dedicated in 3 B.C. to Augustus and his son-in-law Agrippa by two rich freedmen, Mithridates and Mazaeus. The inscription, which originally stood above the gate, is now placed along the side of the agora. This Mithridates has, of course, no connection with the famous king of Pontus. In the wall between the gate and the court-yard is an inscription of the third century A.D. praising a certain market-inspector for keeping down the price of bread: 'Fine bread', it says, 'was sold at 4 obols [perhaps about sixpence] for a 14 ounce loaf; inferior bread at 2 obols the 10 ounce loaf.' A century earlier prices had been about half of these; in the meantime the currency had been debased, and inflation had done its work. Inscriptions of this kind bring the ancient city to life more vividly perhaps than many more imposing monuments; so, too, does a graffito roughly scrawled in a niche of the same gate on the opposite side: it says 'Whoso relieves himself here shall suffer the wrath of Hecate'.

Behind the library to the west are the ruins of the Temple of Serapis, built in the second century A.D. Serapis, the sacred bull Apis, was an Egyptian deity; but Ptolemy I built him a temple at Alexandria in which the god's statue was given features resembling those of Pluto, the Greek god of the under-world. This was an attempt to establish a cult which should be acceptable both to Egyptians and to Greeks; the Egyptians, in fact, soon dropped it and reverted to the old worship, but its success with the Greeks, and even with the Romans, was remarkable. Under the Empire almost every city of note in the eastern provinces had a cult of the composite Serapis, fre-quently associated with Isis and other Egyptian deities.

The Serapeum at Ephesus is notable especially for its massive architecture. It had columns only in front; eight in number, these were formed each of a single block of stone. The diameter is nearly 5 feet, and the height about 46 feet, so that each column must have weighed not far short of 60 tons. The achievement of transporting and erecting these monoliths, and of placing on them the capitals and the heavy entablature, all with the utmost precision, is impressive in the extreme. Of the richness of the decoration an idea is given by the block lying in front of the temple-steps. Quarter-circular grooves in the floor show where the heavy double door opened into the interior. Several of the surviving stones, including the columns, show traces of the red paint with which they were originally coloured; temples and statues were normally painted in antiquity. Red and blue are the colours most used; of these the red pigment employed was the more durable, and not infrequently survives, whereas blue is rarely to be seen.

Opposite the library the paved street turns to the east and rises gently to follow the south foot of Mt. Pion to the Magnesian Gate. This part of the city is in process of excavation by the Austrian archaeologists at the time of writing. Among the new discoveries the visitor's eye is perhaps most attracted by the Temple of Hadrian, fronting the street on the north side (Pl. 32). The façade has been re-erected from the architectural fragments found. This is the temple which earned for Ephesus its second 'Temple-Wardenship'. In the fourth century the building was damaged by fire or by an earthquake; the reliefs in the porch, or pronaos, belong to the restoration which was then undertaken. (Those now in position are casts; the originals are in the museum.) That on the right (east) side is particularly interesting. It shows a group of thirteen figures; on the extreme left and right stands Athena with her round shield; after her on the left come six other Greek deities, then a group of five representing the Emperor Theodosius and his family on either side of a figure of Artemis. If we remember that Theodosius was among the fiercest opponents of paganism, this acceptance of the pagan goddess, as it were, into the bosom of the royal family is remarkable indeed, and leaves no doubt of the strong hold which Artemis still had upon men's minds, even at this late date.

Further evidence to the same effect was found by the excavators in the temple of Hestia Boulaea adjoining the Odeum higher up towards the Magnesian Gate. In this sanctuary burned the eternal fire, which was never permitted to go out; it formed the political centre of the city. This building was found, when excavated, to have been systematically despoiled in antiquity and its contents removed; nevertheless it still contained two statues of Artemis carefully preserved where they lay. The statues might be overthrown by the

AT—M

Christian destroyers of the temple, but respect for the goddess still forbade that they should be carried off to the lime-kiln.

The despoiler of this sanctuary is, as it happens, known. Behind the temple of Hadrian are the so-called Baths of Scholasticia. This lady, commemorated by a statue found in the building, restored the baths in the fourth century, perhaps after the same earthquake which damaged the temple of Hadrian. She used for the purpose material taken from the temple of Hestia Boulaea. That this is so is especially clear from the thick solid columns which stand in the front hall of the baths. These are covered with inscribed lists of members of the College of Curetes; similar lists are found on the outer walls of the temple of Hestia, to which accordingly it is safe to suppose that the columns also originally belonged.

Adjoining the Baths of Scholasticia is a room identified, from inscriptions and from the erotic character of certain figurines found in it, as a brothel (Aşkevi on the notice-board).

Among the inscribed stones lining the street, about 30 yards below the temple of Hadrian, lying flat behind the upright row, is a statue-base erected by the Sacred College of Silver-smiths—the same to which Demetrius belonged.

Just above the temple of Hadrian is the elaborate Fountain of Trajan, and farther up the paved street other buildings are being brought to light. On the saddle at the top of the rise the Odeum has long been known; it is a small theatre-like building, in very decent preservation, used for musical performances and perhaps for lectures and rehearsals.

Opposite the Odeum is a large fountain, or Nymphaeum, which served for the distribution of water to the city. It was fed by an aqueduct of which a part remains, crossing the valley three miles to the south of Selçuk, immediately below the present main road. It is a handsome structure in two storeys, and is dated by its inscription to the time of Augustus. Farther on still is the Magnesian Gate, of which hardly anything is left, and close beside it the Girls' Gymnasium—so-called not be-cause it was for the use of young women but because of the numerous female statues found there (Pl. 41).

If the visitor will continue from here round the east foot of Mt. Pion, he will come in about half a mile upon an impressive necropolis in a gully of the hillside. In addition to numerous single graves, large vaulted halls of brickwork have been constructed, with sepulchral niches and chambers in their walls, often in two or more storeys. The whole installation is of Christian date, and grew up around the burial-place of the famous Seven Sleepers of Ephesus. These young men, so the story ran, were Christians who lived in the time of the Emperor Decius, about A.D. 250. To escape the obligation of having to perform sacrifice in the temple of the emperor they left the city and lay down to sleep in a cave. When they woke up and went back into the city to buy bread they found that they had slept not one night but close on two hundred years, and that Christianity was now the accepted religion of the Roman world. The emperor, Theodosius II, was informed of this remarkable occurrence and at once recognised in it a proof of the doctrine of bodily resurrection, a question which was at that time agitating the Church. When the young men eventually died their bodies, miraculously preserved from decay, were given splendid burial and a church was built over their resting-place.

Excavation has, in fact, revealed a small church, and beneath it a rock-cut gallery with chambers opening off it, on the walls of which are scratched invocations to the saintly young sleepers. From a desire to be buried as close as possible to them the surrounding necropolis was gradually extended in subsequent centuries, and the place has ever since been regarded as holy.

The excavations continue. The last few years' work has already made a great change in the appearance of the site, and a vast amount remains to be done. It is calculated that the parts of Ephesus so far dug comprise in area only a twentieth part of the whole city.

PANAYA KAPULU

Just outside the city on the south a recently made road leads to the so-called Panaya Kapulu, or house of the Virgin Mary, Meryem Ana in Turkish. This is a small building now converted

into a chapel, set in a pleasant spot with terraces and an
abundant fountain. Whether this is really the Virgin's home,
and even whether the Virgin really lived and died at Ephesus,
are hotly debated problems (Pl. 44).

The canonical tradition holds that Mary died in Jerusalem
at the age of 63. But the foundations of this tradition are
neither very early nor very strong. The principal evidence is a
passage of St. John of Damascus, written in the eighth
century, which relates that in A.D. 458 the Empress Pulcheria
wrote to the Bishop of Jerusalem asking him to send the body
of the Virgin to Constantinople. The bishop replied that he
was unable to do so, as according to a reliable tradition she
was buried at Gethsemane, and the tomb was found empty,
three days later, by the apostles. There is reason to suspect,
however, that this passage has been interpolated into the text
of St. John; and it is curious that earlier writers such as
Eusebius and Jerome make no mention of this tomb at
Gethsemane. The scriptures themselves are completely silent
concerning the latter part of the Virgin's life.

The rival tradition, which goes back at least to the Council
of Ephesus in 431, maintains that Mary came with St. John
to Ephesus between 37 and 48, lived there and died there.
Christ on the Cross entrusted His mother to His beloved John;
'and from that moment the disciple took her into his home'.
It is to be assumed, say the Ephesian partisans, that from that
time on the two were inseparable; when John came to Ephesus,
Mary must have been with him. John was certainly in Asia
from 67 onwards; but if Mary died at the age of 63 she cannot
have lived until that date, and it is necessary to suppose that
John paid an earlier visit to Ephesus. This must have been
before 48, in which year he is known to have been in Jerusalem.
Between 37 and 48 we have no information as to where he was
or what he was doing, and this silence is well explained by the
theory that he and Mary were at Ephesus, far from the centre
of events in Palestine. We can then understand how it happened that St. Paul in the 'fifties found churches already
established in Asia.

Nothing therefore prevents our believing that Mary lived
for some time, and died, at Ephesus, and a tradition that she

did so recurs repeatedly from the fifth century onwards. But the situation of her house and of her tomb was, of course, unknown, and the house was likely to have perished long since. Its discovery, against all probability, was due to the publication in the middle of the nineteenth century of a Life of the Virgin as revealed in visions to a certain Catherine Emmerich. This invalid German lady, who for twelve years had not left her bed, and had never in her life been near Ephesus, placed the Virgin's house on a mountain above that city and described its appearance in considerable detail. In 1891 a search was organised by M. Poulin, Superior of the Lazarists, in the hills around Ephesus, and resulted in the discovery of a ruined house which answered exactly to the description—so exactly that, in one observer's opinion, the house and its surroundings might have been laid out according to Catherine Emmerich's directions. This was the Panaya Kapulu. The masonry of the house is agreed to be characteristic of the sixth or seventh century, but competent scholars have been prepared to say that the foundations might quite possibly go back to the first century. Moreover, the search-party learned that every year, on 15 August, the Orthodox Greeks of the neighbourhood, and even from a considerable distance, had long been in the habit of assembling there to celebrate the Dormition of the Virgin, whom they believed to have died at that spot. This belief had been inherited through the generations, and might well be very ancient.

Such is the case for Panaya Kapulu. It at once won the approbation of the Archbishop of Smyrna, who in 1892 authorised the celebration of the Mass in the building and pronounced it a place of pilgrimage.

Since then numerous wonderful cures have been recorded, and in a corner of the chapel are collected the crutches, sticks, leg-braces and other implements dedicated by grateful sufferers who have been enabled to discard them. Faith in the healing powers of the place continues still; when the present writer was récently there an old gentleman sorely afflicted with rheumatism was painfully exercising his crippled limbs inside the chapel, until obliged to return to his wheel-chair. Until lately there were also to be seen in the chapel hundreds

of fragments of cloth hung up by visitors either in gratitude
for a cure effected or in hope of a cure to come. This practice is
observed in many places in Turkey which are reckoned holy.

As for the Virgin's tomb, it was declared by Catherine
Emmerich to be at a distance of something over a mile from
the house, but all efforts to find it have so far been unsuccessful.

BELEVI

Some ten miles from Ephesus, near the village of Belevi on the
Izmir road, are two monuments of comparatively early date,
well deserving of a visit. They stand about two miles from the
village beside the rough road leading to Tire.

The first, which is close beside the road on a slight eminence,
is a mausoleum of most unusual construction. The core of the
monument consists of a cube of living rock about 80 feet
square and nearly 50 feet high, formed by cutting away the
hillside from around it. This was faced with solid marble
blocks, with steps at the foot and a Doric triglyph-frieze at
the top. On this massive base was erected a chamber, also of
marble, surrounded by a Corinthian colonnade. Along the top
of this colonnade stood winged lions arranged in pairs on
either side of globular urns. The roof over the chamber was
probably of pyramidal shape, with perhaps a chariot-and-
four at the summit (Pl. 38).

The grave itself was not in this chamber, where it might be
expected, but was secreted in the rock-cube on the south side
facing the hill. To form it, the rock-cube was cut away from
top to bottom, the two sides of the cut sloping inwards towards
the top; the grave-chamber was then installed in the lower part
of this cut, leaving a trapezoidal area above it. Inside is the
sarcophagus, elegantly carved and decorated with a relief
showing eleven Sirens; the detail of the wings and birds' feet
is finely rendered. On the lid of the sarcophagus the dead man
is represented reclining on his elbow. This chamber was completely invisible from outside, as the marble facing was carried
without interruption across the cut in the rock (Pl. 42, 45).

Only one man was ever buried in this tomb, and in view of
the vast expense incurred he must have been a distinguished

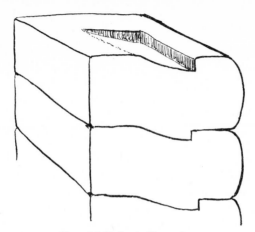

FIG. 35 Belevi. Tumulus

personage; but no trace of an inscription was found, and it is
not known who he was. At first it was conjectured that he
might be Antiochus II of Syria, who died at Ephesus in 246
B.C. under suspicion of having been poisoned by his wife
Laodice. It would be normal for the king's body to be taken
back to Syria, but in the conditions of war prevailing at the
time it might possibly have been decided to bury him near
Ephesus. However, the more recent opinion is that the mausoleum dates to an earlier period, probably in the fourth century
while the country was still under the Persians. The form of
the winged lions in particular suggests Persian influence. The
occupant of the tomb will then have been a local dignitary of
wealth and position; it is not possible to say more.

The second monument is also a tomb, but of utterly
different character. It stands on the hill next to the west of
the mausoleum. It has the form of a tumulus, but the tumulus
in fact consists merely of the summit of the hill itself. Round it
runs a wall of elegant cushioned ashlar masonry. To resist the
thrust of the earth each block has in its upper surface a groove
into which fitted a corresponding projection on the under-side
of the block above. The entrance, on the south, leads to a
tunnel 20 yards long running into the hill, at the end of which,
nearly at the centre of the tumulus, are two grave-chambers.

The ring-wall was carried past the entrance, which was accordingly invisible from outside. Both tunnel and grave-chambers were constructed by cutting down through the rock from above, then lining with masonry and roofing over with large slabs. The tunnel is at present encumbered by piles of earth and stones thrown up by treasure-seekers. The chambers are rectangular, and the roofs are carefully built to prevent collapse. In the outer room the roof-span is reduced by laying blocks obliquely across the corners; in the inner room the roof is formed of a 'corbelled' arch, each course on either side projecting beyond the course below. Above the ceiling of each room is a relieving chamber to reduce the pressure from above; these were not originally accessible, but a hole has been cut in the roof of the inner chamber by tomb-robbers. No sarcophagus or other trace of the actual burial has been found, nor is there any inscription. On the top of the hill are lying a number of squared blocks, showing that some kind of monument stood there. The quarry from which the wall-blocks were cut adjoins the tumulus on the south-west (Pl. 43).

Very varying dates have been proposed for this tumulus, which, like the mausoleum below, must have been the tomb of no ordinary person. The latest opinion is disposed to place it in the fourth century B.C., perhaps a little earlier than the mausoleum.

CHAPTER EIGHT

Colophon, Notium, Claros

THESE THREE places lie close together in the same valley and were always closely associated; Colophon and Notium were cities, Claros was not. Colophon was a member of the Ionian League; its foundation legend concerns Claros and will be recorded below. Notium, on the other hand, was not in origin Ionian at all; it is included by Herodotus in his list of the Aeolian cities. Some scholars have found it surprising to have an Aeolian city isolated so far south from the rest, and have suspected either that Herodotus is in error or that he refers to another city of the same name. The name Notium, meaning 'southern', is one that might well recur on the map. No second Notium is actually known, however, in this region and the tradition need not be doubted; Magnesia on the Maeander was also an Aeolian foundation, equally distant from Aeolis, and like Notium was never included in the Ionian League. The name Notium may indeed refer to the situation of the city far to the south of Aeolis proper. (The alternative is that it means 'south of Colophon'.) However this may be, Colophon and Notium were certainly in close relations from very early times, as indeed they must be if both were to survive. When the Colophonians led a colony to Myrleia (now Mudanya) on the sea of Marmara they must have sailed from Notium; and, in fact, we hear that Colophon in early days possessed a powerful fleet.

Colophonian territory extended to the east over the great plain of Cumaovası, perfect country for cavalry; it is no surprise that the city was famous for its horses. So much so that in any doubtful engagement the intervention of the Colophonian cavalry was at once decisive; hence, says Strabo, the expression 'to put the Colophon on it', meaning to settle the

matter out of hand. The explanation is dubious, as the word
colophon means a summit or culmination (whence its use in
English for the end-plate of a book), and there need be no
reference to the city.

In battle the Colophonians used squadrons of dogs, finding
them, says Pliny, the most reliable auxiliaries, with the addi-
tional advantage of not requiring pay. If the animals were
anything like the Anatolian sheep-dogs of today, we may well
imagine they were formidable adversaries. The dog played
another part also at Colophon, for there as at Sparta, and nowhere else in the Greek world, it was used as a sacrificial
animal. So at least Pausanias tells us. When the Greeks
sacrificed an animal the flesh was normally eaten afterwards
by the animal's owner and any whom he might invite; a speci-
fied portion was the priest's perquisite, and the god received
some of the hair or fat or other part which made a fragrant
smell, this odour being fortunately what the gods particularly
enjoyed. The Greeks rarely ate meat except after sacrifice—
that is to say, they sacrificed their meat before eating it. To
offer a dog was therefore a sacrifice in every sense, not merely
an occasion for a good meal. At Colophon the custom was to
offer a black bitch by night to Hecate, that strange three-
headed deity of the underworld, sender of ghosts and haunter
of cross-roads. At Sparta the offering was made to the
war-god.

Rich territory and a strong navy together brought great
wealth to Colophon, so that before long it could be quoted as
a city where the rich were actually in a majority. Affluence had
its common effect, and the Colophonians sank into luxury and
effeminacy; as many as a thousand of the citizens, we read,
used to attend the market-place in purple robes worth their
weight in silver and drenched with perfume; this and their
extravagance at table caused them to be compared with the
notorious Sybarites of southern Italy. By this profligacy, say
the historians, they and their city were ruined; in the early
wars with the Lydians, Colophon was the only Greek city
besides Magnesia that Gyges was able to conquer. Later, of
course, it fell to Persia with the rest, and never afterwards
regained its former prosperity. When the Persians were

expelled after Salamis and the Delian Confederacy established, we find Colophon paying a normal tribute of three talents, only half as much as, for example, Teos.

In these early times little is heard of Notium. Thucydides calls her 'Notium of the Colophonians', and her assessment in the confederacy was as low as one-third of a talent, or less than was paid by many of the small Carian townships. It was always paid separately from Colophon. During the Peloponnesian War an incident occurred which is interesting for the light it throws on the ideas and methods of the time. Not all Colophonians were content to be tribute-paying members of the Athenian maritime confederacy; many preferred the old conditions under the Persians. These therefore banded together and called in the Persian forces, who occupied the town. Their opponents, the anti-Persian party, fled for refuge to Notium; but before long similar trouble arose there too, and the city was divided into two camps. The pro-Persians walled off a large part of the town and called in those of the same mind from Colophon; the other party applied for help to the Athenians. The Athenian commander Paches thereupon invited the commander of the Persian party, by name Hippias, to a conference, promising to return him safe and sound to the city if no agreement was reached. When Hippias responded Paches put him under detention, and by an unexpected assault captured the city. He then restored Hippias according to the letter of his promise, and as soon as he was inside the walls seized him and put him to death. Notium was given back to the pro-Athenian party, but Colophon remained in Persian hands, and continued so almost without interruption till the coming of Alexander.

Aristotle, writing in the fourth century, quotes Notium and Colophon as an example of faction arising owing to the ground not being suitable for a single city, presumably because the places were too far apart; it is a fair inference that before his time Colophon was joined in a political fusion with Notium, so as to form one city. This was certainly the case in the third century. The year 299 B.C. was important for Colophon; having the temerity to resist Lysimachus, the city was captured by him and destroyed; its population was transferred to help man the great new city of Ephesus which he had just founded. The tomb of the Colophonians who fell in this battle stood, says Pausanias, on the left of the road as you go to Claros— possibly one or both of the two tumuli still visible about a mile north of the village of Çile.

After the death of Lysimachus in 281 Colophon was restored, with a new wall several miles in length. But the new city was never of very much account; in Hellenistic times the emphasis was on seaborne commerce, and apart from Notium Colophon was nothing. The two cities were now one; Colophon was called the Old Town, Notium was New Colophon or Colophon-on-Sea, and her own name fell into disuse. Even the two combined, however, could not compete with Ephesus, and soon ceased to play any part in history. Such prosperity as they had was almost entirely due to the fame of the oracle at Claros.

The three sites are easily visited by motor transport in a day from Izmir. The road is good as far as Cumaovası, after that poor. The ruins of Colophon at Değirmendere, apart from one or two stretches of the Hellenistic wall, are scanty, difficult to find and unrewarding when found. Most travellers will be content to pass on to Claros and Notium.

NOTIUM

Notium is a typical early Greek settlement site, on a hill directly above the sea, with a river close at hand and a modest territory in the valley. The ruins are not spectacular, as very little is actually standing, but the site is very attractive. The hilltop is about a kilometre in length and comprises two eminences with a saddle between. The whole is surrounded by a ring-wall over two miles long, of similar date to that at Colophon; considerable stretches of this are quite well preserved.

On the western eminence is a small temple (A), with an altar in front on the east and surrounded by a stoa; surprisingly, the stoa is not parallel with the walls of the temple. This building was at one time conjectured to be the temple of Clarian Apollo; when excavated by French archaeologists in

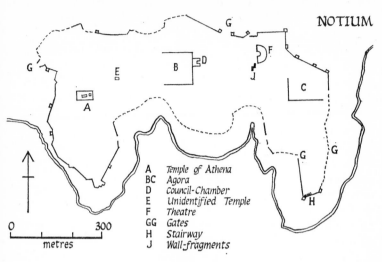

NOTIUM

A   Temple of Athena
BC   Agora
D   Council-Chamber
E   Unidentified Temple
F   Theatre
GG   Gates
H   Stairway
J   Wall-fragments

0   300
metres

FIG. 36 Plan of Notium

1921 an inscription was found proving it to be a temple of Athena.

The agora (B) is on the slope towards the saddle; adjoining it on the east, at D, are the scanty ruins of a building containing rows of seats, which the excavators suggested might be a court of justice. The arrangement of the seats on three sides of a square, as also the situation close to the agora, are strongly reminiscent of the council-chambers at Priene and Heracleia,[1] and it seems more probable that this was the function of the present building also.

On the eastern eminence is a second agora (C) now featureless, and the theatre (F). This is small, with only twenty-seven rows of seats, and has never been excavated. The form of the cavea is Greek, being rather more than a semicircle, but it has been reconstructed in Roman times; part of the southern retaining wall is preserved, with a vaulted passage. There are considerable remains of the stage-building, but they are now buried.

It would be interesting to identify the wall built by the pro-Persian party, during the principal appearance of Notium in

[1] Below, pp. 205, 255.

history (above, p. 187), to fence themselves off from their opponents. Its approximate position is hardly doubtful; it must have run across the waist of the site between the theatre and the agora B. A few scraps of wall are now to be seen here, in particular at J, close to the theatre; but they are scarcely convincing. It appears highly likely that the wall was removed, as an unwanted impediment, immediately after the crisis was ended.

On the western slopes of the hill next to the north of the town is a fairly extensive necropolis; the tombs are either sunk into the ground, or cut horizontally into the rock, or in a few cases constructed of masonry above ground. To the west of the town, on the opposite side of the river and close to the shore, is a cave some 50 feet wide and deep and about 10 feet high. At the back is a spring of poor but drinkable water with an arched coping above it and various niches cut in the rock near by. This spot was probably sacred in antiquity, but we have no information concerning it. In 1963 its floor was strewn with tin cans, old newspapers and other rubbish, for an attempt is being made to convert Notium into a bathing resort, and two restaurants are now installed on the beach, where the visitor may refresh himself with a scanty meal at extortionate cost.

CLAROS

South of Colophon, and about one mile from Notium and the sea, is the site of Claros. There was never a city here; the site is on the territory of Colophon and contains the famous temple and oracle of Apollo with its associated buildings. Like most of the great temples of Asia Minor, it stands on flat ground; but the explanation is not in this case that the Ionic order appears to better advantage in such a position, for the architecture is, surprisingly, Doric. The sanctuary lies in the valley of a small stream called in antiquity the Ales or the Halesus, and said to be the coldest in Ionia; this now overflows every winter, and in the course of centuries had buried the ruins deeply under its silt, and until recently the exact site of the temple was unknown.

The Colophonians maintained that the sanctuary and oracle

of Clarian Apollo were very ancient. Our earliest mention of the sanctuary is in the Homeric hymn to Apollo, which may perhaps date to the seventh century B.C.; a second mention in the short hymn to Artemis may be a good deal later. Neither of these refers to the oracle. Nor was Claros among the oracles consulted by Croesus in the sixth century, and, in fact, there seems to be no recorded activity of the oracle before early Hellenistic times.

On the other hand, the spot was traditionally associated with divination from the remotest antiquity. Even before the Trojan War, it was said, the Sibyl Herophile came there and uttered her predictions, one of which was that Helen would be the ruin of Europe and Asia. The original Carian inhabitants were first displaced by Greeks from Crete; later a party of Thebans, including the prophetess Manto, came to settle, and Manto married the Cretan leader. Their son was the famous seer Mopsus. After the Trojan War the equally famous seer Calchas arrived at Claros, and a contest in divination took place. 'I wonder,' said Calchas, 'how many figs there are on this tree; can you tell me the number?' Mopsus replied, 'Ten thousand; and if you measure them with a bushel measure, there will be one over which you cannot get in.' This answer was judged to be correct (nothing is said of the method of judging), and Calchas thereupon died of grief, as he was destined to do when he should meet a greater seer than himself. An alternative version made Calchas put before Mopsus a pregnant sow and ask how many young she was carrying; Mopsus replied, 'Three, including one female.' This also proved correct (and much less disputable than the other), with the same melancholy result.

Virtually nothing is heard of Claros in classical times, though the sanctuary certainly existed. The temple seen today was built early in the Hellenistic period; one of Apollo's first responses from his new house may have been the advice he gave to found the new Smyrna across the Meles.[1] Like so many other sanctuaries, Claros suffered from the pirates; the oracle seems to have declined for a while, but revived brilliantly under the Roman empire. The temple was rededicated

[1] Above, p. 44.

by Hadrian towards the end of his reign. At this period delegations came regularly from many parts of the world—Caria, Phrygia, Pisidia, Pontus, Thrace, Crete, and even Corinth—to consult the god and to sing hymns in his honour. Records of these visits are carved in hundreds on the steps of the temple, on the Propylaea, on the bases and even in the flutes of the columns, and elsewhere; Ionia is represented only by Chios and Phocaea, and it seems that the neighbouring cities for the most part preferred to give their custom to Didyma.

For the method of consulting the oracle we have Tacitus' description of a visit paid by Germanicus, the adopted son of Tiberius, in A.D. 18. 'There is no woman there as at Delphi', says the historian; 'rather a priest, after hearing merely the number and names of the clients, goes down into a cave; there he drinks from a secret fountain and, though generally illiterate, issues responses in verse concerning the various matters in the consultants' minds.' This trick of answering the enquirers without hearing their questions seems peculiar to Apollo at Claros. Pliny also mentions 'a pool in the cave of Clarian Apollo, a draught of which inspires wonderful oracles, but shortens the life of the drinker'. From the inscriptions we learn that the envoys sent to consult the god were commonly initiated into the local mysteries, but as to the nature of these mysteries we have unfortunately no information. The Clarian oracle was one of the last to survive in Christian times; the temple was finally overthrown by an earthquake and the ruins gradually buried under the river mud.

All remained to be rediscovered. In 1826 the Rev. F. V. J. Arundell saw two marble columns just projecting from the earth; by 1907, when the Ottoman Museum undertook an excavation, these had completely disappeared, and were only found again when a peasant reported that he frequently struck his plough against a block in the ground. The excavation revealed a building which was thought to be the temple, but proved later to be only the Propylaea or entrance gate to the sanctuary. Nothing more was done; the river got to work again, and when the writer visited the site in 1946 all that could be seen was an overgrown hollow and the tops of one column and one pillar. A thorough excavation was finally undertaken by the French in 1950; the temple of Apollo was found and cleared, and a number of other buildings brought to light.

From the words of Tacitus and Pliny quoted above it was naturally thought that the oracle was not in the temple of Apollo but in a cave outside. Just opposite the sanctuary a side valley opens on the east from the main valley, and about half a mile up this is a cave high in a cliff, accessible only with tackle. When entered in 1913 it was found to contain a spring of water and numerous stalactites, also sherds of pottery ranging in date from the third millennium to the Roman empire. This cave was confidently hailed as the oracle of Apollo. Tacitus' words 'goes *down* into a cave' might perhaps have caused misgivings, and, in fact, the oracle has now been conclusively located inside the temple. Nevertheless, the cave was evidently important, and probably sacred, in antiquity; and if anyone cares to believe that this was the original holy place at Claros, before the temple was built, he can hardly be contradicted.

The French excavations were conducted under difficulties owing to the high water-table, and pumps were necessary for the lower levels; it is to be feared that the mud will before long cover the site again. At the time of writing the water is already up to the level of the temple pavement.

From the Propylaea a Sacred Way, lined with monuments but only partially excavated, led north-west to the temple. The latter is large, and of the Doric order; its east front is the best preserved, the blocks at the west end having been largely robbed for later buildings. Towards the west end was placed the colossal cult-statue of Apollo, of which fragments were found and remain on the temple platform; the right arm measures over 11 feet. The god was represented seated, with a laurel branch in his right hand, just as he is shown on imperial coins of Colophon. On his right was Artemis, his sister, on his left Leto, his mother; the three figures also appear on coins. Fragments of the female statues also were found (Pl. 47, 60).

But the most interesting part of the temple is certainly the adyton, or holy of holies, where the oracles were delivered. This part was especially difficult to excavate, but the work was fortunately helped by the occurrence of two exceptionally dry seasons in succession. All this part has now filled with water again, but in 1963 the plan was still visible on the spot (Pl. 48).

From the east front a stairway leads down on either side, with a double bend, to a narrow corridor running under the length of the temple. Making four more right-angled turns on the way, this leads for 100 feet to the two oracular chambers, roofed with vaulted arches and barely high enough for a man to stand. The inner chamber, directly under the statue of Apollo, held at the back a large basin of water contained by a breast-high parapet; here the prophet entered alone to draw inspiration from the sacred water. This then is the 'cave and secret fountain' which deceived explorers for so long. The outer chamber, joined to the inner by a passage through a thick wall, was probably for the use of the clergy attached to the temple. Clients were not, it seems, admitted to the adyton itself, although the circumbendibus by which it is approached seems naturally adapted to bewilder a suppliant and reduce him to a fitting state of humility in presence of the god. The titles of the clergy are known from the inscriptions; in addition to the prophet they included the priest of Apollo, a thespiode and one or two secretaries. The function of the thespiode was to render the oracles into verse; it appears that Tacitus was deceived in thinking that this was done by the illiterate priest. In this outer chamber a remarkable discovery was made, namely a stone some 2 feet 3 inches high, of bluish marble, in the form of half an egg. This is the omphalos, or navel-stone, of Apollo, which is properly a feature of Apollo at Delphi. Legend said that Zeus, to determine the centre of the earth, set two eagles to fly from its opposite ends; they met at Delphi, which was accordingly known as the navel of the earth. A navel-stone was in fact found there by the excavators, similar in shape to the one at Claros. It appears that in course of time the omphalos came to be regarded as belonging to Apollo rather than to Delphi, and similar stones have been found in other places where he was worshipped (Pl. 46).

Some 30 yards from the front of the temple is the great altar of marble, 58 feet long. On its surface were found the marks of two separate tables for offerings, one for Apollo, the other for Dionysus. This sharing of the worship is again reminiscent of Delphi, where during the three winter months Apollo withdrew to enjoy the sunshine with the Hyperboreans beyond the north wind, and Dionysus reigned at Delphi in his place. Lying near the altar is a well-preserved sundial dedicated to Dionysus.

A little to the north-west of the main temple is another smaller temple in the Ionic order, belonging to the Clarian Artemis. It was identified by an archaic statue found by the altar in front of it; on the statue is an inscription in letters of the sixth century dedicating it to Artemis. Since the dedicator himself was the first priest, the foundation of the temple will be of that period. No cult-statue has been found in this temple, but it appears from the coins that Clarian Artemis had a distinctly un-Greek form, reminiscent in its general outlines of the Artemis of Ephesus (Pl. 60).

A certain number of responses by the Clarian oracle are recorded. The god's advice concerning the foundation of New Smyrna has already been mentioned. Germanicus in A.D. 18 was warned of his approaching end; and, in fact, he died in Syria the following year, poisoned (as was believed) with the connivance of his adoptive father Tiberius. We read in Pausanias that when the Roman emperor diverted the course of the river Orontes in Syria there was found in the dry bed a gigantic coffin and a skeleton more than 11 cubits in height. The Syrians applied for enlightenment to Claros, and the god declared it to be the body of Orontes, an Indian by race. This Orontes being utterly unknown, Apollo's pronouncement had the great advantage of being unverifiable while at the same time providing an origin for the name of the river. At the time of a severe pestilence in the second century A.D. the men of Pergamum sent to Claros (rather than the neighbouring Gryneum) in the hope of relief. Apollo's advice was characteristic: divide the citizens into four groups for the worship of Zeus, Dionysus, Athena and Asclepius; offer to these certain prescribed sacrifices and prayers for salvation. This is by far the commonest form of oracular advice: sacrifice to particular deities. It does not appear that the French excavators have brought to light any new responses, but at the time of writing their full publication is still awaited. When it appears it may perhaps enlighten us also concerning a curious statement of Tacitus; that the Colophonians normally chose a Milesian to be priest of Apollo—a surprising allegation for which no supporting evidence whatever has hitherto come to light.

CHAPTER NINE

Priene and the Panionium

F o r m a n y travellers Priene is perhaps the most attractive of all the ancient sites on the west coast. Not only are the ruins comparatively well preserved, and admirably excavated for the visitor's benefit, but above all they give a feeling of intimacy greater than is easily found elsewhere. Priene is small, and its buildings are small likewise; they date for the most part to the earlier days of the city's existence, and the massive Roman structures familiar on so many sites are conspicuous by their absence. The visitor, wandering among the public buildings, streets and private houses, can feel himself back in the days of Alexander. Priene is above all a *Greek* city.

The present site beside the village of Turunçlar is not, however, the original site. Where that may have been is quite unknown. Tradition said that the city was founded during the Ionian migration by Aepytus, a grandson of Codrus, the last king of Athens, who was later joined by a party of Thebans under one Philotas; Priene, in fact, always looked to Athens as her mother-city. This early city was from the first a member of the Ionian League, but no trace of it has ever been found; it lies no doubt deep under the Maeander mud. Its history, too, is scanty in the extreme. We know that it suffered severely from the Persian conquest, and for a time hardly existed; it recovered, however, sufficiently to provide twelve ships against the Persians at the battle of Lade in 494 b.c. No inscriptions, and only a single coin, of the old Priene are known.

Two circumstances, however, gave the city an importance disproportionate to its size. In the first place it produced one of the Seven Sages of antiquity, namely Bias, who is famous for two pieces of advice which he gave. When Croesus had overrun Ionia and was beginning to build a navy to attack the

islands also, Bias, hoping to save them, went to Sardis and
reported (falsely) to Croesus that the islanders were preparing
a force of cavalry to attack him. The king was delighted:
'Nothing would suit me better than that islanders should
engage the famous Lydian cavalry on land.' 'What then,' said
Bias, 'do you imagine the islanders are thinking, when they
hear that the land-power of Lydia is intending to engage them
on the sea?' Croesus saw the point and abandoned his ship-
building. Later, when Persian rule had replaced the Lydian,
Bias advised the Ionians assembled at the Panionium to
abandon their cities and sail in a body to Sardinia, where they
might found a new city and prosper in freedom. The Phocaeans had, in fact, already followed similar counsels, and the
Teians did so shortly afterwards, but the Ionians as a whole
could not bring themselves to leave their homes. So great was
Bias' reputation that there was afterwards in the new Priene
a building called after him, the Biantium; a similar honour was
given also at Priene to Alexander, and at Smyrna to Homer.

In the second place, it happened that the site chosen for the
Panionium lay on the territory of Priene, and the Prienians
were largely responsible for its management; they had, for
example, the privilege of appointing the president at the
various meetings. The coastal strip on which the Panionium
lay was, however, claimed also by the Samians, and this
quarrel lasted for centuries, with Priene on the whole getting
the better of it.

All the while the silt of the Maeander was pushing the
coastline farther to the west, and for this reason no doubt it
was eventually decided, towards the middle of the fourth century B.C., probably at Mausolus' instigation, to refound the
city on a new site, where its ruins now stand. It appears that
this new site was the same which had previously served as the
harbour of Priene, called Naulochus; Strabo says that Priene
was originally on the coast, and that in his own time it was
forty stades, or rather over four miles, from it. If this is correct, the rate at which the coastline was advancing at that
period must have been (as indeed is natural enough) much
greater than it has been since. (See below, p. 219).

The new town was still in process of building when Alexander arrived in 334 B.C. Finding the temple of Athena, the main sanctuary of the city, still unfinished, he made the same proposal that he had already made at Ephesus, which was to undertake the cost of the building in return for the privilege of making the dedication. The Prienians were less proud and independent than the Ephesians—or perhaps they were merely less wealthy—and the offer was accepted; Alexander's dedication was found by the first excavators and is now in the British Museum. It stood on the temple wall; the architrave over the columns would have been a more natural place, but the building had perhaps not yet reached to that height.

In the second century, while Priene was under the rule of Pergamum, a peculiarly undeserved misfortune befell her. Ariarathes, king of Cappadocia, was deposed from the throne by his brother Orophernes; the latter, in the course of his reign, deposited 400 talents, or perhaps half a million sterling, for safe keeping at Priene. Later, when Ariarathes, with the help of Attalus II, succeeded in expelling Orophernes, he demanded the money back. The Prienians replied that they were bound to return it only to the man who had deposited it, whereupon Ariarathes, with Attalus' consent, sacked the Prienian territory. The citizens appealed to Rome; they had, says the historian, high hopes of keeping the money themselves, but they were disappointed, being required to give back the 400 talents to Orophernes, and having meanwhile suffered severely for their loyalty to him.

As a city of the Roman province of Asia, Priene, like the others, had much to bear from the tax-gatherers and from the hardships of the Mithridatic Wars; and when better times came under the empire, Priene, for whatever reason, did not share in the general upsurge of prosperity. The harbour Naulochus had by then been long since unusable; even if another had succeeded it, the city must have suffered from the competition of her mighty neighbour Miletus. However this may be, Priene sank into insignificance. No gigantic structures rose to overlay the simpler buildings of earlier times, and Priene remains as the best example we have of a Hellenistic city.

The town is situated on sloping ground at the south foot of a mighty cliff of rock. Above this, on the mountain-top, is

the acropolis, called in antiquity Teloneia. It housed a permanent garrison, whose commandant, elected for a period of
four months, was forbidden to leave it during his term of office.
Nothing remains on the summit except some ruins of the
fortification-wall, and the chief reward for making the climb
is a superb view over the city and the plain, with the Maeander
meandering into the distance. The ascent may be made by a
narrow rock-path up the precipitous cliff-face; the path is not
exactly dangerous, but calls for a good head for heights. On
the way up it passes an attractive little sanctuary containing
rock-cut reliefs and statue-bases. The alternative route is by
the valley on the west.

The principal sanctuary of Priene is that of Athena; when
the temple was standing it dominated the town. The English
excavators in 1868–9 found the temple walls still in place to
a man's height, but the blocks were later plundered by the
local inhabitants, and until recently little more than the foundations was to be seen. For the building Mausolus supplied his
own architect, the Carian Pytheos, who also worked on the
Mausoleum at Halicarnassus; he afterwards wrote a book,
taking the Athenaeum at Priene as a model of temple-
construction. This book was still used as a textbook in Roman
times.

The plan of the temple is, in fact, typical of Greek temples
of the classical period. The antechamber, or pronaos, on the
east, is entered between two columns; from here a door leads
into the main chamber, or cella, at the back of which stood
the cult-statue. At the rear, but not communicating with the
cella, is a third chamber, the opisthodomus, also entered between two columns. In many cases this rear chamber was used
to house the temple treasures, in which event the spaces
between the columns and side walls were closed with grilles or
marble slabs; traces of such a closure can still be seen at
Priene. The whole building was surrounded by a single row
of Ionic columns; the drums of these, being less convenient
for house-building, have not been removed by the villagers,
and many are lying on the temple terrace and on the slopes
below, where they were thrown apparently by a violent earthquake. In 1964 a number of them were re-used in re-erecting

half a dozen of the columns; this has resulted in a great improvement to the appearance of the temple.

Ancient temples were not used, like modern churches, for congregational services. The building was conceived as a house for the deity, and on ceremonial occasions was entered only by the priests and others who had a special function to perform; the congregation remained outside.

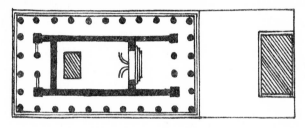

FIG. 37 Plan of the Temple of Athena

As was said above, the temple at Priene was dedicated to Athena by Alexander in 334 B.C. Later a second dedication was made to Augustus, so that the temple henceforth belonged jointly to him and to Athena. Architrave blocks carrying this new dedication are still lying on the temple platform. At this time also was built an entrance gateway on the east of the precinct; one side of this is still standing. The altar is in the normal position in front of the temple on the east; in its general form it was similar, though on a smaller scale, to the great altar at Pergamum, but the existing remains give little idea of its former appearance (Pl. 52).

The theatre is another building that goes back to the early days of the city's existence. The alterations to which, like all the rest, it was subjected in Roman times have not destroyed its Greek character; it gives an excellent idea of what a Hellenistic theatre was like.

Only seven or eight rows of seats in the cavea were originally excavated; within the last year several more have been cleared, but the appearance of the theatre has been little if at all improved. The front row consists of five marble thrones of honour spaced at intervals round the orchestra; similar thrones in the theatre at Athens were reserved for the priests,

and the same may have been the case here. In the middle of
the fifth row is a 'Royal Box', but this is not a feature of the
original theatre. In the middle of the front row is the altar of
Dionysus, to whom sacrifice was made whenever the theatre
was used. The cavea is more than a semicircle and is supported
at the ends by retaining-walls (analemmata) of handsome
cushioned ashlar, well preserved. Between these and the flanks
of the stage-building on either side are open passages (parodoi)
which served as entrances for the public and, during the performance, for the chorus; at other times they were closed with
gates. An interesting feature, peculiar to the theatre at Priene,
is the water-clock which stood at the west corner of the
orchestra. Only the base remains in position; the cuttings in it
provided for the flow of water, but it is not easy to see exactly
how they worked. We hear nothing in literature of any time-
limit on dramatic performances, and it is more likely that the
clock was used during the public assemblies which also took
place in the theatre. A time-limit on speeches was certainly
normal practice in the law-courts at least—and, in fact, it is
not impossible that the theatre was actually used as a court
of law (Pl. 49).

The stage-building consisted of two parts, a rectangular
two-storeyed building containing the property-rooms, dressing-
rooms and the like, and a narrow single-storeyed structure
projecting in front. This latter is the proscenium; nowhere else
is a Hellenistic proscenium so well preserved as here. Its front
consists of a row of twelve pillars, ten of which have Doric
half-columns attached, surmounted by an architrave and
triglyph-frieze; from this stone beams were laid across to the
front of the main building, and wooden boards laid between
the beams. The eleven spaces between the columns were variously filled: the two at the extreme ends were closed merely by
iron bars forming a very wide-meshed grille; the third, sixth
and ninth held double folding doors; and in the remainder
were inserted painted panels of wood. The holes and sockets
for these various fixtures may still be seen on the pillars.
Numerous traces of colour, blue and red, survive on the epis-
tyle; but the red colouring of the columns and capitals was
done at a much later period (Pl. 53).

PRIENE

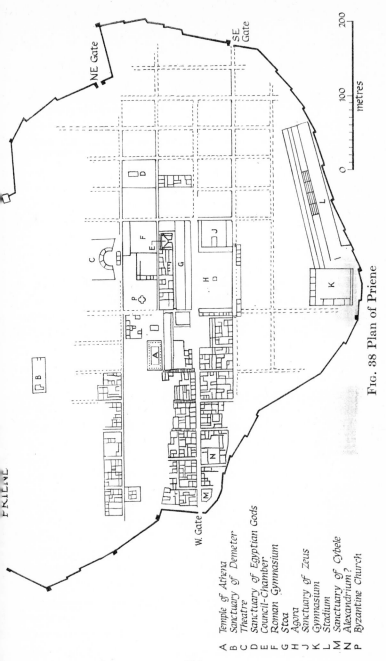

Fig. 38 Plan of Priene

A Temple of Athena
B Sanctuary of Demeter
C Theatre
D Sanctuary of Egyptian Gods
E Council-Chamber
F Roman Gymnasium
G Stoa
H Agora
J Sanctuary of Zeus
K Gymnasium
L Stadium
M Sanctuary of Cybele
N Alexandrium?
P Byzantine Church

What was the purpose and use of this proscenium building, which dates from the third century B.C.? On this question scholars are not yet agreed. We know from inscriptions that tragedies were produced at Priene in the fourth century; in these, actors and chorus alike must have performed at orchestra level in the classical fashion, and it is commonly supposed that even after the erection of the proscenium this continued, for some time at least, to be the case. The three doors then served for the actors' entrances and exits, and the painted panels between the columns could represent the scenery. The flat roof of the proscenium would be useful for the appearance of the *deus ex machina*, or when it was required to show a character on the roof of a building. Others, however, maintain that the proscenium roof *looks* like a stage (which can hardly be denied) and must always have been used as such. Many visitors to Priene will probably share this feeling; on the other hand, the doors and panels between the columns then become rather meaningless. It has also been argued against this opinion that the marble thrones in the front row must have been intended to give the best view, which they would only do when the performance was on ground level; but, in fact, with so narrow a stage, the loss of view is negligible. It is interesting to test this on the spot, remembering that the actors wore high buskins.

At all events, it is generally agreed that by about the middle of the second century B.C. the performance took place on the proscenium roof, the actors entering by three wide doors in the front wall of the upper storey of the main building. At this time probably the 'Royal Box' was installed to restore to the previous occupants of the marble thrones the slight advantage of a horizontal view. The high stage made the actors better visible and better audible to the spectators as a whole, but it had one inconvenience in the awkward separation of the actors on the stage from the chorus down below in the orchestra. Not that this mattered in the dramas produced by the contemporary playwrights, which made little or no use of the chorus; but down to quite a late date the tragedies and comedies of the old classical masters were regularly revived, and in these contact between chorus and actor is frequently required. However, in case of necessity, it was always possible for one or more performers to mount to the stage from the orchestra by a stairway, which still remains in part at the west end of the proscenium.

At either end of the proscenium are bases which carried statues. The stone slabs let into the earth in front of the proscenium supported other offerings; they are not remains of a pavement for the orchestra, whose surface was merely of beaten earth. Other statues stood on the newel-posts at the foot of the cavea on east and west and on another base on the east side. These last must have impeded the view from certain of the seats.

In or about the second century A.D. the theatre was altered to suit Roman requirements by doubling the depth of the stage. This was done, however, not as usual by bringing the stage forward into the orchestra and building over the parodoi, but by removing the front of the stage-building and re-erecting it farther back. In this way the Greek character of the theatre has been preserved. At this period the spaces between the columns of the proscenium were permanently closed with a solid filling of which a small fragment survives at the west end, painted red and yellow on white.

One of the most attractive and perhaps the best-preserved building in Priene is the Council House. It consists of a single chamber resembling a tiny rectangular theatre, with rows of seats on three sides. The fourth side contains two doors, one on each side of a rectangular recess in which are stone benches, probably for the presiding officials. In the middle is a decorated altar for the sacrifices with which every public assembly began. There is no platform for the speakers, who presumably addressed the meeting from the ground. The chamber had a wooden roof supported on pillars; the pillars stood originally at the top of the seats, but the span of 47 feet was found to be too great, and stronger pillars were later installed nearer together (Pl. 51).

That this building was used for meetings of the City Council is beyond doubt. The Council, or Boule, was the chief instrument of government; the normal practice was for the Council to prepare measures for submission to the general assembly,

or Ecclesia, whose decision upon them was final. The Chamber
has seats for 640 persons; the Council in a small city like
Priene can certainly not have numbered so many—even at
Ephesus it was only 450—and it is likely that, at least in the
early days, this building was also used for the general assembly.
It is perhaps surprisingly small for the purpose: 600-odd
enfranchised citizens would imply a total population of some
3,000: but we have no reason to suppose that Priene in the
fourth century was any larger than this. In later times it is
probable that the general assembly was held as usual in the
theatre.

Visitors who are not unduly pressed for time should make
the short climb to the Sanctuary of Demeter and her daughter
Core, that is Persephone. This, too, dates from early Hellenistic times, and possesses a number of unusual features; for
Demeter, the Earth Mother, was not like the other Olympian
gods, and her sanctuaries have a character of their own.

The entrance is on the east. Just beside the gate stood two
statues of priestesses, one of which was found and removed by
German excavators; the base of the other remains. The central
part of the sanctuary is an open space; though it contains no
rows of seats as at Pergamum and Eleusis, it may be assumed
that mysteries were celebrated here also. The temple stands,
as at Pergamum, at the west end of the enclosure, but its form
is highly exceptional. In front is a porch with three Doric
columns between the side walls, forming a kind of pronaos.
From this the main room, or cella, is entered; its length is
strangely from north to south. At the north end are two small
rooms side by side, of which the eastern opens into the porch.
Along the west wall of the cella runs a high stone bench, used
for displaying votive offerings, as is shown by the sockets cut
into its surface. The east wall is broken by a double right-
angled turn. Round the temple, between it and the enclosing
wall of the sanctuary, runs a narrow passage. Almost every
feature of this building is alien to the normal form of a Greek
temple; and not less interesting is the sacrificial pit sunk in the
ground outside the temple on the south-east. It is square and
carefully lined with masonry, and was covered by planks, laid
across between stone blocks of flat triangular shape, one of

Fig. 39 Plan of the Sanctuary of Demeter and Core

which remains. Pits of this kind served for pouring offerings, especially the blood of sacrificial victims, to the deities of the underworld, among whom Demeter and Persephone were pre-eminent; the custom is familiar, but the actual pits are very rarely preserved. At a much later time an altar of normal form was installed, towards the east end of the sanctuary on the north side; its Roman date is shown by its inferior masonry. Until then the victims were apparently slaughtered at the mouth of the pit.

The stadium lies close against the southern wall in the lowest part of the city. It was constructed in the second century B.C.; but there must have been a stadium at Priene from the beginning, for in the inscriptions a front seat at the games is awarded as a privilege to benefactors from the fourth century onwards. The word stadium denotes originally a measure of length equal to 600 Greek feet, or rather less than 200 yards (called in English a stade); this being the length of the sprint, the shortest distance run in the official games, the word comes to mean a foot-race of this length; finally it is used of the arena in which the races and other games took place.

At Priene the stadium is exceedingly simple in construction. The course is a level space 20 yards wide and something over a stade in length. Spectators sat on the north side only, owing to the nature of the ground; for the same reason the stadium had not the usual rounded end. Stone seats were provided only in the middle part; at the two ends either wooden seats were installed or, as at Olympia, none at all. All races finished at the eastern end, and to improve the view of the finish from the far end the western part makes a slight angle with the rest.

The starting-sill for the stadium race is partially preserved at the west end. It consisted originally of a row of ten square pilasters with Corinthian capitals and an architrave. The bases remain in position, resting on a long stone foundation; the cuttings in these present an interesting problem: how was a simultaneous start obtained? In the surface of the long foundation, through all its length, even under the pillar-bases, is a channel 9 inches wide and 6 inches deep; in the open space between the two central columns, which is wider than the others, two short side-channels turn off it at right-angles. The bases have in their sides, over the channel, rectangular cuttings about 4 inches by 6; these are found on both sides of the two central bases, on the inner side of the two end bases, and on the outer side of the other six bases. A narrow ledge cut along the upper rim of the long channel suggests that some sort of covering was laid over it. Fragments of the entablature over the pillars found by the excavators showed a similar horizontal channel and vertical perforations.

How are these facts to be interpreted? No complete explanation has been advanced, but certain possibilities suggest themselves for consideration. In most Greek stadia where the starting-sill is preserved we find that two grooves are cut in the sill one behind the other, from 4 to 7 inches apart, to hold the runners' toes at the start; their closeness together argues an ancient starting-technique different from the modern. Since the sill at Priene is, as it stands, utterly unsuited for a start, it seems likely enough that boards or stone blocks carrying grooves of this kind were fitted over the long channel between the pillars; a breadth of 9 inches allows ample room for grooves only 4 inches apart. Place would thus be provided for eight runners; the central space was not used for this purpose. The long channel itself is nothing more than a drain, to avoid the danger of a slippery start in case of wet weather. To the further question, how the starting-gate was manoeuvred, the evidence will hardly furnish a complete answer, but here again a suggestion may perhaps be offered. The function of the

vertical cuttings in the bases was apparently to hold upright
wooden posts against the sides of the pillars; we may suppose
that these posts held horizontal bars working up and down
like signal-arms; cords attached to these arms could then be
passed up through the hole in the entablature and along the
channel to the central space where the starter stood; holding
the ends of the cords in his hand he could, by releasing them,
drop all the eight 'signal-arms' simultaneously. A method
exactly similar in principle to this was certainly used at the
Isthmian Sanctuary at Corinth, where clear traces of it were
found by the excavators. It may be noted, however, that no
function is thus assigned to the extra cuttings in the middle
and end bases. (See Fig. 41 and Appendix V.)

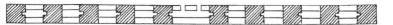

FIG. 40 Starting-sill in the Stadium

In any case it is certain that this comparatively elaborate
starting-sill was not in use in very early times, and at Priene
is probably not earlier than Roman. In the fifth century B.C.
there was no physical obstacle in Greek stadia holding back
the runners at the start; before the battle of Salamis in 480
B.C., Themistocles, who was eager to engage the Persians
without delay, was rebuked by the Corinthian general: 'At
the games, you know, Themistocles, those who "jump the gun"
get a stroke of the rod.' And even at Priene, where the stadium
is not older than the second century, we have apparently the
remains of an earlier and simpler starting-sill. Some 6 feet in
front (to the east) of the sill described above is a simple line
of eight square stone slabs let into the ground; in the centre of
each is a square hole evidently intended to hold a post.
Nothing more survives, and the details of the starting-method
employed are no longer recoverable.

The athletic events contested in the stadium at the official

AT–O

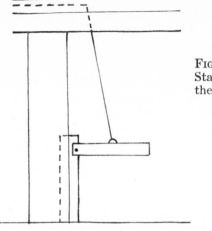

Fig. 41
Starting-gate in
the Stadium

games in the Greek cities were: foot-races, wrestling, boxing, the pancration and the pentathlon. Horse and chariot races were held separately in the hippodrome. All athletic events were divided into age-groups, generally men, youths and boys.

Foot-racing was in three categories, the stadium-race, the diaulos and the long race. The first was a simple sprint from one end of the course to the other. The diaulos was a double stadium, that is, up the course and down again, with a hairpin turn at the end. For this a second starting-sill was required at the other end of the stadium, but at Priene this has not been found. The long race seems to have varied in length at different times and places; we hear of seven stades and twenty-four. Time-keeping was of course unknown, water-clocks and sand-glasses being obviously inadequate, so that we cannot tell what sort of standards were achieved. Victory was the thing that mattered; second prizes for athletics were rarely given.

Wrestling was of the 'upright' kind—that is, a fall was counted as soon as any part of the body above the knee touched the ground; the bout was not continued on the ground. The contest was probably best-of-five, three throws being necessary for victory. The so-called 'Graeco-Roman' style of wrestling is not, however, ancient. The pancration was a form of unarmed combat, not unlike all-in wrestling; it was not decided by falls, but continued on the ground until one man

FIG. 42 The pancration, from a vase-painting. One man has his thumb in the other's eye; this being a foul, the steward stands by ready to administer a stroke of the rod

surrendered. Punching, kicking and strangling were permitted —indeed, all means except biting and gouging. One pancratiast had a trick of winning by breaking his opponent's fingers, and this device was even copied by a wrestler.

Ancient boxing was very different from the modern. The gloves used had a ridge of hard leather over the knuckles, and were intended not merely to protect the striker's hands but to render the blow more severe. There were no ring and no rounds; as in the pancration the bout continued until one man admitted defeat. Classification was by age only, not by weight; hence in practice only heavyweights competed in the men's class. The rules also were probably different from ours, though we have, of course, no actual statement of them, and the vase-paintings may not be reliable evidence. If these could be trusted, it would appear that blows were aimed almost exclusively at the head; in general the hands are held high. On the other hand, there is some rather uncertain evidence that kicking may have been permitted.

The pentathlon was a combination of five events, three peculiar to the pentathlon, namely the jump, the discus and the javelin, and two, running and wrestling, which had their own separate events as well. In the discus and javelin only distance counted: there was no question of aiming at a mark: it was only required that the missile should not fall outside the level arena into the spectators' seats. The javelin was thrown with the aid of a thong wound two or three times round the shaft and allowed to slip from the hand at the moment of throwing; this use of a thong permits slightly better performances than the ordinary modern method.

The jump was a long jump; high jumping was not an event in the games, and seems hardly to have been practised by the ancients. But it was not a simple long jump as we know it today, and its nature has been much disputed. In the first place jumping-weights were used, made of stone or metal and weighing from 2 to 9 lb, held one in each hand throughout the jump. In the second place jumps of 55 and 52 feet are recorded, admittedly exceptional. Since a long jump of even 30 feet has never been achieved in modern times, it has been thought that the ancient jump was really a hop, step and jump, and it was on this supposition that this event was included when the Olympic Games were revived in 1896. The present world record is 55 feet 10¼ inches. But experiments have shown that a triple jump *with weights* is exceedingly cumbersome and that 35 feet is about the limit of possible achievement. For a *standing* long jump, on the other hand, weights are a distinct advantage, and a recent theory is that the ancients practised a fivefold standing jump, that is five successive leaps, each from the spot where the previous one landed. Ten feet being a very good single jump under these conditions, a world record of 55 feet is possible enough.[1] This theory is attractive at first sight; on the other hand ancient vases exist which seem clearly to show a jumper *running* with his weights.

[1] More like 50 feet in reality, the Greek foot being slightly shorter than the English.

In this case a standing jump is excluded, and the latest suggestion is that of a double jump—that is, a step and a jump.[1]
No such jump is ever practised nowadays, so that no records
are available, and the effect of carrying weights is uncertain;
all the arguments cannot be discussed here, but this last
solution is perhaps the most probable yet offered.

How was the winner of the pentathlon decided? This fascinating problem, too, has been vigorously debated. Again it
is not possible here to present all the evidence and all the
arguments, but a number of points are reasonably assured. It
is quite certain that the modern system of awarding marks
for each event and adding these up was not employed in
ancient times. Victory again was the thing that mattered, and
three outright wins in the five events was always enough to
determine the victor. Recent discussions have further established that the number of competitors—so long as no one had
three outright wins—was successively reduced in three stages;
that is, after the first three events (which were the three field
events peculiar to the pentathlon) only those who by their
performance had earned the right to do so competed in
the fourth event, the foot-race. Again after the foot-race only
a limited number proceeded to the wrestling. As soon as any
one competitor gained three clear victories the pentathlon
came to an end; failing this, the winner of the wrestling was
the final victor. On the difficult question of the principle by
which the number of participants was reduced agreement has
not yet been reached.

Conveniently adjoining the stadium at Priene is the lower
gymnasium. Chance has preserved for us an inscription recording the decision to build this gymnasium; it is dated soon after
130 B.C. A resolution, we learn, had earlier been made to erect
the building, relying on contributions promised by certain of
the kings; owing, however, to changes in their fortunes, the
money had not been forthcoming, and the expense is now
undertaken by a rich citizen named Moschion.

The gymnasium consists as usual of an open palaestra for
athletic exercise, surrounded by a stoa and rooms for gymnastic and educational purposes. Best preserved are the rooms on

[1] H. A. Harris, *Greek Athletes and Athletics*, chap. IV (c).

the north side. In the middle is the ephebeum, used here as a
lecture-room; benches for the students ran round the foot of
the walls. The upper part of the walls was adorned with
Corinthian half-columns. This room can hardly fail to appeal
to any visitor who has ever carved his name on his desk at
school, for the wall is covered with names of students. 'Phileas
son of Metrodorus, his place; Epicurus son of Pausanias, his
place'—more than 700 names may still be read (Pl. 54).

As was seen at Pergamum and Ephesus, it was normal in
Roman times to have full-scale hot baths (thermae) adjoining the gymnasium. At Priene we see the simpler Greek
practice, for the wash-room at the west end is well preserved.
The row of basins at the back survives, fed—with cold water
only—through lions'-head spouts from a channel in the wall.
Two other basins, for washing the feet, stood one on each side
of the entrance. The floor is covered with a paving of smooth
pebbles (Pl. 50).

The other rooms on this side, if they followed the normal
rule, should have been used respectively for the wrestlers to
coat themselves with fine sand, for the boxers to practise with
a punch-bag, and for the athletes generally to anoint their
bodies with oil. Vast quantities of olive-oil were consumed in
this way, and its provision was a favourite form of endowment
by public-minded benefactors: 'So-and-so oiled the citizens
for a year', is the rather quaint expression used in the inscriptions.

The streets and private houses are certainly among the most
attractive features of Priene. The streets are laid out on a
rectangular plan, with main streets running east and west,
joined by numerous lanes running north and south. Owing to
the steep slope of the ground, these latter are frequently
stepped. Each block, or 'island' as the Romans said, contains
normally four houses.

The houses are of a type still commonly seen in Mediterranean countries, being shut off from the street by high walls
affording no view in from outside; these outer walls, which are
still standing often to a man's height, are in general of very
good masonry, comparable with that of the public buildings
and dating from the early days of the city.

The interior arrangements are on the whole remarkably uniform, though not now so easy to follow on the ground as when they were first excavated. The street-door, often set in the side-street, leads through a vestibule to an open court-yard; beside the door stood commonly an altar for family sacrifice and a herm, or truncated image of Hermes, the god of good luck. On the north side of the courtyard is an ante-chamber open in front, and behind this the main living-room of the house; at the side of this and of the antechamber there are generally two more rooms, one of which is the dining-room. Upper storeys are not preserved, but traces of stairs occur in a few houses. There is no indication of separate women's quarters; possibly the women lived upstairs, as sometimes in classical Athens. The rooms were high, as commonly in hot climates, often 15 to 20 feet; they were heated in winter by portable braziers. Kitchen hearths are sometimes found in the antechamber. Only one bathroom was found by the excavators; it is tiny, some 6 feet by 3 feet 6 inches, and accommodates one person sitting with his feet in a basin-like hollow. Latrines occur only in three or four houses, nor have any public conveniences been found at Priene. Windows in the houses are not preserved, but probably only because the walls are not standing high enough; light was also admitted through the doors from the courtyard, but in general the interiors must have been distinctly dark. Wall-decoration is simple, and mostly imitates architectural forms; wall-painting consists merely of plain geometrical designs.

The early date of these houses is proved by the many coins found in them, most of which are of the third century B.C. Some of the houses were later converted to the 'peristyle' type favoured in Roman times, but for the most part they remain as they were when the city was first built.

Finally a word may be said of an interesting little sanctuary among the houses in the third block from the west on the south side of the main street leading to the west gate. It has the general form of an ordinary house, with an entrance from the side-road on the west into a courtyard; on the left door-post was found an inscription recording the holding of a priesthood, and adding: 'No admittance to this sanctuary except to the

pure, and in white raiment.' On the north side of the courtyard is an antechamber, badly ruined, and beyond this a
large room, in the north-east corner of which is a stone bench
for offerings, similar to that in the sanctuary of Demeter.
In front of this bench, over a natural crevice in the ground,
stood a marble table; its supports were in place when excavated, but have now collapsed, and the whole condition of the
building has been allowed to deteriorate. Among a number of
statuettes found here is one that appears to represent Alexander the Great, and some have accordingly supposed that this
sanctuary is the Alexandrium mentioned in an inscription and
not found elsewhere in the city (above, p. 198.). Alexander-
worship is well attested. On the other hand, the sacrificial table
over a crack in the ground suggests rather offerings to some
subterranean deity, and on the whole it is safer to reserve
judgment.

THE PANIONIUM

Mention has been made above more than once of the Panionium, where in early times the religious assembly of the Ionians
was held and accompanied by a great festival, the Panionia.
The sanctuary was sacred to Poseidon Heliconius, so named
from the town of Helice in Greece where his worship was
established and transported to Ionia. The place being on
Prienian territory, it was under that city's management and it
was customary for a young man of Priene to be appointed as
priest. According to Strabo it was reckoned a good omen here
if the sacrificial victim uttered a bellow during the ceremony,
and some ancient scholars believed that Homer was alluding
to this when he wrote: 'he bellowed as a bull bellows when
dragged to the altar of Lord Heliconius'. They may well have
been right; and their conclusion, that Homer must have lived
after the Ionian colonisation of Asia, was certainly correct.

Some time during the fifth century it became impossible to
celebrate the Panionia owing to the constant hostilities, and
it was transferred to a safer place near Ephesus; Thucydides
refers to it under the name of the Ephesia. Diodorus, who
records the transference, says that nine cities took part, not
twelve; this statement lacks ancient corroboration and has

generally been supposed to be a mistake. For a hundred years, under Persian rule, the activities of the Ionian League were in abeyance; Alexander's conquests brought a revival, and the Panionia continued to be celebrated in its original place down to Roman times. Its importance was, however, diminished by a second Federal festival which the Ionians instituted in honour of Alexander himself, held on the territory of Erythrae; and, in fact, the Panionia never really regained its early brilliance.

The site of the Panionium has only recently been finally determined and excavated. The approximate position is described by Herodotus as on Mt. Mycale facing north, and by Strabo as the first place north of the Samos strait, three stades from the sea. In 1673 an inscription naming the Panionium was found in the village of Güzelçamlı; it was seen again by Chandler in 1764 in a church by the shore, but the church is now destroyed and the inscription lost. The exact site was conjectured by the German scholar Wiegand at the end of last century, when he saw on the hill of St. Elias near Güzelçamlı the remains of eight rows of seats, as of a theatre, cut in the hillside. These seats were still visible when the present writer was there in 1946, but subsequently became hidden and were only with difficulty rediscovered in 1957. In that and the following year excavations were carried out by a team of German archaeologists. The hill has meanwhile changed its name. It was used in the First World War and the ensuing Greco-Turkish war as a machine-gun post, whence its present outlandish name of Otomatik Tepe.

On top of the hill, which is quite low, are the scanty remains of the sacred enclosure. The surrounding wall is partly preserved on the north, west and south, though nowhere to a height of more than three courses; the entrance is distinguishable on the west. In the middle, running north and south, was a long narrow structure some 57 by 14 feet; it is now completely destroyed, and is recognisable chiefly by the cuttings and dowel-holes in the surface of the rock. This was evidently not a temple but an altar, and, in fact, the ancient authorities make no mention of a temple at the Panionium, but speak consistently of sacrifices. These scanty relics are not datable in themselves, but are attributed by the excavators on other grounds to the late sixth century B.C.

Some fifty yards to the south-west of this enclosure is a large cave about 30 feet deep and the same in width. Nothing significant has been found in it, but since the whole site was dedicated to Poseidon, the Earth-Shaker, it is likely that the cave, too, was sacred to him, and may have played a part in the cult.

Below the cave, at the foot of the hill, is the theatre-like building mentioned above. When excavated it proved to have eleven rows of seats, and never apparently had any more; its total diameter is a little over 100 feet. Where the stage of a theatre would be there is only the rock, in part artificially levelled, and where the side-entrances (parodoi) would come transverse blocks are laid across. It is accordingly clear that the building cannot, in fact, be a theatre, appropriate though this would be on the site of a great festival, and there can be no doubt that we have the remains of the council-chamber in which the delegates from the Ionian cities met to take decisions in the interests of the League. Here it was that Bias stood to advise the Ionians to migrate to Sardinia. Thales of Miletus would have had a common council of the Ionians at Teos, nearer the centre of the country, but his recommendation was not adopted. The excavators thought to discern in the arrangement of the front row of seats some confirmation of Diodorus' statement that only nine cities participated, but this is not easy to make out on the ground.

About 200 yards to the west of this spot is a small hill or mound carrying the ruins of a structure of Roman date, apparently a tomb.

★

CHAPTER TEN

Miletus

GREAT CHANGES have taken place in the Maeander valley during the last few years. Whereas formerly the river used to flood the plain every winter, and Miletus was approached by rough track, renewed annually, and a primitive grind across the Maeander, now a large part of the plain has been reclaimed, a fine new road has been driven across from Söke to Milâs, and cars may reach Miletus all the year round. The ancient site was formerly occupied in part by the village of Balat—that is, Palatia, with reference to the Byzantine castle on the hill above the theatre; but this village was destroyed by an earth-quake in 1955, and a new one, Yeniköy, has been built a mile to the south on the road to Didyma.

Miletus tends to produce a sense of strangeness, even of unreality, in the modern visitor. He may feel, as the writer felt on his first visit, 'This is not what I expected.' When the name of Miletus is mentioned the hearer thinks at once of the great maritime city of the archaic period, mistress of the Aegean and birthplace of science and philosophy; but of this city most visitors see nothing. Roman Miletus, whose ruins meet the eye today, was, of course, a great city still, but some-how it does not satisfy as Ephesus, for example, does. This feeling is greatly accentuated by the complete change in the landscape due to the silting process of the Maeander. This river is what Herodotus calls a 'worker'; it has been, and still is, advancing the coastline by an average of some 20 feet in a year, so that Miletus, in classical times a city on a headland at the mouth of a broad gulf, is now nearly five miles from the sea. The island of Lade, of sinister fame, now stands high and dry as a hill on the plain, and the Latmian gulf has become the freshwater lake of Bafa. Standing on the hill above the theatre, it requires a strong effort of the imagination to picture Miletus as it once was.

Miletus has the unique distinction among the cities of Ionia of receiving mention by Homer. It was the home of 'Carians of uncouth speech' who fought against the Greeks at Troy; nothing is said of any Greek settlement. The passage is evidently archaising, for long before Homer wrote in the eighth century Miletus was a Greek city. The colonisation is attributed as usual to Ionians led by a son of Codrus, by name Neileus; they found the place occupied by a mixture of the native Carians and certain Cretans who had migrated from a town of the same name in Crete. The Ionians, says Herodotus, slaughtered all the male inhabitants and married their wives, having brought no women with them; wherefore the women of Miletus, then and afterwards, bound themselves by oath never to sit at table with their husbands nor to call them by name.

Ionian Miletus prospered exceedingly and was in early times beyond question the greatest city of the Greek world. A favourable position, combined with a spirit of enterprise derived from their Athenian founders, gave the Milesians the leading place among the sea-traders of the time. By land the city's communications were poor. It might appear today that Miletus served as a terminal to the great caravan route down the Maeander valley; but a glance at the accompanying sketch-map will show that in antiquity this was far from being the case. Priene and Myus were better placed in this respect; but, in fact, this route seems rather to have led, as it does now, to Ephesus (p. 232, Fig. 45.).

But by sea the Milesians were unequalled. As early as the eighth century, and especially during the seventh, they founded numerous colonies on the shores of the Hellespont, the Sea of Marmara and the Black Sea; the total number is put as high as ninety. Obviously these cannot all have been peopled solely by Milesians; the mother-city must have served as a centre for disaffected persons, exiles and others in search of a new home. These would gravitate to Miletus and join the next group that was sent out. However this may be, preferential terms of trade with these colonies undoubtedly contributed to the wealth of the city.

Material prosperity was accompanied by brilliant intellectual achievement. Not that Miletus was alone in this: Heraclitus of Ephesus, Bias of Priene, Xenophanes of Colophon and others prove the contrary: but Miletus certainly led the way. First and foremost comes the name of Thales. His dictum that 'All things are water', and his prediction of the solar eclipse of 585 B.C. have been mentioned above; he is credited also with diverting the course of the River Halys to allow Croesus' army to cross. When someone taunted him that for all his brains he was still a poor man, Thales' answer was practical and effective: his study of astronomy enabling him to know that next year's olive harvest would be a bumper one, he cornered all the olive presses in Miletus; by letting these out at a high rental he proved that philosophers can if they wish grow rich, but (says the historian) this is not their aim. Thales also, we read, was the first man to succeed in inscribing a right-angled triangle in a circle; in celebration of this he sacrificed an ox— which means in effect that he stood himself a good dinner.[1] Another of his achievements was to calculate the height of the Pyramids in Egypt by measuring their shadow at the time of day when a man's shadow is equal to his height. Among his sayings the most famous is 'Know thyself', which was inscribed on the temple at Delphi. Less acceptable to modern ideas, perhaps, is his remark that he thanked the gods for three things, that he was human and not an animal, a man and not a woman, a Greek and not a barbarian. The list of the Seven Sages in antiquity varied enormously, but three names were unanimously included, those of Thales of Miletus, Bias of Priene and Solon of Athens.

Thales was followed in the field of physical science by his countrymen Anaximenes and Anaximander. The former found in air the basic substance of the universe; by a process of condensation and rarefaction this produced all other forms of matter. Anaximander preferred a different basic principle, which he called the Infinite. Or perhaps—since it was both

---

[1] There is something wrong here. The least mathematically-minded can inscribe a right-angled triangle in a circle. Unless we should read 'equilateral triangle', the meaning is probably that Thales first proved that a triangle inscribed in a semicircle is right-angled.

finite and material—the Unlimited would be a better word: unlimited, that is, by any characteristics or qualities, and so capable of breaking down into the various material substances of the world we see.

Milesian, too, were the fathers of geography. Anaximander produced the first map of the world; based upon supposed principles of symmetry in the disposition of the continents, seas and rivers, it was grotesquely inaccurate to modern ideas, nor does Anaximander himself appear to have travelled. Such was not the case with Hecataeus, whose *Geography* was a commentary on his fellow citizen's map. He travelled a great deal, and could supplement his own observation from the constant stream of visitors to Miletus from all parts of the earth. Where we can check the fragments of his work that survive, they are found to be very reliable. Hecataeus is frequently quoted, and rather uncharitably criticised, by Herodotus.

Intellectual and material prosperity had no softening effect upon the Milesians. 'Once upon a time', said the later proverb, 'the Milesians were brave men.' They successfully resisted the attacks of the Lydian kings Gyges and Alyattes, and even Croesus was content to make a treaty with them. The Persians were too strong for them, but they, too, consented to make terms; Miletus was the only Ionian city thus distinguished. Tribute had to be paid, and the tyrant ruled only with Persian consent, but otherwise Miletus was more or less free.

In the ill-starred Ionian revolt of 500 B.C. the part played by Miletus was bound up with the romantic career of Histiaeus. The story begins in 512, when the Persian king Darius undertook his disastrous expedition against the Scythians; his force included a naval contingent led by the tyrants of the Greek cities, including Histiaeus, tyrant of Miletus. On reaching the Danube he crossed on a bridge of boats, leaving with the Greek captains a cord in which he had tied sixty knots, with instructions to untie one every day, and if he had not returned by the time they were all untied, to sail away home. He then advanced into the wilds of Scythia. The Greeks waited the sixty days, but the king did not appear. While they were hesitating what to do, a party of Scythians arrived and urged them to destroy the bridge, so ensuring Darius' ruin and their own freedom—for the king meanwhile had been suffering serious reverses in Scythia. The Greeks were tempted to fall in with this proposal, but Histiaeus restrained them and preserved the bridge. When Darius arrived hard pressed and found the bridge surviving after the allotted period, he was so grateful to Histiaeus that he allowed him to choose whatever he wished. Histiaeus asked for Myrcinus, a small town in western Thrace with silver-mines close by, which he proceeded to fortify. Darius, however, warned that a Greek stronghold here was highly undesirable, summoned him to the Persian capital on the pretence that so valuable a friend was needed at his side. Histiaeus accordingly languished in Susa for eleven years. Meanwhile his son-in-law Aristagoras was ruling in Miletus in his place; having failed lamentably in an attack on the island of Naxos which he had persuaded the king to let him undertake, his stock was low. At this point Histiaeus, weary of enforced Persian hospitality, secretly sent a slave to Aristagoras bearing tattooed on his head the message 'Rouse the Ionians to revolt'. This he did in the expectation of being sent by Darius to quell the revolt when it should occur. Aristagoras, who had himself been contemplating this same means of retrieving his fortunes, acted accordingly. And sure enough Histiaeus appeared on the scene, professedly sent to help the Persian satrap to suppress the rebel Greeks. The satrap, however, was suspicious and declined to work with him, whereupon Histiaeus fled, and occupying Byzantium turned his hand to piracy. Not long afterwards he was captured and put to death by the Persians. Such is the story as told by Herodotus; modern historians have no difficulty in pointing out its improbabilities.

The battle of Lade in 494 B.C., the collapse of the revolt and the Persian capture of Miletus put an end to the city's golden age. Never before had she been taken by force, and the event was recognised as a major calamity. When an Athenian dramatist put on a tragedy entitled 'Fall of Miletus', the audience burst into tears and the poet was fined 1,000 drachmae. According to Herodotus the city was destroyed, most of the men slain, and the women and children enslaved.

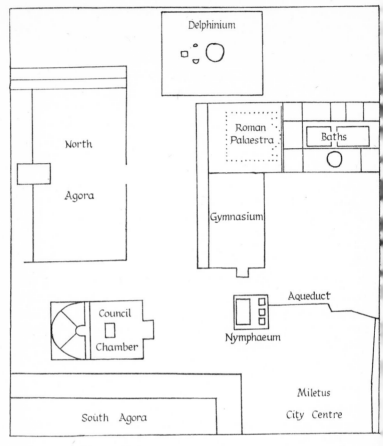

Fig. 43 Plan of the City Centre at Miletus

Nevertheless, within a generation Miletus was on her feet again. Following the defeat of the Persians in Greece and the liberation of the Greeks of Asia, the city was rebuilt on the site which she was to occupy for the rest of her existence, and by the middle of the fifth century was paying five talents a year as a member of the Delian Confederacy, a sum only a little less than that paid by Ephesus. At the same time she was issuing an abundant silver coinage.

Despite this remarkable recovery, Miletus was never again

the force that she had been. The Athenian naval supremacy deprived her of her commanding position as a trading nation, and there was nothing to take its place. In general the city's fortunes followed those of Ionia as a whole. In the fourth century there is evidence of close relations between Miletus and the Carian dynasts Mausolus and his father Hecatomnos, and the city may have been actually in their power for a time; Milesian coins exist bearing the inscriptions EKA(tomnos) and MA(usolus). Be this as it may, when Alexander arrived in 334 B.C. a Persian garrison was in control, and Miletus was the first city to offer him resistance. He at once laid siege to it; his ships forestalled a Persian relieving fleet, and the city fell to a vigorous assault.

In the Hellenistic era Miletus experienced the usual vicissitudes, coming in turn under the power of Antigonus, Lysimachus, the Seleucids of Syria, the Ptolemies of Egypt, the Attalids of Pergamum and finally, of course, the Romans. In the province of Asia, Miletus was a 'free' city, rich and prosperous like the rest, with many fine buildings. But the threat of the Maeander silt was growing serious; some time about the fourth century A.D. the coastline passed the Milesian promontory, and before long Lade, too, ceased to be an island. Mosquitoes swarmed, and the once great city slowly sank to become the fever-ridden village of Balat.

Concerning the earliest, pre-Greek settlement at Miletus a certain amount has been learned from the recent excavations. It lay on the level ground to the south-west of the existing city, and dates back to Mycenaean and Minoan times, about 1600 B.C. The considerable quantity of Cretan pottery found there supports the tradition which said that Miletus was founded from Crete. If this is in fact true, it must have been occupied, not as a trading-station—for, as was said above, Miletus' land-communications were poor—but as a port of call on the route to the further east. During the fourteenth century, about the time when the Minoan power in Crete came to an end, the settlement at Miletus was fortified with a solid wall over 14 feet thick; this may perhaps indicate that the place had passed from Minoan hands into those of some

AT–P

Asiatic dynast, whose descendants may represent the 'Carians of uncouth speech' who fought at Troy.

The subsequent course of events has not yet become clear. The great wall did not stand for very long, and in course of time the archaic temple of Athena was built by the Greek colonists directly over its ruins. Somewhere about 800 B.C. a fortified settlement was built on the hill now called Kalabaktepe, some two miles to the south-west of the present ruins, but the excavators are not now disposed to regard this hill as the acropolis of the early Greek Miletus; it is not, in fact, yet determined exactly where this archaic city lay. The region of the pre-Greek settlement continued to be occupied right down to the destruction of Miletus by the Persians in 494 B.C., as is shown by clear traces of burning found in the excavations; but not enough ground has yet been cleared to show whether this was indeed the site of the city of Thales and Hecataeus. Kalabaktepe was excavated in 1904–8, when strong walls 12 feet thick with gates, and numerous foundations of houses and a small temple were brought to light. By no means all of this can still be seen today. Sherds reveal that the hill was occupied from about the eighth century till the Persian capture in 494, and was not altogether deserted even after that.

Among the ruins of the later city all else is overshadowed by the magnificent theatre. In its present form this was built about A.D. 100, replacing an earlier theatre on the same site. If Priene gives us the best surviving Hellenistic theatre, Miletus undoubtedly has the finest of the Graeco-Roman type. The stage-building is of similar form to that at Ephesus; the cavea is semicircular in the Roman fashion, and the seats are completely preserved up to the first diazoma. The vaulted passages under the seats, and the vaults and stairways of the vomitoria, are also in excellent preservation. The 'Royal Box' is marked merely by two pillars. On some of the front rows of seats, from the third to the sixth, are a number of inscriptions reserving the places for certain persons or groups of persons: in the fifth row is the 'place of the Jews also called the God-fearing', and in the third row the 'place of the goldsmiths of the Blues'—with reference to the factions of the Blues and Greens familiar in Byzantine history. On a block of the wall at the top of the stairway at the west end of the upper diazoma is an interesting inscription relating to a labour dispute which arose in the course of the construction of the theatre. The workmen —evidently free agents, not slaves—became dissatisfied with the terms of their employment and were considering abandoning it and seeking other work elsewhere. The matter was referred to arbitration, the arbiter being Apollo at Didyma. His recommendation, in hexameter verse, was to make proper use of building technique, to seek the advice of a skilled expert, and (characteristically) to sacrifice to Athena and Heracles. In other words, 'Get someone to teach you how to do the job economically, and you will find it will pay you well enough.' The men were not mere labourers for hire, but a group of artisans who, in accordance with the normal ancient practice of paying by piecework, had contracted for the job as a whole; owing (apparently) to their own inefficiency, they found it unsatisfactory and were thinking of breaking the contract. This is about as near to a strike in the modern sense as is found in ancient times. Apollo's advice was presumably followed with success, or the matter would not have been recorded on stone (Pl. 55, 57, 58).

The centre of the city lies to the east of the theatre on the low ground, where the ruins are flooded every winter. The Delphinium, or precinct of Apollo Delphinius, was the principal sanctuary at Miletus apart from the great temple at Didyma. It was also very ancient, for the cult was brought from Athens by the original Ionian settlers. Inscriptions found in it date back as far as the sixth century B.C., having apparently been brought from the earlier city; one may be seen built in under the wall on the south side of the court. The name Delphinius is derived from the Greek word for a dolphin, and has only an indirect connection with Delphi; an early legend, seeking to explain the name Delphi, related that Apollo, needing priests for the temple he intended to build there, espied a Cretan ship on the high sea, and, changing himself into a dolphin, guided the sailors thither. The existing remains at Miletus are those of a Hellenistic building reconstructed in Roman times; the extensive use of a pinkish stone

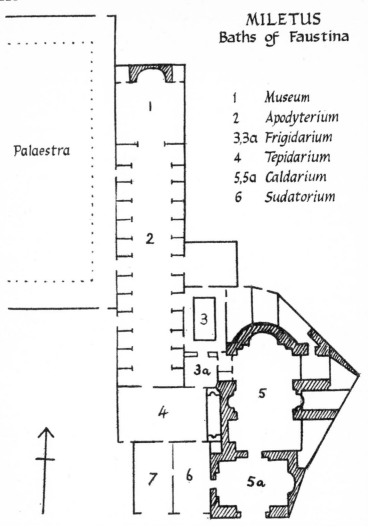

MILETUS
Baths of Faustina

1   Museum
2   Apodyterium
3,3a Frigidarium
4   Tepidarium
5,5a Caldarium
6   Sudatorium

Palaestra

FIG. 44 Plan of the Baths of Faustina at Miletus

gives them a distinctive appearance. In the course of the excavation nearly 200 inscriptions were found of the greatest interest for the city's history.

The Bouleuterion, or Council Chamber, is among the earliest buildings surviving at Miletus, being built between 175 and

164 B.C. It consists of a semicircular assembly hall, fairly well preserved, and a badly ruined forecourt. In the middle of the forecourt are the foundations of a rectangular structure which is believed to have been, not as might be expected an altar, but a tomb. What distinguished person was honoured in this way is quite unknown, and some scholars, in fact, prefer to regard it as an altar (Pl. 56).

Opposite the Council Chamber stood the Nymphaeum, from which water was distributed to the city, but the existing ruins give little idea of this once fine and ornate building. Above the three vaulted niches which now catch the eye were two reservoirs fed by the aqueduct which leads to the building from the rear. From these the water was conveyed partly to channels spreading to various parts of the city, and partly to a large basin in front and below. This basin was framed by an architectural façade of three storeys at the back, with columns, niches and statues, and at either side a two-storeyed colonnade. Of this ornamentation nothing remains but fragments found during the excavation.

Apart from the theatre, the best-preserved building at Miletus is the Baths of Faustina. The Faustina in question is probably the younger of that name, wife of the Emperor Marcus Aurelius, a lady noted for her profligacy with other people's money. The whole complex is really a gymnasium with baths attached in the usual Roman way, and the stadium close by. The palaestra is at the time of writing a cultivated field; from its east side is entered the main chamber of the building (2 in the plan), a long hall running north and south, with small rooms along each side, and an apsed chamber at the north end (1 in the plan). Statues of Apollo and the Muses were found in Room 1, indicating that it was used as a lecture-room; the small chambers of Room 2 served for small classes and discussion. Some of those at the south end may have been changing-rooms for those intending to use the baths. Rooms 1 and 2 together have a striking resemblance to the original Museum which preceded the Double Church at Ephesus.[1] The baths, adjoining on the east and south, comprise as usual a series of rooms heated to varying degrees, much as in a

[1] Above, p. 174.

Turkish bath, which is indeed a direct descendant of the Roman Thermae. Room 3 is the Frigidarium, or cold plunge, a simple rectangular basin of cold water; at one end was placed a reclining statue of a river-god, no doubt the Maeander, and in the middle of one side a marble lion. Water was admitted through the base of the statue and through the lion's mouth. This room is in good preservation and the statues have been left in position. A smaller Frigidarium 3a adjoins on the south. Of the other rooms the coolest was the Tepidarium (No. 4); it was slightly heated by a basin of warm water at the east end. Rooms 5 and 5a are the hot rooms, or Caldarium. They were heated by a hypocaust; that is, the floor was raised some 2 feet 6 inches on supports and the space below filled with hot air from an adjoining furnace. Flues also ran up the walls between the niches. In the hottest room of all, the Sudatorium or Sweating-room (No. 6), flues ran continuously all round the walls. The northern half of this room was later converted into a water-basin, from which the bathers might pass into the cool room 4 and finish with a cold plunge in the Frigidarium. The adjoining room No. 7 was probably similar to No. 6, but has not been excavated.

CHAPTER ELEVEN

Didyma

BEYOND MILETUS, in the extreme south of Ionia, stands what is probably the most impressive single ancient monument on the west coast, the temple of Apollo at Didyma. It is remarkable for its huge size, for its unique plan, and not least for its fine state of preservation. A hundred years ago Sir Charles Newton could write: 'Two giant columns supporting a piece of architrave, and a third unfinished column are all that remain standing of the Temple of Apollo, of which the mighty ruins lie as they originally fell, piled up like shattered icebergs.' Today, thanks to the French and German excavators, the building stands exposed, except for its colonnade, virtually complete. In size it is hardly exceeded by any temple of the Greek world. Planned in Hellenistic times, it serves as a reminder that vastness in architecture was not purely a monopoly of the Romans.

Like Claros, and unlike Gryneum, Didyma was never a city; the temple with its oracle belonged to the territory of Miletus, and its priest was an important official of that city. The name is not Greek but Anatolian, like Idyma in Caria, Sidyma in Lycia, and others; but its accidental resemblance to the Greek *didymi*, 'twins', gave rise to the idea that it referred to Apollo and his twin sister Artemis. Some ancient writers actually use the form Didymi. Artemis had, in fact, a temple and cult at Didyma, but it was of minor importance compared with that of Apollo.

Pausanias says that the oracle existed even before the arrival of the Ionian settlers. It is certainly very ancient; the earliest inscriptions found on the site go back to about 600 B.C., and one of them is a fragment of an oracular response. The clients appear to have asked if it was right for the younger generation

SOUTHERN IONIA
IN EARLY TIMES.

FIG. 45 Southern Ionia in early times

to engage in the practice of piracy, and the god replied, 'It is right to do as your fathers did.' In these early days the cult was in the hands of the Branchidae, a noble family claiming Delphian origin; and Branchidae is often used as an alternative name to Didyma.

When Croesus in the middle of the sixth century was contemplating an invasion of Persia, he thought to take the advice

of an oracle; and to make sure of having the best advice he
devised a preliminary test. He sent messengers to a number
of the best-known oracles, of which Didyma was one, to ask
on a particular day what King Croesus was doing at that
moment; he was, in fact, boiling a tortoise and a lamb in a
bronze cauldron. Apollo at Delphi found the answer, and
another oracle also received honourable mention, but Didyma
failed to rise to the occasion. Croesus was nevertheless a good
friend to the Branchidae and made splendid offerings to the
god—the same indeed that he made to Delphi. These latter
are described by Herodotus; they comprised 10 talents of
pure gold and 226 talents of 'white gold' (electrum), a total
of close upon 2 cubic metres; two huge bowls of gold and silver;
four large jars of silver; two sprinklers of gold and silver; his
wife's necklaces and girdles; and a gold statue, about life-size,
supposed to be a likeness of his cook.

Concerning the form of the temple at this time we know
little or nothing. Visitors were in the habit of landing at the
little port of Panormus on the shore to the north-west and
approaching the sanctuary by a Sacred Way. This road was
lined with statues, many of which, dating from the sixth
century B.C., were still in position till they were removed by
Newton in 1858 and sent to the British Museum. They are
mostly seated figures in the stiff archaic posture, some bearing
inscriptions; they include also a lion and a sphinx. This removal
of ancient sculptures (with, of course, the permission of the
Turkish Government) from the soil of Greece and Turkey for
the benefit of European museums, notably by Lord Elgin,
Sir Charles Fellows and Sir Charles Newton, has been often
criticised. It was not criticised at the time, and was justified
by a double motive, to preserve the monuments from damage
or destruction, and to make them available to scholars and to
the educated public. The Elgin Marbles caused a sensation in
England and produced a revolution in artistic taste. The
present-day visitor to the Parthenon could wish they were
still in place, but in 1800 a visit to Athens, or still more to
Ionia or Lycia, was a great rarity. How many people would
ever have seen the sculptures of Xanthus if Fellows had not
brought them to London? Had these monuments been left

alone, they would inevitably have suffered loss or damage; Mahaffy records how he saw a Greek sitting gun in hand on the Acropolis at Athens and shooting off pieces of the sculpture in the theatre of Dionysus; and Newton notes that a seated figure on the Sacred Way, seen some fifty years earlier by Sir William Gell, had already disappeared. Survival for two thousand years is no guarantee of survival for another hundred. Now that Turkey and Greece are frequently visited and have responsible governments who value these things, the question has reasonably been raised whether they should be given back; meanwhile, as at least a temporary measure, casts can be installed, and in some cases this has been done.

The early phase in the history of Didyma came to an end with the destruction of the temple by the Persians. Herodotus tells us that after the collapse of the Ionian revolt and the fall of Miletus in 494 B.C., Darius sacked and burnt both temple and oracle; Strabo and Pausanias, on the other hand, say that this was done by Xerxes on his return from Greece after his defeat at Plataea in 479. The Branchidae on this occasion were guilty of sad disloyalty to the god; they willingly surrendered his treasures to the Persian king, and to escape the consequences of this treachery they fled with him to Persia, where he settled them on a site in Sogdiana. A hundred and fifty years later Alexander came upon this settlement still existing; after asking the Milesians in his army how he should deal with it, he destroyed it utterly. So, as the historian does not fail to point out, the sons paid the penalty for their fathers' sins. Later still, Seleucus I of Syria found in Ecbatana, the Persian capital, the bronze statue of Apollo that Xerxes had stolen, and restored it to Didyma.

It was long before the oracle recovered from the destruction by the Persians; for the rest of the fifth century and most of the fourth it is silent. With the coming of Alexander, however, we learn that the sacred spring, the fountain of prophecy at Didyma, which had long been dry, gushed again; the oracle, coming to life, announced that Alexander was a true son of Zeus and foretold his victory at Gaugamela. But the real revival of Didyma was due to Seleucus. About 300 B.C. he began to build, on the site of the old temple, the vast structure

which is still standing today. The new sanctuary quickly became rich, but in 278 B.C. it suffered severely from raids by the
invading Gauls. Among the inscriptions found by the excavators is a temple-inventory for the year 277 B.C.; it records that
there survived 'from the war' in the treasury of Apollo one
ornamented bowl and a silvered ox-horn, and in that of
Artemis one censer lacking the support under one of its legs,
two smaller censers and three girdles: nothing more. But the
unfinished building still stood, and for the next two hundred
years the Milesians themselves worked to complete it; a
further plundering by the pirates about 70 B.C. was quickly
made good. The temple never, in fact, received the finishing
touches, as the visitor today may readily observe; for example,
many of the blocks were never finally smoothed, and the
fluting of the columns was not completed.

The plan of this temple is unusual, or even unique, in a
number of respects. The order is Ionic; the type is 'dipteral
decastyle', that is the building was surrounded by a double
row of columns numbering ten across the front and back. The
pronaos, or forecourt, is filled by twelve more columns, making
a total of 120. Between the pronaos and the cella, or main
chamber, is an antechamber containing two more columns;
this has a door opening on to the pronaos, but it was not used
as an entrance, since the sill is 4 feet 9 inches high. This antechamber is a quite exceptional feature, and its purpose will
be discussed later. From it three doors open on to a flight of
stairs leading down to the cella, which lies 18 feet below. The
cella itself is like a great open courtyard, with walls over
70 feet high; its unusual length is due to the absence of a rear
chamber (opisthodomus). Owing to its size, as Strabo tells
us, it was never roofed. From the pronaos the cella is reached
by two sloping tunnels, one on either side, a unique arrangement. It was customary for the cult-statue in a Greek temple
to stand towards the rear of the cella; at Didyma, since the
cella was open to the sky, the statue of Apollo was housed in
a small Ionic temple, of which only the foundations remain;
this temple also contained the oracular spring. The upper part
of the cella walls is decorated with pilasters; between their
capitals ran a frieze carved with griffins and lyres. One or two

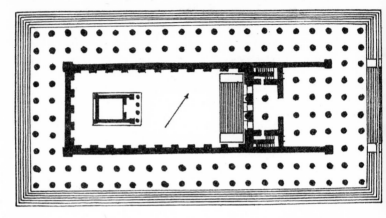

Fig. 46 Plan of the Temple of Apollo at Didyma

fragments are lying against the north wall. A further unusual
feature is the two staircases built in the wall on either side of
the antechamber; they lead up to the top of the cella walls.
The temple was richly and variously ornamented; mention may
be made of the varied decoration of the column-bases in the
pronaos, and of the Medusa frieze which ran above the architrave. At the west end a fallen column has been preserved by
the excavators, with the drums overlapping, exactly as it fell
when overthrown. The temple platform is not exactly horizontal, but slightly raised in the middle; the convexity, though
only of a few inches, is clearly visible by squinting along the
steps. This curvature is normal practice in Greek temples, to
correct the optical illusion by which a long, dead flat line
appears to sag in the middle. It is said that the Parthenon does
not contain a single straight line (Pl. 59, 61).

An ancient privilege of the temple was that of asylum. Just
as Antony extended the asylum at Ephesus, so Julius Caesar
extended that of Didyma by two miles. In spite of this, when
the Emperor Tiberius held his investigation into the claims of
the Greek temples,[1] the Milesians relied not on Caesar's action
but on a letter written by Darius I in the ancient days of the
Branchidae, with the result that Didyma was placed only in

[1] Above, p. 164.

the second class, namely those whose claims were doubtful by reason of their antiquity.

In general the Roman emperors showed themselves good friends to Didyma. Trajan in A.D. 100 paid for the construction of a road from Miletus to the sanctuary, a distance of some eleven miles; hitherto the Milesians had been in the habit of sailing to the port of Panormus. Trajan also paid Apollo the compliment of accepting the office of prophet, an honour which was later repeated by Hadrian. It is not, of course, to be supposed that these emperors listened to the inspired utterances of the prophetess at the sacred spring and turned them into verse for the benefit of the clients; all that is implied is that the expenses attached to the function of prophet were defrayed by the imperial treasury. In the second century, under the 'good' emperors from Trajan to Marcus Aurelius, Didyma enjoyed great prosperity and the oracle flourished; of the oracular texts found by the excavators the majority date from this period.

Decline set in in the third century. In A.D. 262, when the Goths came marauding down the coast, the temple of Apollo was hastily converted into a fortress, of which the ruins remained to be cleared away by the modern excavators. At this time, as we learn from an interesting inscription, the people, penned inside the temple walls, suffered from thirst until Apollo revealed a spring in the sanctuary and so saved them. This can be no other than the sacred spring itself, which must accordingly at that date have been utterly neglected, if not altogether lost. At the time when the inscription was written, about 290, it had once more fallen into decay, and was repaired by order of the proconsul; but again it is spoken of as a quencher of thirst rather than as a source of prophetic inspiration.

The cause of this decline was unquestionably the spread of Christianity, which seems to have taken an early hold at Miletus. The oracles, as one of the main strongholds of paganism, were bitterly attacked by the Christian writers; by the anti-Christian emperors they were naturally defended and patronised. Diocletian sent to Didyma to ask Apollo how he should deal with the Christians, accompanying the question with a present of statues of Zeus and Leto; it is not surprising to learn from our Christian source that the god 'responded as an enemy of the divine religion'. Julian the Apostate was another emperor who, as he tells us himself, was prophet of Apollo; and on learning that a number of chapels of Christian martyrs had been erected at Didyma, he ordered them all to be burnt or razed. But the tide was not to be stemmed by these means, and the end came in A.D. 385 with the famous edict of Theodosius, that 'no mortal man shall have the effrontery to encourage vain hopes by the inspection of entrails, or (which is worse) attempt to learn the future by the detestable consultation of oracles. The severest penalties await those who disobey.' The final humiliation was the erection of a Christian church in the holiest part of the temple itself.

For the actual working of the oracle at Didyma we are moderately well informed. The classical authors speak consistently of a prophetess and of a sacred spring as the source of her inspiration; we learn also that prophecy was by means of words—not as at Ammon in Libya by nods and signs, nor as at Dodona by the rustling of the winds in the trees. Our only detailed account comes from a writer of the fourth century A.D., the philosopher Iamblichus. His words are puzzling. The woman, he says, either holds in her hand a staff 'given by a certain god', or sits on an *axon*, or wets either her feet or the hem of her robe in the water, or inhales the vapour from the water; by all these means she prepares herself to receive the god's inspiration. He adds that she is required to live in the sanctuary, and before prophesying to bathe and to abstain from food for three days. It is hard to know what to make of this, or how reliable the information is. What the *axon* may be is quite unknown—possibly some kind of swivel seat—and the staff is equally obscure. But there is at least no mystery about the spring of water. It was discovered by the excavators in the interior of the cella, where it may still be seen in the little Ionic temple. In fact, three springs or wells have been found inside the cella; the repeated disappearance and rediscovery of the sacred spring in ancient times may perhaps be due to its shifting its position from time to time.

The clients were not permitted to come into the presence of the prophetess; the oracles, rendered into hexameter verse,

DIDYMA 239

were delivered to them in writing by the prophet of Apollo. The prophet was the highest official of all at Miletus; he was appointed for one year by a mixture of choice and lot, and while in office was required to live at Didyma. He was assisted by an official called the *hypochrestes*, the subordinate oracle-giver, whose duties are not explained; it is not unlikely that it was he who put the oracles into verse, a task which not all prophets may have been well qualified to perform. Only one oracle of Didymean Apollo is known to have been in prose. The hypochrestes may also have performed the functions of the prophet in years when that office was held by an emperor.

From the inscriptions we learn further of the existence of a building called the *chresmographeion*, or oracle-office. It is not known where this stood. The French excavator Haussoullier supposed it to be the antechamber at the top of the stairs which lead up from the cella, between it and the pronaos. This room is not a normal part of a Greek temple, so that it was natural to regard it as relating to the special feature of Didyma, the oracle. The German excavators on the other hand believe the chresmographeion to be identical with a building which no longer exists, but whose blocks were found scattered in great numbers in and around the temple; these blocks were inscribed with the names of prophets, who evidently had the right to immortalise themselves in this way. Something like 200 names occur. The original position of this building is uncertain, but there is reason to think it was not in the temple itself. This was no doubt where the versification was done, perhaps also where copies of the oracles were kept. The room between the cella and the pronaos may have been a waiting-room for the clients while the business of prophecy was going on.

The crop of oracular inscriptions revealed by the excavations is disappointingly meagre—hardly more than a dozen texts, and mostly so wretchedly fragmentary as to suggest they were deliberately smashed by enthusiastic Christians. From the literary sources we learn a little more. Under the Branchidae, high though Apollo's reputation was, his recorded responses hardly show him in a very brilliant light. In one case he appears to condone his clients' leanings towards piracy; a second case is his failure—or perhaps his refusal?—to meet the test prepared by Croesus. A third was that of Pactyes the Lydian. After Cyrus' defeat of Croesus this man attempted to raise the Lydians against their Persian conquerors, but was compelled to fly to Cyme, where he asked for political asylum. The Persians at once demanded his surrender. The Cymaeans, torn between respect for a suppliant and fear of the Persians, asked the advice of Apollo at Branchidae, and were told to give Pactyes up. A certain citizen, however, by name Aristodicus, suspecting that the envoys had falsified the oracle, persuaded them to send others, including himself, and ask again. The god's reply was the same as before. Whereupon Aristodicus proceeded to walk round the temple driving out the sparrows and other birds which were nesting in it. At this a voice was heard from the sacred precinct saying. 'What impiety is this—chasing out the suppliants in my temple?' Aristodicus replied, 'Lord, you protect your suppliants, yet urge the Cymaeans to surrender theirs?' Apollo, fairly trapped, did the best he could. 'Yes, I do—that you may for the impiety perish the sooner, and learn never again to consult the oracle about surrendering a suppliant.' The Cymaeans, now in a worse dilemma than before, evaded it by sending Pactyes to Mitylene.

In later times Apollo scored some notable successes. His forecast of Alexander's victory at Gaugamela was mentioned above; at that same time, while Seleucus was still only an officer under Alexander, the oracle hailed him as king. Furthermore, when Seleucus asked about his return to Greece, the god replied, 'Be in no hurry to reach Europe; Asia is for you far better.' And in 280 B.C., when Seleucus crossed the Dardanelles to set foot in Europe for the first time since Alexander crossed into Asia, he was stabbed to death by his enemy Ptolemy Ceraunus. Apollo's advice regarding the labour troubles at Miletus has already been mentioned. When the emperors Licinius and Constantine were fighting each other for the mastery of the world the former approached the oracle at Didyma concerning the outcome; the god replied, 'Old man, youthful warriors are pressing you sorely, while your strength is undone and hard old age is upon you.' This pessimistic estimate was justified soon afterwards, when Licinius was deci-

52   Priene. Supporting Wall of the Temple Terrace.

53   Priene. Theatre.

54   Priene. Inscribed Wall in Gymnasium.

55   Miletus. View towards Theatre Hill.

56   Miletus. Bouleuterion.

57   Miletus. Covered Passage in the Theatre.

58   Miletus. The Theatre, with the former island of Lade in the background.

59   Didyma. Medusa head from the frieze of the Temple.

60 (1) The four 'neocorate' temples at Ephesus.
(2) The two ends of the double temple at Sardis.

61 Didyma. Temple of Apollo.

63   Myus. The site from the south-east.

62   Heracleia. Rock-cut beds for wall-blocks.

64   Heracleia. "Sanctuary of Endymion".

65   Heracleia. The Necropolis.

66   Heracleia. Market Building. Mt. Latmus in background.

67   Heracleia. Temple of Athena.

68 and 69   Heracleia. Walls.

70   Heracleia. Walls.

71   Sardis. Temple of Artemis.

72   Sardis. Ionic Capital from the Temple.

73   Sardis. Temple of Artemis.

74   Sardis. Curious rock-formations in the neighbouring hills.

75   Sardis. Lydian Rock-Tombs. Acropolis in the background.

sively defeated and deprived of the purple. Later, when asked whether Christ was god or man, Apollo is said to have answered, 'He was a man in the flesh.' This judgment was no doubt predictable, and on the whole Didymean Apollo may be thought to have deserved his reputation.

A question which is more often asked than answered is, how did the oracles manage to maintain their reputation for knowing the unknowable? How did they succeed in satisfying a multitude of clients for hundreds of years? The enquirers ranged from kings to peasants, and the enquiries from the highest matters of state to the most trivial personal affairs; even if we bear in mind that in such matters one striking success will make up for many failures, it is remarkable that people continued to be willing to make long journeys to consult the prophetic gods and heroes. With regard to questions of policy there is perhaps no great mystery. The priests of a great shrine like Delphi or Didyma, listening day after day to queries on affairs of state from all over the Greek world, were well placed to know what was going on; even without sending out intelligence agents (for which there is no evidence), they must have been well able to offer shrewd and reliable advice. Oracles have a reputation for obscurity, and it is true that they tended to avoid a direct reply. Croesus on a famous occasion was told that by attacking Persia he would destroy a great empire, and did, in fact, destroy his own, but such downright ambiguity is exceptional; more often the client is given some general advice, or advice which he may interpret for himself. Or again, when a woman asks who has stolen her gold earrings, or who is putting the evil eye on her daughter, she will seldom receive a straightforward answer, but will be advised to sacrifice to this or that deity. Nevertheless, mere evasion and obscurity cannot be satisfactory for long, and it is perhaps not excluded that genuine inspiration may have played a part. At all events, the preparations undergone by the priestess, the abstention from food, the inhaling of vapours and the rest, combined with the general atmosphere of expectation, must have put her in a highly receptive frame of mind.

But the oracle was not the only activity at Didyma. Every fourth year there was celebrated the festival of the Great

AT–Q

Didymeia. Instituted at least as early as 200 B.C., this festival
was especially popular under the empire. In addition to the
usual athletic events there were contests in oratory, music
and drama; these were presided over by the prophet, but the
organisation was, as usual, in the hands of the agonothete.
We learn that the festival was held only partly at Didyma and
partly in Miletus; curiously enough, the contest in tragedy was
held in the sanctuary, where no sign whatever of a theatre has
been found, while the splendid theatre at Miletus remained for
this purpose unused.

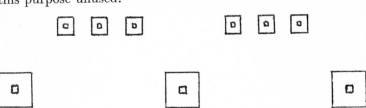

FIG. 47 The Starting-sill in the Stadium at Didyma

The stadium, on the other hand, is still extant. It lies immediately beside the temple on the south side, so close indeed
that the steps of the temple actually served as seats for the
spectators. The lower steps are covered with names carved
upon them to reserve places for particular persons; close on
200 names may still be read, some carefully engraved, some
merely scratched. The names are thickest on the lowest steps,
which were evidently regarded as the best seats. They are all
names of individuals, singly or in groups; no places are reserved for any officials in their official capacity—not even for
the prophet or agonothete, who must nevertheless have had
their special seats.

The starting-line for the foot-races is preserved at the east
end of the stadium. It differs in some respects from that at
Priene. The remains consist of nine stone blocks, three large
and six small, pierced with holes for holding upright posts,
set in a double line across the stadium. The three large blocks
are placed at intervals of about 16 feet; the six smaller ones
are set in two groups of three in the spaces between the large
blocks but a little in advance of them. The adjoining sketch

shows the original arrangement; but as the stones are set merely in the earth those on the north have shifted their positions. The excavators explain that the actual starting-line was formed by a cord stretched across between the three large posts; the smaller posts served merely to space the runners equally at the start. In this way the stadium would accommodate eight runners at a time. But the matter may not be as simple as this. The central large post seems to serve no purpose on this theory; moreover, this block has also a horizontal perforation which remains unexplained. Nor is it clear why the smaller posts were not set in line with the larger in the natural way. The starting-lines of the many stadia in the Greek world show such a variety of forms, and offer so many problems, that it is safer to reserve judgment.

A conspicuous feature of the temple is the letters carved in great profusion on the walls and steps of various parts of the building. Much speculation has been aroused as to their purpose. They fall into three groups: (1) the letters IE, (2) one or more abbreviated personal names, and (3) both of these together. Various explanations have been offered, but it is now proposed to regard the personal names as those of slave-owning citizens of Miletus who hired out their men to the temple authorities to work on the construction of the building. IE then denotes slaves of the hieron or temple itself. Where two or three marks appear on one stone, slaves of different owners worked on that block—not necessarily all in the temple itself, perhaps also in the quarry or the workshop where the stones were trimmed. The purpose of the marks is then to indicate to whom payment is due for the handling of that particular block by his slaves; payment was made, as usual in antiquity, by piecework. The marks were, of course, intended to be shaved off when the stones received their final dressing; but the temple was not finished, and this stage was never reached.

★

CHAPTER TWELVE

Myus and Magnesia

AMONG THE twelve cities of the Ionian League Myus was probably the poorest and most insignificant; Lebedus alone might rival her in this respect. The site now lies solitary and deserted beside the Maeander, well away from normal traffic routes, and is scarcely ever visited. The surviving ruins indeed may be thought not to justify the trouble of reaching them; but anyone who is attracted by out-of-the-way, end-of-the-world places will find the excursion rewarding. Myus lies half an hour's walk to the north-west of the village of Avşar, and may be reached by a rough jeep-road from Sarıkemer; there is also an alternative approach from the village of Özbaşı, crossing the river by a ferry. The site was dug by the Germans at the time of the excavation of Miletus; in 1964 the work was continued on a small scale, but without producing any striking change in appearance.

Myus was founded, according to legend, by yet another of the sons of Codrus; but the site was poorly chosen and it is likely that almost from the beginning the city was affected by malaria. It may well be due to the depressing and enervating effects of this disease that Myus played no part in the great flowering of Ionian civilisation, nor ever, so far as we know, produced a famous citizen.

A story is told that when Themistocles, the Athenian hero of Salamis in 480 B.C., later fell into disgrace and exile, he made the friendship of the Persian king, and was given by him three towns to supply him with a livelihood—Magnesia for his bread, Lampsacus for his wine, and Myus for his *opson*. This Greek word has no equivalent in English; it is translated in Turkish by *katık*, and means 'something to eat with your bread', whether meat, fish, cheese, olives or anything else. It illustrates an interesting difference in dietary habits: whereas we eat bread with our meat or fish, the ancient Greeks, like the modern Turks, ate meat or fish with their bread. Bread was indeed the staff of life; and a Turkish countryman will seldom eat less than the equivalent of half a loaf with his meal. In the case of Myus the *opson* supplied to Themistocles was no doubt mainly fish, for, as the historian Diodorus rightly says, the sea around there was rich in fish; the *dalyan* or fishery a few miles to the south-west will bear witness.

Curiously enough, this was not the only occasion when Myus was given as a present by a king. In 201 B.C. Philip V of Macedon was overrunning Asia Minor with his army; being short of supplies, he approached the Magnesians, who gave him a quantity of figs, for they had no corn. When later he laid his hands on Myus he presented it to the Magnesians in payment for the figs. There can surely not be many free cities which have suffered the indignity of being twice given away to others.

The history of Myus is in the main the story of the Maeander silt. In 499 B.C. a fleet of 200 warships could anchor there, although five years later at the battle of Lade the city could provide no more than three ships, a figure equalled only, among those who were present at all, by the half-city of Phocaea. In the Delian Confederacy, Myus paid a normal tribute of one talent, again equal to the lowest among the Ionian cities. In 390 B.C. she was still at least an independent city, for she was involved in a quarrel with Miletus over a piece of land; by 201 B.C. she was sufficiently reduced to be given away in return for figs; and early in the second century she appears as a mere dependency of Miletus, for we find that city claiming a piece of territory on the grounds that it was sacred to Apollo Terbintheus, the principal deity of Myus. Malaria and the Maeander mud were steadily doing their work; the population became so reduced that by Strabo's time Myus was no longer able to function as a city and was fused in a political union with Miletus. At that date Myus could no longer be reached by sea, but by sailing in small boats some three miles up the river. Pausanias tells us graphically what finally happened. 'There was close to Myus a small inlet of the sea'—now represented apparently by the Azap Gölü—'which the Maeander converted into a lagoon by blocking the entrance with mud; as the sea receded and the water of the lagoon became fresh, such innumerable swarms of mosquitoes arose from it that the inhabitants were obliged to abandon the city. Taking with them all their movable property, including the statues of their gods, they moved to Miletus, and when I was in Myus there was nothing there but a white marble temple of Dionysus.'

The foundations of this temple may still be seen today, but virtually nothing is standing. The site is marked by a conspicuous Byzantine castle on a knoll beside the river; the lower slope of this hill has been fashioned into two rock-terraces one above the other. The upper of these is flanked by a rock-wall containing a shallow chamber or niche with a number of cuttings. This terrace carried a large temple in the Doric order, some 56 feet in width; this was probably the temple of Apollo Terbintheus, Lord of the Terebinth. The foundations of one side-wall survive in part, and a row of round holes parallel with it, as if to hold the columns of the peristyle. Supporting this terrace and flanking the lower is a wall of large blocks in the 'Cyclopean' style; on this lower terrace stood the temple of Dionysus seen by Pausanias. There remain only a part of the foundations, a supporting wall, and a single white marble column-drum.

The main habitation was on the next hill to the east, on which are numerous rock-cut houses, tombs and cisterns.

The extreme scarcity of cut blocks on the site, despite the excavation and the absence of any considerable modern building in the neighbourhood, is explained by their removal to Miletus for constructional purposes there. Be this as it may, it is certain that no other excavated site in Ionia offers so little to the visitor's eye. Myus had presumably public buildings like any other city, but apart from the scanty fragments mentioned no trace of them has come to light (Pl. 63).

MAGNESIA ON THE MAEANDER

Cicero remarked that all the Greek colonies in Asia were washed by the sea, with the single exception of Magnesia. The statement is not quite accurate, as Colophon and the other Magnesia are also some way from the coast, but inland settlements are certainly the exception. In actual fact the original site is not known, for Magnesia, like Priene and so many others, changed its position in classical times. The city is remarkable in another way, too: though situated in the heart of Ionia it was, like Notium, founded by Aeolians, and was never a member of the Ionian League. These founders came from the original Magnesia in northern Greece; they are said to have travelled first to Delphi, then to Crete, and finally to Asia. In a later inscription the Magnesians claim to have been the first Greeks to cross into Anatolia.

The scanty history of the early city is mainly a series of calamities; and, in fact, the 'sufferings of the Magnesians' became proverbial. In the seventh century, when Gyges, king of Lydia, was attacking the Ionian cities, Magnesia contrived for special reasons to incur his particular enmity. The story was that a foppish poet of Smyrna, named by a coincidence Magnes, in the course of his travels aroused by his good looks the affections of many men and women, and especially of King Gyges. In Magnesia he made a particular hit with the women, many of whom he seduced; their menfolk thereupon, on the plea that Magnes had slighted their city in his poems, set upon him, tore his clothes, cut off his long hair and generally beat him up. Enraged by this treatment of his favourite, Gyges repeatedly attacked Magnesia and finally captured it. Yet worse was to follow; soon afterwards the city fell to the Cimmerian invaders and was almost annihilated.

But the principal fame of Magnesia in early times lies in its connection with Themistocles. Of the three towns presented to him by the Persian king Artaxerxes,[1] Magnesia was the one which he chose as his residence. It was to supply him with bread; as we learn that the king had been drawing a revenue of fifty talents a year from the city, Themistocles had certainly no reason to go hungry. He was, in fact, greatly honoured by the citizens; he built a temple of the Mother Goddess and appointed his daughter as priestess. Of his death various accounts are given; Thucydides says he died of disease, but

[1] Above, p. 244.

others say he deliberately took poison because he felt himself unable to fulfil his promises to the Persian king. The later version was that while sacrificing a bull to Artemis he collected a bowlful of the blood, drank it and so died.[1] He was given public burial at Magnesia, and a handsome monument to him was erected in the market-place.

Chiefly owing to its inland situation, Magnesia was never a member of the Delian Confederacy, and its next appearance in history is in 400 B.C., the year following the adventure of Xenophon's Ten Thousand. The Spartan general Thibron, attempting to secure the freedom of the Asiatic cities, succeeded in capturing Magnesia from the Persian satrap; seeing that it was unwalled, we are told, and fearing that the satrap might retake it during his absence, he transferred the city to the neighbouring Mt. Thorax (the present Gümüş Dağı). The site chosen, where the ruins now lie, was the little town of Leucophrys, 'Whitebrow'; it is militarily a very weak one at the foot of the mountain, and moreover the city continued to be unwalled. If greater security was really Thibron's motive for changing the site, he must have been relying on the sanctity of the place, for there was there an ancient and venerable shrine of Artemis, surnamed Leucophryene—the same, in fact, at which Themistocles was sacrificing when he met his end. It seems, however, probable that, as in the case of Priene, the advance of the Maeander silt was at least a contributory reason for the move.

The new city, of course, fell quickly back with the rest into Persian hands, and remained so till the coming of Alexander, to whom it surrendered without resistance. In the troubled Hellenistic times the city seems to have prospered quietly, without playing any significant part in history. An inscription of Magnesia found near Davutlar, if it is in or near its original position, implies that early in the second century Magnesian territory extended to the west coast beyond Mt. Thorax. If

[1] This method of suicide, though seldom if ever actually imitated, was reckoned perfectly possible in antiquity. Pliny says that bull's blood coagulates and hardens very quickly, and is therefore considered poisonous to drink fresh, except that at Aegira in Greece the priestess drank it before descending into a cave to prophesy. How much truth there may be in this the present writer is not able to say.

true, this is surprising: this land was disputed by Priene and Samos, whereas Magnesia looks naturally to the east: it seems more probable that the stone bearing the inscription has been carried from farther east for the construction of the mosque into which it is built. Stones are often carried considerable distances in this way, and these *pierres errantes* frequently cause trouble to students of historical geography.

From early times the Magnesians were often at war with the Ephesians, fighting best, we are told, when inspired by the song of the cicada. The chirruping of this insect, which many people tend to find irritating, seems always to have had an exhilarating effect on the Greeks. Magnesian cavalrymen, like the Colophonians, took hunting dogs into battle with them; these they used as their first line of attack, followed by their servants armed with javelins; the horsemen themselves formed the third line.

When the province of Asia was overrun by Mithridates, the Magnesians were among the minority who declined to accept liberation at his hands. For their loyalty to Rome they were rewarded with the title 'free', and Magnesia became a leading city in the province and a judicial seat of the governor. On a coin of the third century A.D. she describes herself as 'seventh city of Asia'.

Among the distinguished artists of Magnesia was a certain Anaxenor, a singer to the lyre. This man was one of the crowd of artistic youths with whom Mark Antony surrounded himself in the east; he was highly honoured in his own city, and his statue was erected in the theatre. The inscription on the base ended with a quotation from Homer, and Strabo tells us that the stonemason, for lack of space, omitted the final iota of the last word, thereby converting a dative into a nominative and bringing on his city a reputation for illiteracy. The German excavators, digging in the theatre, had the good fortune to find this base still largely intact—an exciting discovery. They report that there is, in fact, just room at the edge of the stone for a narrow letter, and that the surface actually shows a mark there which might be taken for a badly written iota, but is probably only an accidental defect in the stone. Alternatively we might suspect that some Magnesian, tired of the jeers at his city's scholarship, carved the missing letter with his penknife. The stone itself was taken to Berlin.

The principal excavations took place in 1891–3, but the ground is flooded every winter by the neighbouring stream, the ancient Lethaeus, and most of what was unearthed is now buried again. There is indeed little to be seen apart from the ruins of the temple of Artemis Leucophryene, which lie in a flat heap close beside the road.

Artemis had a temple here from at least the sixth century B.C., for remains of that date were found under the present building. This latter was the work of Hermogenes, architect of the temple of Dionysus at Teos, and dates from the early second century B.C. The plan may be traced, with some difficulty, among the jumble of blocks. Interesting features are the internal columns in the pronaos and cella, and the placing of the external columns at twice the usual distance from the temple walls. To this latter feature the term pseudo-dipteral is applied, as if the object were to give the appearance of a double row of columns without the expense of the inner row. Another peculiarity is that the temple faces west, contrary to the normal rule. It is in the Ionic order and stands as usual on flat ground.

Shortly before Hermogenes' temple was begun, in 220 B.C., there occurred a remarkable epiphany of the goddess. In what way exactly she manifested herself we do not know, but on the matter being referred to Apollo at Delphi the god declared that the city and territory of Magnesia should be regarded as holy ground. The Magnesians therefore decided to establish a great quadrennial festival under the name of the Leuco-phryena, and sent ambassadors all over the Greek world inviting the cities to attend it and to recognise the sanctity of Magnesia in accordance with Apollo's words. The favourable replies of some seventy cities were found by the excavators inscribed on the walls of a hall in the market-place. The inviolability thus conferred finally removed any need for the Magnesians to fortify their city; the walls now to be seen date from early Byzantine times, when Apollo's pronouncements no longer passed current.

The theatre lies at the west foot of the hill just to the south

of the temple, but there is very little to see. The curve of the
cavea remains, and a fragment of the supporting wall, but the
seats are gone; of the stage-building only the top of an arched
door and a couple of column-stumps are visible above ground.
This theatre nevertheless is, or was, interesting, as it is one of
the half-dozen in which a tunnel was installed leading from
the stage-building to the middle of the orchestra. These
tunnels were presumably used for the appearance of actors
rising from the underworld, as is required in one or two of the
surviving Greek tragedies. When the present writer first
visited Magnesia in 1939 the tunnel was visible in the form of
a deep trench, lined with masonry and filled with brambles,
leading out from under the stage into the orchestra and
branching right and left in the form of a letter T. It has now
been filled in, no doubt in order to avoid the nuisance caused
by animals falling into it; that this can easily happen was
proved by the writer's companion, who had the misfortune to
do so himself. The only other tunnel of this kind in Asia
Minor is that at Tralles, the modern Aydın, but long occupation of the acropolis hill by the military has obliterated this
also.

Higher up to the south are some scanty traces of a smaller
theatre or odeum, and farther to the west the outline of a
stadium can be discerned; for the rest the ruins of Magnesia
are once again covered by the mud.

★

CHAPTER THIRTEEN

Heracleia under Latmus

UNTIL THE last few years Heracleia, tucked into the far corner of the lake of Bafa, was highly inaccessible and rarely visited. The writer in 1946, and Freya Stark in 1952, made the journey in a small boat from the west end of the lake; and this may still be done. But the recent opening of the fine new tarmac road from Söke to Milâs has made things easier. Skirting the south shore of the lake, and towards its east end, the road passes a small landing-stage, with a coffee-house across the road opposite; from here a motor-boat may be hired to Kapıkırı and Heracleia. By land a rough jeep-road leads from the village of Bafa in six miles to the site; it crosses at one point a causeway and bridge over a marshy stream. If the bridge is not in good repair, a pleasant half-hour's walk brings the traveller to his destination. The village is deserted in the height of summer, when the inhabitants move to their *yayla*, or summer quarters, about a mile along the shore of the lake.

It is safe to say that no one who makes the excursion to Heracleia will be disappointed. Though situated on the Ionian coast—for the lake of Bafa was in antiquity an arm of the sea—the city belongs, in character as in history, to Caria. The scene is dominated by Mt. Latmus, whose serrated crest has given it the name of Beş Parmak, the Five Fingers. Some 4,500 feet in height, this wild and rocky mountain sends down a spur towards the village of Kapıkırı, and up this ridge run the walls of Heracleia, in beautiful masonry unusually well preserved. They rise, in fact, about 1,600 feet from the lake, but they seem to climb into the sky, twisting and turning in a fantastic wilderness of rocks. The visitor who follows them up and up finds himself, in Freya Stark's words, 'curiously uncertain as to where the confines of reality end or begin'. The contrast with the rich lands and gentle contours of Ionia is complete.

The city was Carian from the beginning. In early times it bore the name of Latmus, distinguished only in gender from the mountain above, and under this name it paid a tribute of one talent a year in the Delian Confederacy in the fifth century. This assessment puts it among the more important of the non-Greek townships of Caria. Mausolus, dynast of Caria in the fourth century, captured it by a rather mean trick, after winning its confidence by a pretence of friendship and enticing the citizens to open their gates as his army marched by. However, he atoned for this duplicity handsomely enough, for it was undoubtedly Mausolus who built the magnificent fortifications which are standing today. This was a part of his great scheme, which he did not live to complete, of reorganising Caria on the Greek model; the change of name from the Anatolian Latmus to the Greek Heracleia was similarly due to him. As a powerful fortress-city on the northern border of Mausolus' realm Heracleia might have had a future; but Mausolus died, Alexander came, and the face of things was altered. Heracleia was never, in fact, a city of much account. With little in the way of territory, its prosperity must come from the sea; and with Miletus at the mouth of the gulf its prospects were poor. As the Maeander gradually converted the gulf into a lake, Heracleia became completely cut off.

Nevertheless, Heracleia-under-Latmus has at least one claim to fame in its association with the enigmatic figure of Endymion. The legends concerning Endymion are confused and contradictory to the point of relating apparently to two different characters. Some say that he was a king of Elis in the Peloponnese, that he set his sons to run a race at Olympia to decide who should succeed him, and in this way originated the Olympic foot-race. But the better-known stories tell how he was loved by the moon Selene and slept eternally on Mt. Latmus. Zeus, it was said, was fond of the handsome lad and gave him leave to choose whatever he wished; Endymion chose to sleep for ever deathless and ageless. The choice appears a strange one; but there was perhaps more in it than

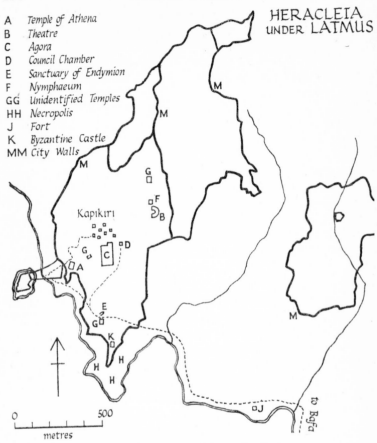

A   Temple of Athena
B   Theatre
C   Agora
D   Council Chamber
E   Sanctuary of Endymion
F   Nymphaeum
GG   Unidentified Temples
HH   Necropolis
J   Fort
K   Byzantine Castle
MM   City Walls

HERACLEIA
UNDER LATMUS

Kapıkırı

FIG. 48 Plan of Heracleia under Latmus

meets the eye. It was whispered that Endymion had an amour
with Hera, and when this came to Zeus' notice it may be that
the choice he offered was similar to that offered in more recent
times between gun, rope and poison-cup. At all events
Selene saw him sleeping on Latmus and came down to him
and kissed him, and some say she bore him fifty daughters.
This might be thought enough to wake him; and, in fact, his
sleep cannot have been really eternal, for the men of Heracleia
pointed out his tomb in a cave on Latmus, and his sanctuary
also on the mountain. A later account rationalises the story.

According to this, Endymion was the first man to discover the true orbit of the moon; having done nothing with his life but study for this, he was said to have slept for thirty years. Let other scientists take note. Later still, certain Christian writers declared that Endymion was a Carian mystic who desired to learn from the moon the name of God; on learning it he died, and his mortal remains were preserved to that time in Caria, where his coffin was opened every year and the bones were observed to emit a humming sound—presumably in an effort to communicate the name of God to man.

The outstanding feature of the ruins of Heracleia is undoubtedly the great city walls. Taken in their entirety they show, still standing intact, almost every feature of a classical fortification. Towers and curtains, roofs and windows, gates and posterns, internal stairways leading to the parapets, all are in excellent condition; here and there, where the wall is gone, the beds for the blocks may be seen climbing the steep rock-faces like stairs (Pl. 62, 68, 69, 70).

But the lower town, too, has much of interest to show. To the traveller approaching from the lake the most conspicuous building is the well-preserved temple on the bluff above the landing-stage. It is identified as the temple of Athena by an inscription still lying beside it. The form is simple, merely a cella with walls standing to their full height, and a pronaos; there were columns in front, but none at the back or sides (Pl. 67).

The little island opposite the landing-stage was a peninsula in antiquity and was included in the fortifications; the remains of the walls joining it to the mainland are now under water, for the water-level has risen since ancient times.

Just beyond the temple of Athena is the agora, or market-place, on which a village school has recently been built. At the south end the open space is supported by a market-building divided into shops; those below the level of the agora were approached from outside. This building also is well preserved. Close to the agora on the east are the scanty remains of the council chamber; one or two rows of seats, arranged on three sides of a square as at Priene, may be made out, and part of the handsome supporting wall. The theatre to the north is in

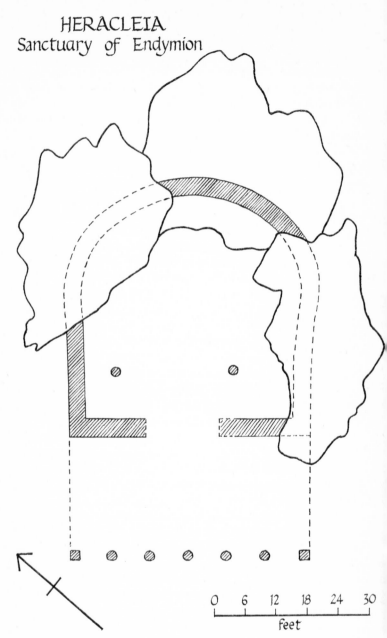

HERACLEIA
Sanctuary of Endymion

0 6 12 18 24 30
feet

FIG. 49 Plan of the Sanctuary of Endymion
256

poorish preservation, and the ruins of the fountain-house, or Nymphaeum, and the temple just above are also scanty (Pl. 66).

In the southern part of the city is an unusual and highly interesting building. It is identified as the Sanctuary of Endymion. The accompanying plan shows the form of the structure; the main chamber is rounded at the back, and its wall fills in the spaces between large outcrops of rock which project into the interior. The wall was originally higher than it is now; beds for the blocks are cut into the surface of the rocks where it ran over them. A cross-wall with originally a door in the middle divides this chamber from an entrance-porch with a row of unfluted columns in front; the row consists, most unusually, of a square pilaster at each end and five columns in between. An odd number of columns, giving a column in the middle instead of a space, is exceedingly rare, and the whole form of the building is exceptional in the extreme. Two other column-bases are visible in the interior; as they are not symmetrically placed, there may originally have been others. The identification of this strange building as a sanctuary of Endymion is very attractive; the entrance on the south-west suits the shrine of a hero or demi-god such as Endymion was; temples of gods and goddesses were entered from the east. As was noted above, Endymion had a sanctuary on Mt. Latmus; either this is a second shrine, or the spot is counted as being on the mountain (Pl. 64).

If the visitor will walk a few minutes south from this sanctuary to the headland beyond the Byzantine castle, he will look down on one of the strangest cemeteries he has ever seen. The graves are of the Carian type, a rectangular hole sunk in the rock and covered with a separate lid. The surface of the rocks is pitted with scores of these tombs, many of them side by side in pairs; a few of the lids are lying close by, but all the graves have, of course, long since been opened and plundered. Some of them are now visible under water, submerged by the rise in the level of the lake (Pl. 65).

But first and last it is the mountain that stays in the visitor's memory. Homer, listing the allies of the Trojans, refers to the 'Carians of uncouth speech who dwell around Miletus and the Mountain of Lice' (Phtheiron); this curiously

AT–R

named mountain was identified in antiquity as Latmus. Some, however, feeling the name to be undignified, understood it as the 'mountain of the Phtheirians', a tribe of men otherwise unknown. The villagers of Kapıkırı deny strenuously that lice are to be found among them. Scorpions there certainly are, and we have it on the authority of Aristotle himself that the scorpions of Latmus never sting strangers, but only the local inhabitants. For this the present writer cannot speak, but he can answer for it from painful experience that the same does not apply to bees.

Latmus was always a holy mountain, and in the Middle Ages it was a favourite resort for anchorites and other holy men. Numerous monasteries and hermitages which they founded may still be seen; but in general they are high up among the wastes of rock, and are virtually inaccessible to the ordinary traveller.

★

CHAPTER FOURTEEN

Sardis

ABOUT THE year 700 B.C. the kingship of Lydia was held by a certain Candaules. This man had the curious fancy to fall in love with his own wife, and it was his habit to extol her loveliness, especially to his favourite minister, by name Gyges. Dissatisfied, however, with the degree of enthusiasm shown by the prudent minister, he was one day moved by an evil genius to address him thus: 'Gyges, it is clear that you doubt what I tell you of my wife's beauty; seeing is believing, so we must contrive that you see her naked.' Gyges was horrified, but the king reassured him: 'Don't be alarmed; she will not even know that you have seen her. I will place you behind the bedroom door; there you can watch her as she disrobes, and as she walks to the bed with her back towards you do you slip out without being seen.' Gyges, seeing there was nothing for it, reluctantly consented, and all took place as the king had arranged—except that as the minister left the bedroom the queen caught sight of him out of the corner of her eye. With great self-control she neither screamed nor gave any sign; but next morning, in the presence of the most faithful of her retinue, she summoned him to her and said: 'Gyges, you have seen me naked; you must therefore choose one of two courses. Either you must kill Candaules, marry me and be king of Lydia, or you must perish here and now.' Finding entreaties vain, Gyges elected to save himself. That night the queen installed him behind the selfsame door, dagger in hand, and when the king was asleep he crept out and struck him dead. In this way the throne of Lydia passed to a new dynasty. Not, however, without disturbance; many of the citizens took up arms in the cause of their murdered sovereign, and civil war was imminent. Finally it was agreed to abide by the decision of the oracle at Delphi, and this proved to be in Gyges' favour. The vast 'Gygian treasure' of gold and silver afterwards preserved in Apollo's sanctuary testified to the new king's sense of gratitude.

The new dynasty, thus (according to Herodotus) inaugurated, lasted for a hundred and fifty years, during which period the Lydian nation enjoyed its great age of prosperity. Of its earlier history little is known with certainty. Homer makes no mention of Lydians; but among the allies of Troy he speaks of certain Maeonians who lived about Mt. Tmolus and Lake Gygaea—that is, in the later Lydia. Herodotus says that these Maeonians voluntarily changed their name to Lydians at an early date, but this is now generally agreed to be an error. Much more likely the Lydians were a separate nation who at some unknown period invaded and occupied Maeonia; even in antiquity the two races were regarded by some writers as distinct.

A strong tradition, led by Herodotus, said that Etruria in Italy was colonised from Lydia. In consequence of a long famine the nation divided into two halves, one of which stayed in Asia while the other sailed to find a new home in the west. Modern research has, in fact, tended to confirm this colonisation from the east, and dates the settlement to about 800 B.C. At that time Rome was not yet founded, and for centuries the Etruscan civilisation was far in advance of any other in Italy.[1]

Of Lydia and its capital Sardis under Gyges and his successors a good deal has been said above. The gradual subjugation of the Greek cities of the coast by Gyges himself, Ardys, Alyattes and Croesus is already familiar. Despite these generally hostile relations the two races entertained a mutual respect and admiration, and each learned much from the other's civilisation. Lydia had relations with Assyria too: Gyges is readily recognisable in the 'Gugu of Luddi' who sent ambassadors to Assurbanipal.

Lydian customs, says Herodotus, were much the same as the Greek, with one notable exception. Girls normally earned their dowries by prostitution, a practice which carried no reproach. The Lydians claimed to have invented all the games

[1] See also below, p. 272.

which were common to them and to the Greeks—not athletic games, but such pastimes as dice, knucklebones and ball. The very ancient game of *pessoi*, a kind of draughts or chess, they did not claim as theirs; and the claim to the invention of ball-play was certainly not justified; ball-games were familiar, not only to Nausicaa in the *Odyssey*, but in early times in Egypt. Rather surprisingly, we hear next to nothing of them in classical Greece.

A more important invention which was attributed, apparently with justice, to the Lydians is that of coined money. Certainly earlier civilisations such as the Hittite and Egyptian seem to have made no use of coinage, though metal bars and rings were used in some places as currency; the Greek word 'drachma' meant originally 'a handful' of these. But of actual coins of precious metal guaranteed in weight by the government stamp we know no earlier specimens than the Lydian. These, with very few exceptions, bear no inscription, but merely the lion's head which was the royal emblem of Sardis. They were made at first of 'electrum', an alloy of gold and silver; tests have shown that the gold content varied from about 36 to 53 per cent. This variation may have shaken public confidence, and it was perhaps for this reason that Croesus, the last Lydian king, introduced coinage of pure gold and pure silver. The new invention was at once adopted by the Greek cities of the coast, and indeed spread rapidly over the whole world.

The gold for these Lydian coins was obtained, in part at least, from the River Pactolus, a small stream which flows down from Mt. Tmolus (Bozdağ) through Sardis to join the Hermus. From this and other gold-bearing rivers an early method of collecting the dust was to lay sheepskins in a shallow part of the stream to catch the particles of gold; the legend of the Golden Fleece is supposed to have arisen in this way, for Colchis, too, had its gold-bearing river, a branch of the Phasis. The Pactolus itself was quickly exhausted, and even in Strabo's time had ceased to yield any gold. It had, however, sufficed to make the names of Gyges and Croesus proverbial for wealth.

With Alyattes' expulsion of the Cimmerians from Asia

Minor the Lydian power rose to new heights. Phrygia, disas-
trously weakened by the northern barbarians, was annexed
and Smyrna was destroyed, though Alyattes failed before
Clazomenae and was only partially successful at Miletus.
Under his successor Croesus the Lydian empire was extended
over the whole Anatolian peninsula except for part of the
south coast. Croesus was the last and most famous of the
Lydian kings, and many tales, more or less historical, were
told about him; a number of these have already been related.

The annexation of Phrygia brought the Lydians into immediate contact with the Persian empire, with only the
River Halys (the Kızılırmak) between them. Learning of the
increasing power of the Persians under their new king, Cyrus,
Croesus determined upon an attempt to check it. Encouraged
by his wrong interpretation of Apollo's oracle,[1] he crossed the
Halys into Persian territory. Following an indecisive battle,
he thought it wise to retreat and collect a larger force; but
Cyrus, with unexpected vigour, passed to the offensive, invaded Lydia, and after defeating Croesus' forces outside
Sardis penned them up in the capital. The siege lasted for a
fortnight before the city fell; of its capture Herodotus gives the
following account. An earlier Lydian king, by name Meles,
had a concubine who bore him a lion; the soothsayers, consulted about this prodigy, declared that if the lion were carried
round the fortifications of Sardis the city would be impreg-
nable. Meles therefore had this done, but omitted one part on
the south side which seemed so precipitous as to need no
supernatural protection. It happened that a Lydian soldier
dropped his helmet at this point and had to clamber down the
rock to retrieve it; a Persian observed this, and the following
day, with a large number of companions, scaled the acropolis
at the same place and took the city by surprise (546 B.C.).

Croesus himself was taken prisoner and by Cyrus' orders
placed in fetters on a pyre to be burned alive. As he waited for
the fire to be lit he groaned and uttered three times the name
of Solon. Cyrus' curiosity was stirred and he bade the inter-
preters ask who this Solon might be. Croesus replied that he
was an Athenian who had formerly visited Sardis and made

[1] See above, p. 241.

light of Croesus' wealth and prosperity, bidding him reckon
no man happy so long as he lives, but to wait for the end.
Cyrus, impressed, ordered Croesus to be taken down from the
pyre; but by this time the flames were ablaze and he could
no longer be approached. Thereupon he called on Apollo to
save him, and at once a storm gathered from a blue sky and a
violent downpour extinguished the fire. Convinced by this
that Croesus was more than an ordinary man, Cyrus ordered
his fetters to be removed and bade him sit beside him. After a
long silence Croesus asked, 'What are those men doing over
there?' 'Plundering your city,' replied Cyrus, 'and carrying off
your wealth.' 'Not mine any longer,' said Croesus; 'it is *your*
property they are pillaging.' Cyrus at once ordered the
plunder to cease.

Such is Herodotus' version of the end of the Lydian monarchy. Other ancient accounts differ considerably, but the
existence of these legends, with their miraculous elements,
only a hundred years later, is striking evidence of the impression made by Croesus on Greek minds.

The end of the monarchy was the end of Lydian greatness.
Hitherto formidable warriors, the Lydians are henceforth
regarded, together with the Phrygians, as effeminate and fit
only to be the slaves of Greeks. This was due (again according
to Herodotus) to deliberate policy on Cyrus' part. Angered by
Pactyes' attempt to organise a revolt,[1] the Persian king had a
mind to sell all Lydians into slavery. Croesus, however, interceded and urged him merely to forbid them the use of arms
and make them bring up their sons to shopkeeping and the
practice of music. Thus their warlike spirit was subdued, and
in later times the Lydian and Phrygian were among the principal musical 'modes' of the ancients. The Phrygian was
considered exciting and emotional, the Lydian decorous and
educative, but we do not really know what they were like.
Ancient music is a difficult subject, and was regarded almost
as a branch of mathematics; in general it was simple, its
elements merely melody and rhythm. 'Harmony' to the
ancients meant a scale or harmonious succession of sounds; in
its modern sense of a harmonious blending of sounds it was

[1] Above, p. 240.

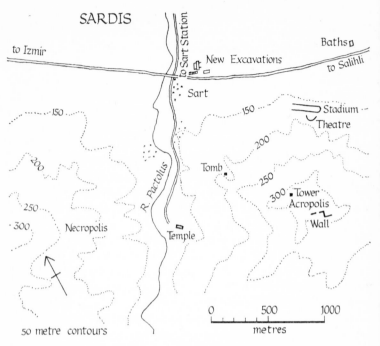

FIG. 50 Plan of Sardis

hardly known to them. One or two ancient hymns have been found inscribed on stone with the musical notation entered above; converted to modern notation (supposing this to have been correctly done) they sound thin and strange to European ears.

Sardis nevertheless continued to be an important city. First as the residence of the Persian satraps, then under the Hellenistic kings, it was always a place of consequence. In 213 B.C. Achaeus, a member of the Syrian royal family, had proclaimed himself king in Asia Minor; hunted down by the legitimate king, Antiochus III, he shut himself up in Sardis. Then occurred an almost exact repetition of the capture by Cyrus. A Cretan named Lagoras in Antiochus' army noticed a precipitous place with a gully below, into which dung and corpses of animals were habitually thrown by the inhabitants, so that the place was constantly full of vultures and other carrion

birds. He remarked acutely that these birds when replete used
to perch on the city walls above, and inferred that the walls
must normally be unmanned at that point, which was accordingly selected for a surprise attack. It is not now possible to
identify the place, or places, where these attacks were made.
The soft friable rock of the acropolis has crumbled and washed
away, carrying most of the fortification with it. The knife-edge
hills so characteristic of the region are due to this peculiarity
of the ground.

In the province of Asia, Sardis was the capital of a district
(conventus) and a judicial seat of the Roman governor. Destroyed by the great earthquake of A.D. 17, the city was rebuilt
by the generosity of Tiberius. Christianity was early established there, and in Revelation Sardis is one of the Seven
Churches of Asia. But there had been backsliding: 'I know thy
ways; thou art called alive, yet art dead.' Nevertheless Sardis
was later an important bishopric, ranked sixth of all those
subject to the Patriarch of Constantinople. Sacked by Tamer-
lane in 1401, the city never recovered. Gradually buried under
the soil washed down from the acropolis hill, the ruins lay
deserted; even the little village of Sart is a creation of the
twentieth century.

Since 1958 the American excavation of Sardis has been resumed, and the appearance of the site is changing from year
to year. For the ordinary traveller, however, the most striking
monument is still the well-known temple of Artemis. This lies
up the Pactolus valley, away from the main area of habitation
by the modern highroad. The temple has long been known. In
the early eighteenth century six columns were standing above
ground, with the architrave still in place; five of these were
seen by Chandler in 1764, but by 1812 the number was down
to three. In 1824 von Prokesch saw only the two which were
still erect when the American archaeologists undertook the
excavation in 1910–14. The task was a vast one, requiring
the removal of a 30-foot depth of earth at the east end; the
original ground-level may still be seen (Pl. 71, 73).

In 499 B.C., during the course of the Ionian revolt against
the Persians, Sardis was sacked and burned by the Greeks; on

this occasion Herodotus mentions that the temple of the native goddess Cybebe (that is Cybele) was destroyed by fire. Cybele being the principal deity of Sardis, her temple would surely be rebuilt, and the early explorers in modern times supposed the extant building to be no other than this. It was therefore something of a surprise when the first excavations revealed numerous inscriptions, in Greek and in Lydian, proving the temple to be that of Artemis. More remarkable still, one of these inscriptions refers to 'those who dwell in the sanctuary of Artemis *and Zeus*'. And in fact the building proves to be indeed a double temple, divided into two nearly equal parts by a cross-wall, close to which are the bases for two cult-statues, back to back. It was accordingly supposed that the two halves belonged respectively to Artemis and Zeus—Artemis on the west and Zeus on the east. Much later, in the second century A.D., the cult-statues of these deities were replaced by statues of the Emperor Antoninus Pius and his wife Faustina, to whom the temple was presumably re-dedicated. The latest investigations, however, have caused these views to be reconsidered. Zeus' share in the temple is now discredited, and the partition of the cella is believed to have been first made by Antoninus Pius, who joined a cult of the deified Faustina to that of Artemis. An interesting coin of Sardis, struck under the Emperor Elagabalus (A.D. 218–22), shows two temple-fronts, each of eight columns, seen obliquely; above each is its cult-statue in a shrine. One statue is female, the other of uncertain sex. It is probable that this coin shows the two ends of the double temple of Artemis and Faustina (Pl. 60).

The building is in the Ionic order, standing as usual on low ground, with eight columns at the short ends and twenty on the sides. There were also fourteen interior columns, none of which remain, and a further six in each pronaos, two of which are slenderer than the rest and stand on high pedestals. These four are the only columns actually found whose fluting was carried out. The high pedestals are unique in Greek architecture, except possibly in the Artemisium at Ephesus, and may be a Lydian feature. Of all these columns two are still complete, and thirteen others stand to a part of their height.

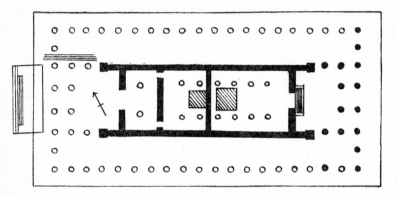

FIG. 51 Plan of the Temple of Artemis at Sardis

The temple was pseudo-dipteral on the flanks, with the columns at twice the usual distance from the cella walls. The Ionic capitals are among the most beautiful known, and the decoration on the bases is reminiscent of that at Didyma (Pl. 72).

At the west end, just outside the line of the north wall of the cella, excavation revealed a flight of steps which may still be seen. They belong without doubt to the existing temple, but their position is utterly abnormal. The arrangement of steps at the west end was evidently unusual; a conjectural attempt at a restoration was made by the excavators, but the question is so uncertain that on the plan, Fig. 51, it has been thought wiser to show only the steps whose position has actually been determined by excavation.

Also at the west end of the temple is an earlier structure which was evidently an altar. Since it is not quite in alignment with the temple walls, it was formerly thought that it must be the altar of an earlier temple on the same site; but this view also is now disputed. The present belief is that the altar, constructed probably about 400 B.C., stood alone during the greater part of the fourth century; for generations the worship of Artemis was centred only upon this. The existing temple—the only one ever to have stood on the site—was begun about 300 B.C. Contrary to the normal rule it faced towards the west;

given the already existing precinct this was natural, or even inevitable, to avoid making it look eastward into the slope of the hill.

By the end of the third century the cella at least was built and in use; a long inscription of about that date carved on the cella wall relates to a loan of money issued by the temple treasury. In the second century construction continued and a start was made upon the surrounding columns; but the work proceeded very slowly, or perhaps came to a complete halt, until the Roman Imperial period. It was no doubt set back by the severe earthquake of A.D. 17, from which Sardis, we are told, suffered more than any other city. A metrical inscription on the base of the fourth column from the north at the east end records that that column was the first to be erected; since the style of the script indicates the second century A.D., it is likely that the work was restarted by Antoninus Pius (138–161) when he joined the cult of his wife to that of Artemis. Even then the temple was never quite finished, as appears from the absence of fluting on the columns.

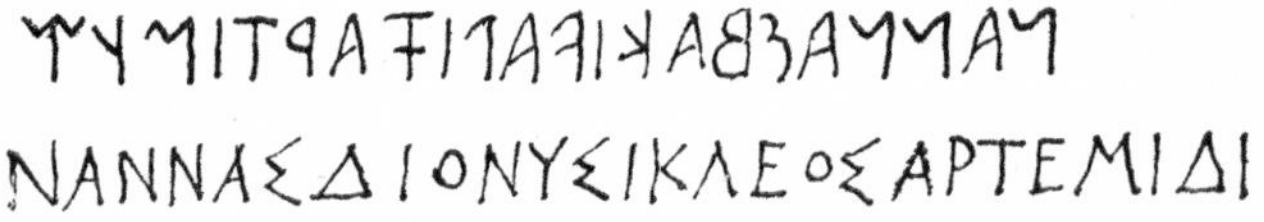

Fig. 52 Inscription in Lydian and Greek

The temple of Faustina was entered from the east by a door still partly preserved. Its threshold lies 6 feet above the level of the temple platform, and was approached by a flight of six steps between projecting wings; the rough steps now installed are merely for the convenience of visitors.

Standing on the north side of the temple, towards the west end, is a tall pedestal bearing an inscription in Greek in honour of a woman who is described by the Lydian word *kauein*, a priestess. Lying on the slope to the north of the temple, farther to the east, is a statue-base of the fourth century B.C. with a bilingual inscription in Lydian and Greek (see Fig. 52 and Appendix IV).

Close beside the north-east corner of the temple is a small

church or chapel which may date back to the fourth century.

The hills around Sardis, and especially those to the west of the Pactolus, contain hundreds of Lydian tombs, the earliest of which belong to the seventh century B.C. Many of these were cleared by the first excavation party, but most have become buried again by the constant shifting of the soil. The standard type comprises a passage leading to a door about 6 feet high, closed by a slab or slabs of stone; at the outer end of this passage stood tall stelae with floral decoration and probably painted inscriptions. Inside the door is the burial-chamber cut out of the solid hillside, with gabled roof and funeral couches on either side and at the back. These couches held tub-shaped sarcophagi of terracotta, painted red, white and black. A group of three tombs recently re-excavated may be visited by following up the side-valley which opens on the west about a quarter of a mile to the south of the temple; the tombs are on the south side of the hollow in which the valley ends, close above a vineyard. (But it is advisable to take a guide.) This excursion is worth while if only for the attractive views of the acropolis which it affords, and for the remarkable pinnacles and buttresses into which the soft rock has been eroded (Pl. 74, 75).

A tomb of quite different type stands on the west slope of the acropolis hill. It has the form of a stepped pyramid, but only the lower part is preserved. The style of the masonry shows that it dates to the period of Persian domination in the fifth to fourth centuries B.C. Perhaps 900 years later than this is another tomb in the east bank of the Pactolus some 500 yards south of the main road. It consists of a vaulted chamber with wall-paintings of peacocks and other birds.

The recent excavations have taken place chiefly in the Pactolus valley by the modern village and on the plain to the north. Lydian remains have come to light in every part, and it appears that the city of Croesus was actually greater in extent than the Hellenistic and Roman cities which succeeded it. At the time of writing the principal excavations are on the north side of the main road some 200 yards east of the Pactolus bridge. The buildings revealed will be more arresting when the contemplated restorations are complete; the small finds are full of interest, and it is intended eventually to exhibit them in the museum at Manisa.

The chief building-complex immediately beside the road comprises a gymnasium and adjoining structures. The gymnasium has a north and south hall, with an impressive entrance building on the east; farther to the east was the open court of the palaestra. The gymnasium as a whole dates to the second century A.D.; the marble facing was added under the Emperor Caracalla in A.D. 212. A Byzantine reconstruction of the fifth or sixth century is recorded by a metrical inscription written round the walls.

Immediately to the south-east of the gymnasium is the Jewish synagogue, identified by the inscriptions found in it; this building appears to have been originally constructed in the third century and repaired about A.D. 400.

Adjoining the gymnasium on the south is a row of Byzantine shops, and between these and the present highroad the excavators have uncovered a stretch of the ancient street, a part of the great Royal Road which led up from the coast to the interior of the Persian empire. The street, of late Roman date, is about 30 feet wide and paved with marble blocks; it had a colonnaded sidewalk on either side. This road was later superimposed by another of Byzantine date, and this in turn by the Ottoman road which remained in use till the construction of the present highway in 1952.

Nearly a mile farther to the east, again close beside the road, is a vast structure of Roman date which the recent excavations have shown to be a bathing establishment. Of the theatre and stadium the positions are recognisable, but nothing remains standing. The numerous fragments of city-wall which are visible in various places belong to the fifth century A.D., when it seems that the city was deliberately reduced in size. The early fortifications have almost entirely disappeared, but on the north side of the acropolis, not far from the top, a handsome Hellenistic tower is preserved in its lower part. It is thought that this may have been built by Antiochus III to remedy the weakness by which his own army had been enabled to capture the citadel.

In 1965 an interesting and unusual feature of the city came
to light. Enclosed by a high wall, the excavators found an area
half an acre in extent occupied by shops and workrooms—a
striking anticipation of the *souqs* and oriental bazaars familiar
today. Not least remarkable is the date of this complex, which
belongs to the period following the expulsion of the Cimmerians
in the early part of the seventh century B.C.

In the last year or two several interesting tunnels have been
discovered leading down the north face of the acropolis hill.
They are thought likely to be of Lydian origin, but their date
and purpose remain to be determined by further excavation.

BIN TEPE

Some six miles to the north and north-west of Sardis, on a
ridge between the Hermus plain and the Gygaean Lake (now
Marmara Gölü), is the great Lydian necropolis called by the
Turks the Thousand Hills. These tumuli are conspicuous from
the Sardis road. A thousand is an exaggeration, but there are
probably over a hundred. They are more easily visited now
than formerly, since the construction in recent years of a new
bridge over the river just to the east of Ahmetli. Beyond the
bridge the roads are bad and only fit for a jeep; except in
summer they may be impassable.

Three of the mounds are noticeably larger than the rest.
The largest of all, at the east end of the ridge, is identified with
the tomb of Alyattes described by Herodotus, who was much
impressed by its vast size. The base, he says, is formed of
huge blocks of stone, the upper part being a mound of earth;
on the summit are five pillars. He estimates the circumference
at over three-quarters of a mile. The monument was erected
by the tradesmen, artisans and prostitutes of Sardis, and the
five pillars were inscribed with a record of the work done by
each class; the prostitutes' share was found to be the largest.

The existing mound answers very well to Herodotus' description. Its general appearance must have resembled that of
the 'Tomb of Tantalus' at Smyrna; there is in each case a
circular wall of masonry at the base, surmounted by a conical
pile. Of the inscribed pillars, however, nothing has been found;

instead, there lies on the summit a spherical stone, 10 feet in diameter, attached to a rectangular base. This is thought to be a sort of phallus, such as frequently stood on sepulchral tumuli. The mound was first examined archaeologically in 1853, when a marble burial-chamber was found in the interior, approached by stone-lined passages; it had, as usual, been plundered. The excavators have recently closed the entrance to these passages, and the tomb-chamber is not ordinarily accessible.

Herodotus' description is not the only ancient notice of this monument that we have. A fragment of the satiric poet Hipponax, who wrote perhaps a hundred years before Herodotus, is addressed to a friend in Lydia bidding him join the poet in Ionia. The fragment is corrupt and difficult, but according to an accepted text it says: 'Traverse, Tearus, the whole road to Smyrna; cross through Lydia past the tomb of Alyattes and the monument of Gyges and the great city and the stele, past the memorial of the great king Tos, turning your belly towards the setting sun.' On the strength of this passage the three largest mounds have been called respectively the tombs of Alyattes, Gyges and Tos, in order from east to west. But the last two of these names are not really more than a convenient means of designating those particular tumuli. It has been suggested alternatively that 'the stele and the monument of Tos' refers to the Hittite figure in the Karabel Pass. To the present writer this suggestion is unattractive; see above, pp. 55–8.

In 1964 the Americans began an exploration of the second of these, called the tomb of Gyges. Here, too, a circular wall exists within the mound, and the architecture is interesting as resembling that of some Etruscan tombs. Future discoveries here may well be of great importance. A number of the smaller mounds also have been examined and found to contain a sepulchral chamber, situated generally away from the centre to make discovery more difficult. Some of them have more than one chamber. Whether there was in all cases a circular retaining wall at the base does not seem to have been determined.